Death
at the
Podium

Death at the Podium

Robert Barclay

LOOSE CANNON PRESS

NATIONAL LIBRARY OF CANADA CATALOGUING IN PUBLICATION DATA
Barclay, Robert
Death at the Podium
ISBN 978-0-9867879-2-8
Revised Edition

Printed in the United States of America
and in the United Kingdom

Published by
LOOSE CANNON PRESS

loosecannonpress@rogers.com
www.loosecannonpress.com

Note to the Reader

This is a work of fiction. The characters are all products of the author's imagination and any resemblance to real persons, living or dead, is not intended. Although many of the places described exist, all the incidents, actions and other aspects of the storyline are fictitious.

Acknowledgements

My thanks go to those who read the entire manuscript, or parts of it. In particular, I acknowledge the following: my good friend Richard Seraphinoff who provided many anecdotes and detailed views on some of the things that go on during an orchestra rehearsal; James and Ellie Duffin, and Anna and Zac Ezekiel who gave valuable advice on location and context; Peter Whitworth for the intricate details and subtleties of flying and navigation in a light plane; Frédérick Hodgson who kindly reviewed sections on the oboe and provided wonderful inside views of that instrument's craft; my son David for his always valuable editing and review; and finally my wife Janet whose insights into the way people think and feel are so much keener than mine. Any errors or omissions are entirely my responsibility.

Robert Barclay
Ottawa 2013

Intrada

It's a small thing; a little over a foot long and weighing only a few ounces. But it has enormous power. Point this thing at one person in eighty and induce fear, anger, embarrassment. Point it at another of the eighty to cause elation, joy or pride. It can be used to whip eighty into a frenzy in an instant, or it can lull the same number into gentle compliance. It zeros-in on individuals; it castigates masses. It leads, it dictates, it whips, it cajoles, it caresses. What kind of weapon is this? What single weapon could embody such science fiction powers?

Is it a gun; a sword; a whip; a magic wand?

None of these things.

It's the maestro's baton.

It's a lightning rod.

MAESTRO DIES ON STAGE
Roberto Cortisone
Arturo Bertolli, maestro of the Sinfonia di Luna, died suddenly from an apparent heart attack while conducting in Rome. It is reported that the attack took place during the concluding movement of Mahler's Eighth Symphony. "It was awful," said a stunned violinist. "He fell off the podium and just crashed right into the violas." The performance was terminated immediately and concert-goers filed quietly to the exits. Emergency staff performed CPR on Bertolli, but with no success. This is the third instance this year of a maestro collapsing during a performance. It shows what an emotional strain it must be to lead an orchestra so selflessly through these great works of musical genius. The funeral will be held in Bertolli's home town of Milan although the date and location are not yet announced.
AP – London

MUSIC TAKES TOLL ON AGEING MAESTROS
Conductor collapses at podium
Roger Newel
The sudden death of Arthur Simmons, conductor of the Clapham South Ensemble, during a concert rehearsal raises yet again the question of the physical fitness of these performers. It is unarguable that they lead strenuous lives and that few of them are still young. Simmons, well known for his flamboyant and energetic style at the podium, is typical of those who throw themselves into a task for which, as younger men, they may well have been equipped. But time takes its toll, and with great age comes great responsibility. It is understood that healthcare and physical fitness training will be the theme of a meeting of professional musicians, which will take place next month in Rome.
The Daily Telegraph

Concert Overture, Opus 26

These musicians are party animals, figured Jonathan Rycroft. It was probably the high intensity battles they waged each day, the emotional output of intense classical concerts, and the serious need to wind down. Also, most of his cadre were unmarried, or at least unattached, on account of the constant traveling, the difficult hours, and their devotion to the business. This party was as noisy as they usually were, with the constant thump-thump-thump of some most un-classical music emanating from the wafer thin Bose speakers, the roar of voices and the clash of cutlery, glass and crockery. It was a small two-bedroom apartment on the ground floor, and the party was spilling out front and back, into the small backyard and the sloping forecourt. Early spring weather made open doors a refreshing change.

Looked like most of the orchestra had showed up; at least, the ones who could actually stand each other's company when not scrubbing, blowing or banging in adjacent chairs all day. The Maestro's toadies were conspicuously elsewhere; probably some genteel swah-ray with light string music and tinkling, empty headed chatter.

Jonathan played the oboe, the first of the two in the East Gladstone Symphony Orchestra. He had won the audition when the previous first oboe had retired. The present second oboe had also auditioned for the job, but on that day at that particular time Jonathan was better. So, no love lost there. Auditions are always a huge crap shoot and people rarely got jobs purely on merit. It was just the luck of the draw.

Jonathan was in a foul mood tonight, brought on by a major difference of opinion with their beloved Maestro, and the glass of red wine in hand wasn't doing its work. Why couldn't I just swallow my pride and shut up, he thought. But then, damn it, why should I bow down to such an ignorant, arrogant fraud? Making music under his baton was becoming tiresome.

As he looked around him he realized that most of his fellow players just sat down at their chairs and did what they were told. So many of them were no longer the idealistic students, glowing in anticipation of their future in music. All of them, he would bet, had been attracted at first by the thought of the tricky solos in front of packed houses, the travel, the romance... But once they had finally achieved that rare privilege of winning an orchestra seat in a competition that was as fierce as any on the planet, they were damned well going to do what it took to keep it. So, once actually seated in a concert hall and surrounded by silent thousands awaiting the uplifting moment, it wasn't all that long before the gloss wore off the apple. The tricky solos in front of packed houses, if one ever achieved that status, were recipes for antacids and tranquilizers. The travel soon became a royal pain in the ass, as different cities blended into a continuum of bland hotel rooms, tough rehearsals and too many drinks after the show. And the romance? Well, enough said about that!

So, cynicism soon set in, and what was once glorious became commonplace, what was once a calling became a job. How many of this lot, he wondered, are just uninspired lunch-pail workers counting their paycheques? The majority, was his view.

There was old Bill Baines, bassoonist, sitting on the chesterfield and chatting with horse-faced Annie what's-her-name who plays the flute. Old Bill just plays his handful of notes day in and day out, year after year, the picture of contentment. Am I supposed to find that horrific vision of the future fulfilling?

Basically, if you want to keep the chair you're sitting in—and job openings in the symphony orchestra world are as rare as rocking horse shit—you just shut up and played the music the way you were told to. But it simply wasn't that easy for him, and he didn't seem to be able to make it so.

Here was a straightforward 'if-then' proposition, he thought, as he sucked at his wine: if you like playing music professionally so much, then why are you so determined to make it difficult for yourself? God, he wished he could answer that one!

Everybody here knew everybody else; that's the way it is in an orchestra. They tended to stick together, party together. People who routinely come together as one in the creation of something greater than the sum of its parts, will always share close feelings. They will also tear each other apart. Over his short time with the group he must have had conversations of some sort with all eighty of them. He nodded to Liz Straker, a cellist, as he wandered through the room, and came upon Steve Mah, a trombonist, who always had an unkind word or two about their Maestro. It was their shared bond.

"Hi, Jon." Mah gave him a sidelong glance and a sly smile. "Great party."

"Yeah, great." He loathed being called Jon but in all fairness perhaps he had never mentioned it to him. The sly smile made Jonathan wonder how many of them knew about his most recent argument with the Great Man.

As he swam amongst the jabbering mass he half-listened to the chatter bursting in pockets around him.

"Well, he may be a hands-on type of conductor, but I wish he'd keep his hands off me. Touchy-feelie, yuk!"

"Yeah, he keeps doing the old Elgar, doesn't he?" This was the musicians' not-so-private code phrase. Translation: Hand of Grope and Horny.

"...of *course*, it was B flat! Which bar were *you* on?"

"...tried using lanolin but it gums up the slides..."

"...his stick technique is the shits. He should take a course..."

"...minor second? Oboes playing in unison!" followed by roars of laughter, not at all betraying the age of the joke and the number of times they had all heard it before. None of them noticed Jonathan but even if they had, he thought, they were all brass players so they wouldn't give a shit anyway.

Jonathan, slid between a pair of violas comparing notes, his nearly empty glass spearing the way, and searched the throng for Kate Heinrichs, the one musician whose beautiful ear he most liked to bend. Kate was one of twelve second violins, consigned to the back row and unlikely to graduate forward in the hierarchy any time soon. He spotted her slim back over by the drinks table and took the opportunity to top up with a not-at-all-bad Baco Noir from Niagara. He was still in a shit mood, and his face showed it.

Kate swung round to him and held out her glass. "Hey, what about me?"

He splashed some red into her glass and offered a mock toast.

"Another wee contretemps with our sweet boss?" she offered, seeing the thunder on his brow.

"News gets around."

"Hardly news! Half the orchestra could hear you buggers slagging each other off in the hallway. You don't exactly keep it a secret, do you? What was it this time?"

"You remember when we were working on the Beethoven One? It's that quick segue he wants from the minuet into the trio; you simply can't do that without a breath at the end of that bar. Nobody could. As if a fiddle player knows shit about the oboe."

"But why did he get so mad?"

"Because I told him, okay if you don't want me to take a

breath there, would it be alright if I broke the following phrase?"

"Oh, you idiot! Why wave a red flag at him?" God, he was so darned frustrating!

"Yeah, well, it's the way he points that fucking baton at me. Maybe he thinks I can't read music. Does he think I can't count? I don't need some asshole telling me when to come in. Why stare straight at me?"

"Oh, you're just being paranoid; he does the eye contact stuff with everybody." Like the rest of them, Kate knew that their illustrious maestro was a monstrous control freak, and kept the players on a very short leash.

"No, it's more than that. He's got it in for me."

"Look, we all get pointed at; we all get the old hairy eyeball..."

"Yeah, but it's the way he looks. Seen his eyes?"

Kate took a long pull at her wine, nodding approvingly. "Well, you better just try to get along with him. What's the alternative? Wanna go looking for another job?" She placed her hand gently on his wrist. "I'd... we'd really miss you, you know."

Not that there was a hope in hell of landing another permanent job in a symphony orchestra in these constrained times. Once you had a chair, no dynamite ever made could blast you from it. But you could be sacked of course. There were musicians lining up to fill vacant spaces at a ratio of about a hundred to one. Jonathan annoyed her, although she wouldn't let it show. Why risk sacrificing a great, hard won job to satisfy... what? Not ego, exactly...

"I know, I know... I'll just have to control myself if I can. Screw it, let's talk about something else."

They moved through the press around the drinks table and found a small oasis near the bathroom door.

It was funny the way Kate and Jonathan had drifted together. When you looked at them they were the most unlikely couple. Well, not really a couple at all; he drew an imaginary line that she was at a loss to understand, but she repeatedly skated as close to it as she could. Testing. He hadn't missed the "I'd... we'd..." or the slight pressure of her hand on his wrist. Yes, he wanted to get closer and, yes, she was inviting, but he simply couldn't let her; it was impossible. He often wished their eyes hadn't met on his first day with the orchestra. Why did he keep gravitating to her?

Jonathan Rycroft was a little under 40 and stood a shade under six feet. He was the kind of guy who favoured tee shirts, jeans and sneakers, although he looked well in the formal black-and-whites the orchestra demanded. This was an off-duty day and the jeans were about the tattiest he had. His dark, close-cropped hair was beginning to thin; his face was not handsome—too long in the nose and narrow of eye—but, when not in a foul mood, his expression spoke of charm and worldly experience. He seldom laughed out loud, but a rare smile could make radiant changes. He was relatively new to the symphony orchestra circuit, having had a profound change of career somewhat late in life.

Kate's head reached just above his shoulder. She was 27 but people thought her much younger. She had soft, light brown hair to shoulder length, which she held back with a band across her forehead; black for concerts, gorgeously multi-coloured when off duty. Grey-green eyes in an oval face, and full lips with a teasing corner to them, smiled at the world. She carried her emotions near the surface and was quickly capable of laughter or tears, although laughter always predominated. But below the general sunniness there was resilience; she had wanted to be an orchestral musician as far back as she could remember, she had worked damned hard, and now here she was.

Jonathan was devoted to his music; that's what stood out from the other guys Kate had known. She had the same drive, and its lack in others had soured her past relationships. You had to share her with her music—it was the whole package—and if you didn't understand that, you didn't understand anything. And it did no good to get jealous about it. She knew from sad experience that dating non-musicians was futile; they would never understand the marriage that music demanded of her. Love and music were inextricably linked; music *was* a love affair, and the *ménage a trois* that resulted had been satisfactory to neither partner. She knew Jonathan would be utterly different; like her, he was absolutely wedded to his music. But for some reason he wouldn't let her into his world. How wonderful it would be if only she could break through. It would be a sharing for life and she ached for it.

He was 12 years her senior, and volatile and moody, while she was more generally sunny and a stranger to bad moods. If either of them thought of their differences of temperament or their age disparity they said nothing. And while their relationship was in this platonic and fixed orbit perhaps there was nothing much that needed to be said. This didn't still the many wagging tongues, of course.

"Hey! Jonah! Heard you again today!" One of the trumpeters,

clearly flying high on liberal booze, banged him on the back. "Gonna to put paid to another one, are you?"

Oh, not again! His reputation wouldn't lie down. Some of the shit-heads in the orchestra—and this asshole in particular—had nick-named him Jonah after the death of the previous maestro during a Beethoven symphony. It was Jonathan's misfortune to have had a row with him just before that fateful concert. So, after the maestro had dropped off the perch, this creep ragged him with causing it. How he thought this was funny he could not divine, and the only excuse for his behavior he could think of was that he spent his entire life drinking beer and making farting noises into a length of brass tube.

It was such a bugger. Sure, the old maestro had been a real drill sergeant, but at least with him you knew where you stood, and his musical ideas were sound. The argument Jonathan had had with him was hardly earth-shaking and should have gone unnoticed. Lots of musicians argue with their conductors. This one had just been bad timing. It's a standing joke that the maestro is a complete asshole and that the entire orchestra cracks jokes behind his back, but really! So, a brief spate of heated words, a concert, and then... death. Right there on the podium in the middle of the Third Symphony. It was awful; he had had a sort of riveting spasm, clutched his chest and tumbled off the podium carrying the music stand with him. There he was, lying amid a flutter of score sheets, baton still gripped in his hand, and gone from this world.

"Oh, for Christ's sake!" muttered Jonathan, and elbowed his way out into the fresh air, with Kate following in the vacuum of his passing. There was no way he was going to confront some drunk who would never have said such things sober. The anodyne of having Kate at his side had been blown to hell and now the foul mood was on him again.

"Come on," said Kate. "Let's get our coats and get out of here."

The town of East Gladstone is situated on a large lake between the Ontario farm belt to the south and the rocks of the Canadian Shield to the north. There is no West Gladstone, although according to the local historians of the East Gladstone and District Museums Association, there once was, but it never prospered and the area upon which its few buildings stood has been reclaimed by the forest. This is cottage and vacation country, far enough away from the larger cities of Southern Ontario to be isolated, yet not so far as to be inaccessible. It's a pretty town; it has attracted writers, painters and musicians since its founding in the early 19th century, and it had developed into a tourist destination through much of that period. It is rare that a town of this size—only 40,000 souls—can afford to support a full-size symphony orchestra, but thanks to a vibrant arts community, a very energetic board of trustees and lots of tourist dollars, it is just about possible.

There are several key ingredients in assembling and maintaining a large group of musicians, and the board of trustees and their management team needed to attend energetically and continually to them all. Clearly, the first item on the agenda was a concert hall. The Centennial of 1967 provided a boon not seen since, and heritage money from both federal and provincial coffers flowed liberally. The East Gladstone Centennial Centre, jutting into the lake on a rocky promontory, arose from this source and was completed the following year.

Ontario architects love wood. It was the material of necessity for many of the earlier colonial structures, from log cabins to barns to meeting halls, and it has entered their psyche to the point where it sometimes supplants other cheaper and more workable materials. Stone and brick structures are impressive and speak of solid, reliable eras when erecting a public building marked a cultural coming of age, and every small town, East Gladstone included, has a four-square town hall, a stone-built church and a solid bank along its main street. But, always, in the background, construction in wood has been the quintessence of what building for comfort, charm and beauty is all about. The Temple built in Sharon in the 1820s by the Children of Peace is a fabulous example, and in modern times the architect who designed the renovation of the Art Gallery of Ontario in Toronto did wonders with wood.

Nowadays, the arching interior space of a large concert hall can be roofed with steel or reinforced concrete at a reasonable cost and with a fair degree of simplicity. In cities this type of construction would be the norm, especially for sports facilities where the aesthetic bows to the utilitarian. Who looks up at the construction of the roof, unless following a fly ball or a high second tier home run? The East Gladstone Centennial Centre was done in wood, as befitted a small town that had its roots in agriculture and had grown to maturity in art. Huge beams of laminated pine soared from the edges of the side aisles, over the 1,500 seat auditorium in sweeping organic curves, tapering to their culmination in a branching, tree-like nexus above the stage. Wood was used liberally in the horizontal, slatted infill between the supports and in the finishing of floors, railings and barriers. Below the sloping, leaf-shaped auditorium were the workshops, dressing rooms, meeting spaces and storage areas that a busy public structure needs.

Once a beautiful performing space is ensured the next item on the agenda is bums on seats; no great building, no amount of funding, interest and support will be effective if the orchestra is not playing to full, or at least nearly full, houses. The take at the door is critical to success, and even though private benefactors may be topping up the bank account, empty halls are a death knell. Heavy tourist presence in the town in the summer months, and a tour schedule for the long winter season, went a long way to filling the seats, and then when the planners added all sorts of festivals in the spring and fall months to the orchestra's activities, the formula for success was given a fairly sound footing.

The East Gladstone Symphony Orchestra comprised some 80 full-time members and was quite capable of performing any or all of the great classics in the concert repertoire. In composition it was mid-way between the early romantic orchestra, which was the ensemble of Beethoven's time, more or less, and the later much enhanced body that developed during the 19th century. (The composition of the modern classical orchestra has scarcely changed in over a hundred years.) Because the EGSO was a relatively small ensemble—compared with the mighty orchestras of cities like Montreal, Toronto and New York—it was often necessary to bring in players on contract, which is an expensive proposition in a smallish town remote from the musical action of the big cities. Money was always tight.

Attracting competent musicians to a place like East Gladstone might not sound easy. In fact, it is not as hard as one would imagine. Music schools throughout North America are filled with enormously talented young musicians, all of whom dream of the great symphony job. One in fifty of them will actually win an audition with an orchestra of any kind, and go on to practice the craft as a professional. It isn't just because the symphony orchestra is in world-wide decline—although that is part of it—it is due also to a system that ties university and college funding to numbers. So, rather than foster a small, very talented and ultimately employable cadre, the schools turn them out *en masse* and throw them into the arena to fend for themselves. The EGSO players were content to be where they were, and hung onto their seats because they knew that there are always substitutes waiting in the wings.

Attracting a great maestro to lead the East Gladstone Symphony Orchestra was the final and vital ingredient for success. While the musicians had been relatively easy to come by, getting the right man for job—it is almost always a man; usually a middle-aged white one—was an order of magnitude more difficult than any other single aspect. It is absolutely essential to embellish the very top of the pyramid of this orchestral enterprise with a flamboyant, attractive, personable star; one who can woo audiences, charm rich donors effortlessly, attract interest like a magnet and, most important of all, be seen by the arts community as a prime focal point. Money will help to attract such a candidate; an idyllic setting (at least in summer) in which to practice his craft will also help. But the true tipping point in the board of trustees' campaign to find a candidate was the cunning expedient of exhibiting fawning adulation during the interview process, cherishing his every utterance as if it were holy writ, and promising by action and example that he would be the central star in the artistic firmament of the town. No true maestro can resist such blandishments.

Carlo Mascagni was their candidate. His interview had been a high cholesterol affair; lots of oil and butter, with a good dollop of syrup thrown in. His musical capabilities were never assessed; he was clearly highly successful internationally and that was good enough.

He was actually quite incompetent.

A conductor is *de facto* an ego maniac; anyone who believes he can impose his will upon 80 mature, well-trained and dedicated individuals must be so. He will steer the orchestra with an iron hand, and impose his musical shaping and interpretation on his musicians. Good conductors are, of course, musical geniuses, and orchestra members will cooperate with their idiosyncrasies—differing tempos, dynamics, note lengths, placement of accents, and so on—even if individually they might have strong reservations. Someone has to be in charge of those concepts, and if they are good musical ideas everyone will acknowledge them and move on. However, Mascagni's ideas were not founded in good musical sense, but seemed merely to be random concepts calculated to enhance his performance and feed his ego. And it really annoys musicians to have a conductor suggesting things that don't make good, expressive musical sense. Or things that are impossible actually to accomplish.

The majority of musicians in the orchestra just wanted to get on with it, and were flexible enough and sociable enough to go with the flow. So they tolerated Mascagni's ego-driven musical posturing just to keep things on an even keel. After all, it was a real job in tough times.

There were a principled few, like Jonathan, who argued with their Maestro. Chief among the arguers was the poor concertmaster, Stefan Kulikofski. He had been in the doghouse from the word go. The orchestra's first violin is *de facto* the concertmaster. But, before he took up the baton, the Maestro himself had been a violinist—and a very good one—and you just can't have any competition in that department. The concertmaster's eminence was, of course, a challenge to the Maestro, the *true* leader of the orchestra, so festering pettiness took the place of mature accommodation.

It was such a pity; there are some wonderful human beings out there conducting orchestras, but the musicians of the East Gladstone Symphony Orchestra got saddled with a maestro.

Unknown to the Maestro, most of the musicians shortened the orchestra's acronym to EGO as being much more appropriate to the case. It was a marvel the orchestra ever got the job done. It's a testament to the majority of players that they just buckled down night after night and played the notes.

It was a fine day in late spring, not long after the party that Kate and Jonathan had left so abruptly. The snow was finally off the fields and the ice had retreated on the lake. Under the lowest of bushes and shrubs there were still traces of snow where the spring warmth had yet to penetrate, but the ground elsewhere was moist and spongy. Daffodils and crocuses were finally optimistic enough to thrust their heads upwards. The town streets had been swept of their residues of salt, gravel and dog shit left by the retreating snow, and café owners were moving furniture onto sidewalks again.

Fine weather notwithstanding, the musicians were all seated

on the stage of the Centennial Centre amid the din of scales, tuning and chatter, preparing for the day's rehearsal. The concert platform was the only place in the whole of East Gladstone large enough to accommodate the entire orchestra, and this meant very flexible rehearsal times, depending upon who else was using the facility. It was nine on a Thursday morning and they would have to be out by twelve.

Before the Maestro could make his appearance the orchestra manager, Harold Gropius, stepped onto the platform to greet them. He was a short fussy little man whose limited stature culminated in a bald cranium fringed with the last wispy traces of his once-brown hair. He dealt with the day-to-day management of the orchestra and was, surprisingly, quite unsophisticated regarding the repertoire. He focused almost entirely upon the routine operation of the ensemble; as long as the musicians had the right music at their stands for both rehearsals and concerts, the brochures and programs were printed correctly, the whole ensemble got where it had to go on time, had sufficient music stands when it got there, and operated like a well-oiled machine, he was satisfied. What they played once his operations had come to their fulfillment was, quite simply, the business of the Board.

"I have some excellent news for you," he began. "As some of you may know, our maestro has secured a guest conductorship in Dallas this weekend."

This was, indeed, cause for celebration—just to be shot of the bastard for a while—but the scattering of applause was premature as the little man wasn't finished yet.

"Of course," continued Gropius, "this rather sudden arrangement meant that we... ah, the Board... would be obliged to find a temporary replacement. Well, we are indeed very fortunate that Sir Arthur Compton is visiting Canada and has graciously accepted our invitation to conduct here this Saturday."

This was genuinely good news. Few, if any, of the musicians had encountered the gentleman at first hand, but his reputation was widespread. He carried the same aura as Adrian Boult or Thomas Beecham or Andrew Davis; he was of the old school, and by reputation a scholar, a tough master and an irrepressible wit. This should be fun.

What had happened was, Sir Arthur's agent had secured three Canadian engagements for him during his North American tour —Montreal, Toronto and Vancouver—but had allowed a little too much time between the two widely separated venues. Perhaps she had visualized a slow progress by train, just like in the good old days of whooping Indians and wigwams. Whatever the case, Sir Arthur had some days to kick his heels in Toronto and had asked if there were a smaller orchestra that he might conduct. East Gladstone won the lottery.

The program for the weekend concert included Mendelssohn, Brahms and Beethoven, none of the pieces a challenge to the musicians and thus feasible for a guest conductor to handle in a flying visit. The Brahms Third symphony was the toughest, but familiar, Beethoven's Sixth symphony, *The Pastoral*, they could practically do in their sleep, while Mendelssohn's *Hebrides*, or *Fingal's Cave* as it is popularly known, was a delight. Yes, this should be fun.

Meanwhile, the same program was to be rehearsed today under the baton of Carlo Mascagni, and not a few of the musicians harboured a secret delight that, once he was off to his guest thing in Dallas, they could pretty well ignore everything he had said. But they still had to get through the next three hours.

Sir Arthur was introduced to the orchestra at the East Gladstone Centennial Centre on Friday morning, having driven up from Toronto with the entourage assigned to him for the tour. The sixty-one-year old conductor was familiar to all of them, of course, as a commanding and enduring presence in their world, but seen in the flesh, he was shorter than what his public image revealed. He was at least three inches less than six feet, round about the middle, and with a fine head of silver hair which was allowed to do what it wished. His pink, clean shaven and almost cherubic face fooled nobody; the eyes were intelligent and magnetic and the mouth was firm. When he looked at you, you knew you were under analysis. But the tiniest hint of amusement would turn a serious demeanor into a chuckling Falstaff, but only upon his terms. He knew what he wanted out of the music, he knew what he wanted out of his musicians, and he knew they would rise for him.

He took charge straight away, while the entourage left with their clipboards and I-Pads and Blackberries to do whatever entourages do between bouts of celebrity handling.

"Now, let's see what we have here. There's damned little time to do much, but I'm told you people know these pieces like the back of your hand, yes?"

He scanned the orchestra showing that gift of the great communicator by making all 80 of them feel engaged and personally addressed.

"Let's have a crack at the Mendelssohn, shall we? What d'ye say?" He sorted out the *Hebrides* score, leaned down for a few quiet words with Stefan Kulikofski the concertmaster, and then tapped his baton.

It was plain sailing for the greater part of the piece until he suddenly called a halt.

"Yes, yes, just back a little. Now, let's look at this little phrase; it's rehearsal letter C, twentieth and twenty-first measures... got it? Dee, dum, di-da—dee-dum you see? The bit that everybody knows, right? Well, let's make the third beat strong instead, shall we? So that the first two are pick-ups to the third. Let's try dee-dum, di-da-*Dee*-dum. And keep those dotted crotchets crisp and in good rhythm."

He chuckled when the North American-trained players were briefly confused. "Ah yes, well, the dotted eighth sixteenth figure then. So, let's do this again..." and off they went. Then he halted once more.

"Well, what about that, eh? And you know," here he paused with his forefinger along his cheek and thumb under his chin, "I'm sure that if Mendelssohn was listening to that he'd say 'You know, Sir Arthur, I think that's jolly good'."

Light laughter at a rehearsal was a rare as rain in February.

They realized how clever he had been; 'the bit that everybody knows' now had his unique imprint. Those who knew the piece well would sit up at this. Sir Arthur's brief visit would surely be remembered.

The session continued this way, with many stops and starts and much penciling on scores, but all of it done with humour and charm. But, when the musicians looked back upon it they realized that, for all the apparent lightness, the medicine had been tough; he had asked a lot of them, but they had indeed risen to his challenge. It was a heady wine for people more used to being shouted at for failing to produce nonsensical phrasing, randomly placed accents, and inappropriate tempos.

At lunch break the usual groups of orchestra members congregated in the cafeteria by habit, and they were amazed to find Sir Arthur circling their tables with a paper cup of tea in his hand, sharing anecdotes and comments. He approached Kate and Jonathan's table, swung a chair backwards and sat with his arms across its back.

"Nice work with the oboes there. Lovely tone! And, you know," addressing the table at large, "I'm very pleasantly surprised at the quality of this group." He took a sip at his tea and winced. "Damned sight better quality than the tea, at any rate!"

Kate Heinrichs surprised herself when she remarked, "I've been hatching up ways of kidnapping you and never letting you go." She coloured a bit when she realized how forward she had been, but the old boy seemed to provoke such things.

"Hah! Might be very nice at that, young lady. What's your instrument?... Ah, fiddle. Sorry I didn't pick you out from the crowd, but there are so many damned fiddles, aren't there? Anyhow, it would be lovely to stay a while but commitments, duties... In all sincerity, this is a big town orchestra in a small town; nice surprise. But let's see if we can't raise the bar even higher this afternoon, eh?" and he was off to the next table.

Kate fell in love with him right there. What *must* it be like, she thought, to have a chair in *his* orchestra! Just before they headed back to the stage she met him very briefly at the door of the cafeteria and had what she later saw as a premonition.

"I wonder, Sir Arthur, do you have a business card? I've never been to London, but..."

"Of course, of course. There you are," delving into his vest pocket. "Do get in touch." He laughed quietly to himself. "Kidnapping..." and trotted off for the afternoon's session.

Symphony No. 8 in C Minor

Stan Ward was on the subway heading to work from his house in the Toronto Beach area. He liked the subway, he liked the street-cars, and he even liked the buses. Let someone else do the driving! You could sit yourself down, turn the world off and let your mind expand. Many of his research insights came while trundling along rails in Toronto, below the busy streets or along the bustling surface, brain in neutral but searching, like the probing beam of Cape Spear Light among the clutter of his experience.

Stan was in his late sixties but still with a straight back, a lean composition, and a head held square and challenging upon his shoulders. The face had fallen away from that of the youth who looked so appealing in the Varsity rowing team shots of the 1960s, but dammit he still had that old charm. The eye was bright, the white moustache and beard neatly trimmed, the whole face saying: Come on, ask me anything, anything at all, and I'll give you something to make you think. I'm not done by a long way, damn yer eyes. He dressed very traditionally, inasmuch as he would wear a tie on all occasions, but did draw the line at wearing suits. That would be retro enough (ghastly term) as to be *in* fashion, and that would never do.

Dr Stanley Ward was a research scientist in the Department of Physiology at the University of Toronto—promoted to Professor Emeritus on his sixty-fifth birthday, and very proud of it—specializing in human energy consumption. He was the grey eminence of a team of researchers whose aim was a detailed characterization and modeling of the mechanisms of energy use in the body, and their accurate measurement. The chemical paths of energy consumption in the human body are enormously complicated, and it has been the holy grail of his branch of physiology not just to understand them, but to measure them with greatest accuracy. His team had worked for nearly a decade on this problem, and was now close to the goal of monitoring energy consumption in a human being to the finest possible degree and, of greatest interest, actually watching it in real time. Before the advent of remote electronic sensors, imaging systems and, of course, extremely fast computing power this aspiration was considered impossible.

Today's meeting would be extremely important. The results of their work were almost ready for publication and the team meeting today would lay out the agenda for submission of a paper to one of the leading journals in the field. Time was of essence as there were others elsewhere on the globe engaged in the same race. Stan had some misgivings; there were anomalous results that needed to be discussed before a final decision was made. As a team member he had but one vote, and the other five were pressuring to publish. Well, we would see. Perhaps his Emeritus position and natural predisposition for caution would count for something.

He emerged from the subway station at Queen's Park, old leather briefcase under his arm, and was quickly bathed in early May sunshine. The green of the trees played fine music with the pink sandstone of the Ontario Legislature as he strode quickly up the diagonal path to the entrance of the Medical Sciences Building, a concrete slab structure from the 1960s that had, in that lost architectural wasteland, surprisingly maintained some of its presence. It wasn't attractive, but by now it had grown into its place, and to the younger generation it simply 'was'.

The labs of the Physiology Department were on the third floor. Stan emerged from the elevator and met Makharam Khan the team member responsible for the electronics of the project. Khan wasn't a physiologist; he had devoted his university career in San Diego to the finer arts of electrical engineering and now, in his mid-30s, was their expert on all things to do with sensors, monitors and software. He had a finely boned face the colour of a medium roast with a dash of half-and-half, framed by large prominent ears, a thin well trimmed moustache, and black curly hair which he kept short. His gold/brown eyes examined the world from an alert and enquiring intellect.

"Hi!" greeted Khan cheerily in an accent of pure Southern California. "All set for the great decision?"

"Good to see you. How was your weekend?" replied Stan, avoiding direct mention of the impending issue.

"Great, great. Here..." as he ushered Stan ahead of him into the office of the Chief of Department, Professor Ken Livermore, who was to chair the meeting. It was a small enough space for six people, and the piles of journals, ring binders and old fashioned computer print-outs that occupied much of the floor space didn't help. Although it is a mark of academic achievement to have shelves of journals and books, scatterings of papers, and certificates in wonky frames on the wall, increasingly these days such signs speak of the passing of time, as so much is now available on the Web, and so much can be compressed into computer files, that hard copies are no longer needed. The filing cabinet will soon be relegated to the scrapheap; an icon of past times.

Stan always arrived early to whatever engagement he was invited to. His wife Sandra professed to be annoyed with his—as she called it—anal-retentive over punctuality, but he stood by it. Many was the party they had attended to find the hostess with her make-up half on and the man of the house still laying out wine glasses. He just didn't understand the concept of fashionably late.

But the room was already full, a sign of the impending excitement. Once Khan had taken his seat on the remaining five-wheeled swivel chair, and Stan had eased down into the one softer chair in the room—as befitted his status—the whole team was assembled. Livermore sat behind a desk piled with papers, with post-doc student Robin Tokarek and biochemist Celia Wong on his left. John Rolfe, a specialist in sports medicine from the Toronto General Hospital, perching on a chair near the door, completed the team.

Coffee, the essential meeting lubricant, was dispensed by Ken Livermore, delaying the meeting agonizingly by enquiring solicitously after their preferences for cream, milk or sugar, and carefully pouring and spooning same ponderously into a mismatched set of mugs brought in from beside the sink in the lab. This making of coffee in-house represented a last bastion against the pernicious invasion of Starbucks.

"Okay, let's roll," began Livermore, sipping from a faded blue Toronto Maple Leafs mug. "Good to see you all here. I think we can all agree that we're ready to go ahead and submit, but let's hear views from all of you first. Robin?"

"No question. Maggini in Milan is working along the same lines. Who knows how far he's got?"

"Yeah," piped up John Rolfe. "Met him in Tampa at the conference in September. He clammed up, but he's scary close."

"Same with Wu Song and Davis. Their paper in Seattle had me wondering. Right Celia?"

"No question. They've got a handle on a lot of the interface between biochemical modeling and electronic monitoring. Don't know if they're as good as us with the electronics..." with a smile at Makharam Khan (there was something going on there) "...but they're a smart bunch."

"So," continued Livermore. "Are we agreed that we have to move this thing along? Yes, Stan?"

"Well, I am a little concerned about the anomalous data from Subject 27. You know that was my pet idea, and though the choice of subject did buck the trend, we all agree that the numbers simply don't add up."

Subjects for the team's experiments were drawn from the student population. It has been a university tradition of long-standing that the experimental subjects most fitted for physiological research were athletes. They were young, in fine physical condition, and were willing to sweat for hours on treadmills and exercise bikes for the measly stipend that the lab's grant could afford. It paid for pizza, with perhaps a little left over for books. Subject 27 had been a departure. It was funny how it came about; while Stan and his wife were attending a pub performance by a Celtic fiddler, he realized that expending vast amounts of energy in some pursuit was by no means confined to sports, and had invited the musician to be run through their process. And at the end of the first session the results had been equivocal enough that a repeat was necessary. Again, the numbers didn't make sense.

"Sure, it's anomalous data," said Livermore, "and we should try to nail it down, but the time factor is critical."

"I vote we drop the data from the set," suggested John Rolfe. "We can always state in the preamble that our experimental subject set is athletes. And even state in the conclusions that we're doing further refining. 'S only the truth."

Rolfe had a predisposition to athletes as he had been sports medicine consultant to the Leafs, the Raptors and the Argos. He knew his athletes.

"You can't exclude data because you don't like 'em," rumbled Stan. This was going in the wrong direction.

"No, no, no, I don't think we'd even suggest that, Stan," replied Livermore. "I guess you find the optics problematic?"

Stan concealed his cringing reaction to this dreadful abortion of language behind a neutral mask. At least, he hoped he had. Good God, the Hubble Space Telescope had problematic optics.

"I don't think it looks good, if that's what you mean."

"Yes, well, I can see where you're coming from." (Stan resisted the urge to peer sarcastically over his shoulder) "It's just that this one single exception needs more work, and I don't think we have the time to hold up publication."

"Perhaps a week or two more?" suggested the Emeritus. "Just to be sure."

"I don't think you need to worry, Stan," put in Makharam Khan. "I don't think it's a physiological anomaly. I've been banging my head against this as well. I'm now convinced it's interference in our sensors and monitoring rig-up."

"Interference how?" asked Livermore.

"It may be acoustic. I know we screen the whole apparatus from electromagnetic radiation, but it may be that we're picking up the sound waves in one of our components as an electrical signal. That would really screw things up."

"Could that happen, do you think?"

"Absolutely! How do think the pick-up on an electric guitar works? Vibration directly above an electromagnet and, bingo! I'm thinking of the small impedance coils on some of our circuit boards."

"Well, that would certainly explain a lot," sighed Livermore in a relieved tone. "And, of course, the production of music is the only variable."

"Look Makharam," Stan asked. "Would it be possible to nail this down, just to put my mind at rest? If the data are tainted then, sure, we can justifiably exclude them."

"Yeah, sure. I'm almost a hundred percent certain, but no harm in running through it again."

"So!" Livermore rubbed his hands together and swiveled his gaze over his colleagues. "We finish work on the paper and submit!"

"Once we are sure of the source of problems in Subject 27," reminded Stan gently.

"Yes, yes, of course! We'll deal with that and, I don't doubt, exclude those data. Now, let's get down to details..."

Discussion centered on the minutiae of the publication process. Where to publish was always a key issue, and these days with internet journals springing up regularly the choice was difficult. They mooted the American Physiological Society's *Journal of Applied Physiology*, the *Journal of Physiological Sciences* or the *Journal of Exercise Physiology*, but decided to shoot higher and submit to *Nature* or *Science*, as the research was indeed of world-class importance.

The meeting ended on a high note. Although not one of them would dare to express it, there was huge potential for a Nobel Prize in their research. What the team had achieved here at the

University of Toronto was—to use a phrase that would have had Professor Emeritus Stanley Ward gnashing his teeth in anguish—paradigm changing.

Stan had a modest and rather lonely lunch in the cafeteria of the Medical Sciences Building then set off for his walk round King's College Circle and Hart House, a routine of long standing. There was a gentle breeze this lovely May day, and some researchers, still in white lab coats, had brought lunch to eat out on the grass. Two kite enthusiasts had their latest creations floating high above the field, green and red specks against flawless blue. A Frisbee swung through the air in effortless arcs.

He was not happy.

Intuition plays a large part in research. It's nothing mystical or magical or arcane; there's a lot of supernatural rubbish talked about intuition and instinct, especially by those who know the meaning of neither word. No, he thought, it's simply based in experience and wide-ranging attention to a host of allied, interconnected, clamoring details. The mind ranges wide all unbidden, picking up a hint here, a soupçon there, a little vibration somewhere else. Stan's eclectic tastes and omnivorous absorption of information over a long career in academia had supplied his mind with a doubting quality that had stood him in good stead on many occasions. In him it came out as caution.

Frankly, he smelt a rat. He didn't like Khan's glib assurance that what he was seeing was merely an electronic artifact, but at first he couldn't put his finger on why. It just didn't feel right. Then, as he rounded Hart House Circle and passed the old observatory at the furthest point of his customary route, the answer came to him

Obvious! Makharam was talking about acoustic pick-up, but surely any sound in the lab would interfere if that was the case. There was the hum of the computer cooling fans and the sound of the exercise bike, and they didn't have a policy of working in silence anyway. So any noise could be picked up; it didn't have to be musical. Clearly, the system wasn't sensitive to sound waves.

And the way the project was now unfolding, the paper would be submitted to the publisher before Khan could get around to sorting out the bugs he guessed were in the system. And Stan now believed there weren't any. Nothing would be found to account for the discrepancy.

Where was Subject 27 then?

No, he was not happy.

A couple of weeks after the excitement of Sir Arthur Compton's visit it was business as usual for the East Gladstone Symphony Orchestra. This morning they had to get to grips with Bruckner's Symphony Number Eight in C minor, and as always it was hard slogging.

At one juncture a halt was called when at least half the players misread a tempo direction.

"Are you quite incapable of following the baton?" the Maestro yelled.

"Yeah, floor-door-window-ceiling," came a mutter from one brass player to another.

"Perhaps, Mr Mah," came the acid response from the podium, "you would choose to share your observations with the rest of your colleagues?"

"I just said I could understand your feeling."

The stare could have sliced sheet metal.

And so, after three endless hours of the *Apocalyptic* (highly appropriate, most thought)—with the Maestro stopping and starting, then stopping again, shouting contrary instructions and providing opaque advice to players whose instruments he wouldn't even know which end to blow in—they paused for the lunch break. Rehearsals were always a damned sight harder than the concerts. The Maestro could howl and rage after a concert, criticizing their playing *ipso facto*, but he could hardly stop in the middle. In a rehearsal, of course, he could stop as often as he wished. And he did.

A core group of players, who usually hung together, sat around a long table in the concert hall cafeteria. There was a lovely view over the lake, and a row of doors led out onto a patio where, in good weather, there were chairs and tables with umbrellas. There wasn't time to go further in search of food, but some wiser souls had brought packed lunches that they ate on the patio outside. These less prepared members sat around the table and nibbled at thick white bread with thin fillings wrapped in superfluous plastic. Kate Heinrichs had made a lunch, but sat indoors with the others because she liked to be near Jonathan.

"Hey," observed Graham Swann, second oboe, "have you been reading about these maestros who keep dropping down dead?"

It was a sensitive issue because their previous maestro had done just that only a year earlier.

"Wish ours would," replied Steve Mah, the first trombone and unofficial jester to the group, and one to whom 'subtle' was a foreign word. Bad taste in spades, but there was general laughter anyway; this group were the ones more often criticized than praised, and they tended to hold a united front against their present leader.

"Yeah, but listen," continued Swann. "There really is something funny going on here. They're dropping like flies!"

"I don't think so," replied Pete Lalonde, the younger of the two clarinetists and the group's titular intellectual. "It's a common misconstruction of social dynamics..."

"Ooh, big words!" piped up Mah.

"Big words, big concepts, dickhead. Shut up and listen and you might learn something. Look, what happens is this: two or three incidents can either be harbingers or aberrations. In other words, these incidents can lead to a pattern or they can be just a blip, a coincidence. Okay? Now, human psychology—and the desire to sell news—ensures that the balance is tipped in favour of a pattern. People crave patterns; it's in our nature. Here's a good example: severe weather phenomena. Have there been more severe weather phenomena in the last, say, ten years or so? Everyone, judging by media coverage, would say absolutely yes."

"You're not a climate change denier, are you?" asked Mah. "'cos if you are..."

"Of course I'm not! What do you take me for?"

"Well, I was just wondering 'cos you said..."

"The point I am trying to get across is, *regardless* of whether weather (yes, *thank you* Steve) is more severe, the reporting is biased towards the pattern. So, weather events that would otherwise go unreported get coverage. Who gave a hoot years ago at mudslides in Brazil? Do you see what I'm saying?"

"So, this is a normal trend? Just coincidence?" asked Kate.

"Look," replied Lalonde. "How many thousands of orchestra leaders are there worldwide? Symphony orchestras, baroque groups, ballet and opera companies, you name it. A huge number. Among all those thousands of conductors, how many are in middle or later middle age? Most, because it takes that long to get there. And they're all in high pressure jobs where the emotions run wild. Rehearsals—we all know what *that's* like!—concerts, public appearances. So, they are therefore much more likely to collapse on the job, where the pressure's intense, than sitting in an easy chair going over scores with a blue pencil."

"When you put it that way," observed Kate, "it does make sense."

"See," continued Lalonde, "it's the journalists who are latching onto these things and skewing our perceptions."

"Like when our old guy—yeah, I know, dodgy subject, eh—died in harness?" asked Mah. "Natural causes. Just a plain heart attack."

"Of course. Well, look at it from any other perspective, for Christ's sake. If it's not a normal, natural occurrence, then what the hell could it be?"

"It's a vile plot by Al Qaeda!" chuckled Mah, rubbing his hands together. "Heh, heh, heh."

"Yeah, right Steve," put in someone else. "That's the other part of the human equation, isn't it? The need for mystery and the inexplicable. Maybe it's a death zapper from a UFO?"

"Exactly!" concluded Lalonde as he bit into his sandwich. "Jush wash... just watch and you'll see it fade away as the press gets bored with it. If you want my opinion, what the orchestras need to do is provide healthcare counseling for these people. It's an ageing demographic and they need to look after themselves."

With this pronouncement the subject was considered closed.

In fact, unbeknownst to the colleagues around the table, maestros around the world were not just falling down dead; the symptoms were now becoming much more severe.

Jonathan sat quietly and ate his lunch. Although no one said it, they all knew the razzing he took from one certain trumpeter, and they knew it was unfair. A couple of them had even taken the bugger aside and told him to cool it, but alcohol usually got the better of him. Or, the worst. They were all well aware that the argument that preceded the old guy's attack was entirely coincidental.

Just bad luck to be in the wrong place at the wrong time.

In cities around the world police forces were beginning to pay attention, although it was newspaper and Web journalists who first put two and two together. Even cursory examination of the corpses had revealed far more than just fatal cardiac conditions, and it only took one journalist to report on the mysterious nature of one death to begin a train of speculation. Once the true symptoms were known, the theory based on the statistical probability of the deaths on the job being due to natural causes was immediately blown away. And, now the news was out, police forces took up the challenge and began both to investigate incidents more thoroughly and to revisit coroners' inquests and post-mortem reports.

Because this was a world-wide phenomenon the headquarters of Interpol in the southern French town of Lyon became the coordinating body. These were not believed to be random occurrences; they were now regarded as targeted attacks and were treated as such. How the attacks were coordinated and carried out, how the targets were chosen, and what individual or organization was behind them, all remained mysterious. There seemed to be no pattern to the phenomenon whatsoever, and the only certain factor was that the victims were always classical music conductors. The mechanism for the attacks induced wild speculation, and although Interpol had nothing concrete to offer, the secret organizations of a number of countries became more than a little interested.

Absurd theories abounded, fed by the news media and the bloggers and twitters, and it is hardly surprising that Al Qaeda was accorded the greater part of the credit. Quite why a middle-Eastern terrorist organization would have such a down on the likes of Mozart, Beethoven and Dvorak was never truly analyzed. Besides, several of the countries targeted had explicitly eschewed jumping on the Bush/Blair bandwagon when Iraq was invaded. It made no sense at all.

Over the following months Interpol began work on a database, which it shared with the law-enforcement agencies of its 190 member countries, but no pattern appeared to emerge. From the perspective of the compilers, and with the data they had available, the attacks would continue to appear random. It is unlikely that analysis of the concert programs on the days the attacks took place could have provided any further insight.

Serenade in D Major

A rehearsal of Mozart one Tuesday morning became a grueling session that really shouldn't have been grueling at all. They were going over the *Haffner Serenade*, which features some spectacular solo violin writing, especially in the rondo, and that was where the problem lay. Had the Maestro had any say in the matter he would not have chosen the piece—or any work that featured the violin in any kind of prominence unless he was soloist —but the matter was out of his hands by the time the concert schedule had been established. Stefan Kulikofski, as first violin, was *de facto* the soloist, and so a bitter one-sided contest took place while the remaining 79 musicians sat back as bored onlookers.

It was long, dragging days like this that made them all wonder quite why a seat in a symphony orchestra had seemed such a great goal.

After rehearsal the musicians stood around in groups chatting lightly before picking up their instrument cases and going their separate ways. There were no more sessions until Friday, which was a refreshing change from an often hectic schedule. Jonathan and Kate drifted together as they usually did, feeding the rumour mill, which relished in spreading the word that they were actually much more of an item than they really were.

"It's a bugger," Kate was saying. "My landlord's going to be in my place all evening fixing the wiring. He's been planning it for ever, and now he's got some electrician who can only do the job tonight. Would you believe it? So, I'll have to wander the streets like a waif until about eleven. Maybe I'll hang around the bus station," she concluded mischievously, carefully eyeing his reaction.

Of course, he had to rise to the occasion, as she knew he would. Ever planning for the future, she knew she would have to invent some plausible story about the wiring. There was screw-all wrong with it, but she hadn't been able to think of anything else. Ooh, I am bad. Sometimes I am so cross with myself.

"Well, you know... You... you could always drop round my place. I mean, I don't want to... It's... it's not great, but it is supplied with bottles and glasses..."

She hugged herself with glee, but nothing showed in either

her expression or her demeanor.

Jonathan kicked himself. Why rise to the bait; what possessed him to let her get closer? This was getting out of hand. He had never been this beguiled; not since...

They agreed to meet outside the concert hall at seven o'clock. Jonathan lived in a small lower floor apartment in a divided townhouse. It wasn't far for them to walk from the centre of town. They strolled side by side in the warm June evening, close but not touching, and talked of all the little incidents of their day; the string that broke at a key moment, the stupid practical jokes of the trombone section, the way the Maestro consistently failed to explain what he wanted in terms most of them could grasp.

Jonathan unlocked the door and swung it wide with arm extended so Kate could enter first. He knew his place wasn't much to boast about, but he really didn't need all that much in home comforts, and his personal possessions were limited. Accumulated personal possessions spoke of past lives, and there was little in his past that really needed touchstones. So she would see a rather barren landscape.

"Come in, come in. Here, give me your coat. There's a row of coat hooks behind the door. Not much space to move. You can put your shoes here by air vent. Let me..."

"Okay, okay," she interrupted. "I can manage." Boy, he's wound-up. Nothing to be nervous about; it's only little me.

The tiny foyer led directly into a small living room. She looked around her as she shucked off her shoes and hung up her coat. A boarded-over fireplace with a mantel, on which were a couple of framed photographs (probably his grandparents) and an MP3 player in its dock. An inkjet printer sat where the fire irons would have been. There was a framed print of St Paul's Cathedral in London on one wall, some old and well thumbed books on a shelf, and an ancient oboe lying on the coffee table. No television. His beloved reed-making tools, which he had told Kate he regarded as the oldest friends he had, lay on a side table. Tatty chesterfield, low coffee table, wooden chair; nothing much else that hadn't been bought at IKEA or Home Hardware.

"A bit Spartan, I'm afraid. I am a man of few and simple needs," he said self mockingly, arms embracing the bareness.

Knocking himself down, thought Kate, is something that I keep noticing about him. It's not modesty; look at the way he deals with the Maestro.

"Drink? Would you like something to drink? I've got some

wine, white and red, and there's beer too, if you like. Coffee? Or tea...

"Stop!" She placed her hand gently on his forearm. "Chill out. Look, I'm not the bloody Queen of England. I'm just little Kate Heinrichs from the old EGO. But if you would like to bring me a glass of red wine, kind sir, you will make me your friend for ever."

She looked around her as he darted away and clinked and clattered at the drinks in the small attached kitchen. She heard the *squoink* of the cork being drawn. Music to her ears. It pained her heart to see the sparseness of his life. Who *was* this man? She had chatted with him at parties, at rehearsals and in the green room, but she still knew next to nothing. Well, she thought, here I am in the lion's den, so let's see if we can draw some thorns.

"One glass of red wine, as the lady ordered!" He brought the bottle into the room, juggling two glasses in one hand, and placed it on the coffee table beside the oboe. That's a good sign, thought Kate, there will be top-ups. When he handed her the glass his hand shook slightly. There was a short pause as they both sampled their wine. It lengthened.

"That's a nice looking instrument," said Kate, pointing to the oboe on the coffee table. "May I pick it up?"

"Of course. It's... It's a tool, not a precious object to be handled with kid gloves. Here...," and he handed it to her.

"What's its story?" She clicked some of the keys.

"It's a Boehm-system instrument. Boehm, yes, that's... that's a maker who revolutionized keywork in the 19th century. This one was made by Triébert in Paris; 1860 or so."

"And it plays?"

"Oh, yes. It's lovely. It's in the old French orchestral pitch and the tone is kind of bottom-heavy—bit shrill in the upper register really—but I like because it's a sort of touchstone. Know what I mean?"

"Yeah, my best fiddle's quite old. Well, 19th century French—Cremona knock-off—although it's seen a lot and it just feels right."

"Same with this. Can't use it in the orchestra of course." He laughed, a rare occurrence with him, thought Kate, but nice when it comes. "Can you imagine the Maestro working with historic temperaments? Holy shit, I think he'd burst into flames first!"

"Yeah, he absolutely loathes the Early Music Movement. Calls 'em jobbing amateurs. Tafelmusik in particular."

"It's hard enough for him to adjust to orchestras that tune to A four forty-two. Like when he was in Toronto that time."

"Yeah, two Hertz and he was all pissed off!"

They both laughed at this, and Kate felt the first stirrings of climate change in the room. The wine was going down very nicely.

"So, where did you get it?" she asked, handing the oboe back.

"I found it years ago in a junk shop in London. I'm not all that interested in historic instruments but it just caught my fancy. I was attending a conference on microwave transmiss..."

Suddenly he reddened and his eyes shifted away.

"Microwave transmission? That doesn't sound very musical!"

"No, well... Yeah... Another life... Hey, your glass needs topping up." It didn't. "Look," he continued, nearly filling her glass to the brim, "I've been meaning to ask you, how did you get the job in the EGO? How long have you been with them anyway?"

Wow, thought Kate, that was a pretty tight U-turn. We're on two wheels here. Okay, go with the flow. Let's trot out the old Heinrichs life history and see if he'll chill out and reciprocate.

"I was born in Saskatchewan. Dad and Mum are farmers, wheat mostly. It's a little place near Kindersley. You've probably never heard of it; about a million miles north of Swift Current."

"Heinrichs?"

"Yeah, Germans. From 'way back. Quite a lot of Mennonites out that way. Some German-speaking Russians too."

"You have brothers, sisters?"

"One older brother, Carl. He's at the University of Victoria now, doing poly-sci. Dad thinks he'll take over the farm, but I don't see it any time soon."

"Is he musical?"

"Not passionate, like me, but talented, yes," she thought a moment, twirling her glass. "I think that's the difference between us. He never really worked hard at anything, whereas I worked my butt off. I always loved music when I was a kid, and then my uncle—they have the next lot west of us—gave me an old fiddle of his dad's, my Grampa's. I was only six going on seven. It was an Eaton's Catalogue factory fiddle from Czechoslovakia, with the label that said," here she laughed out loud, remembering in detail, "Antonius Stradivarius Cremonensis Faciebat Anno 1721."

He laughed too; a laugh of relief at the blessed change in direction of the conversation. "You've remembered the label from all those years ago!"

"Yeah, well, kids at that age it's half fantasy really, isn't? I used to sit in my bedroom, not playing all the time but just looking at it, reading the label again and again, and dreaming. Making mystical places and populating them with mystical people."

They sipped their glasses while she paused in thought, childhood scenes playing in video behind her eyes; tiny, at the wrong end of the telescope.

"Y'know," she continued, "it even *smelt* old. It was musty, dusty inside, and when I put my nose right down to the F-holes I could breathe history into my brain. Violins are magic!"

"When did you find out it wasn't a Strad?" he asked bringing her to earth with a thump.

"No, it didn't work that way. I never heard about the Great Stradivarius until much later—I was pretty isolated out there in the prairies—so there was no 'Oh, shit, there's no such person as Santa Claus' moment."

"So that five buck fiddle started you playing?"

"Yep. Never looked back. I had the music in me. Grandad played the fiddle for dances, Mum's a lovely singer. Came naturally. Even as a tiny kid, tuning that fiddle; I didn't have to be shown. It was there. There's pictures of me with that great big thing under my chin. It was full-size, you see. I had a hell of a job getting my little hand around the neck. My wrist used to ache so, but I couldn't stop. When they realized that I was for real they bought me a small one; what they call quarter-size, although it isn't really. Wish I knew what happened to that old fiddle..."

"Maybe it's still at home somewhere?"

"Oh, I do hope so! I'll look in the attic next time I'm back visiting. Christmas maybe. It's not worth anything, but it's so full of memories."

"So where did you study music?" he asked, keeping her front and center.

"I was lucky that our school had a good music program. It's crappy the way so few schools do. Then, after high school I went to the University of Saskatchewan in Saskatoon. This was marvelous because not only did they have a great program, they also had a quartet of classic Cremonas donated by a collector. Terrific exposure. Then, after that, I got accepted to the Conservatory in Toronto, and the rest, as they say, is history."

"Do you like it here in East Gladstone, or is it just a stop on the road?"

"Look, Jonathan, I'll be straight with you. (Top me up will you? Thanks.) I know how good I am, but I also know my limitations. To have got a chair—*any* chair—in a symphony orchestra is, for me, the dream come true. Sure, it's a small outfit in a small town, but that's fine by me. So while I've got it, I'll enjoy it to the full. Tomorrow can wait in the wings."

So, that's my story in précis, she thought, leaving out the boyfriends who never quite achieved the harmony she ached for. Let's see where we can go from here. But before she could attempt to rewind to the bit about microwave transmission, he had launched into a detailed dissertation on the great Cremona violins, the mythology that surrounds them, the 19th century predisposition for romantic associations, and the obscene prices they fetched on the market.

"Yes, it's true," she put it at one point. "The guys who own those things are in one of the most exclusive clubs on the planet. Too rich for my poor little taste."

There was much she disagreed with, and also much common ground, so the conversation was lively. The bottle emptied and another appeared, and the evening wore away very pleasantly enough, but her heart pained in unfulfillment. It was not at a physical level at all; not in the slightest. The closeness she ached for was a psychic one. She ached because she knew that he was in anguish in some mysterious way. But there was a barrier, a distance, she desperately wanted to cross. She knew that this had to be accomplished, because they simply couldn't keep on as they were. You get to a point of no return, then you find a wall as high as the sky in front of you, blotting out the light, and there's nowhere to go. You can't go back; you can't go forward. She cried inside in that place that nobody can ever see.

"It's been a lovely evening. Thank you so much for entertaining me," she smiled brightly as he helped her on with her coat.

"I've really enjoyed this. I hope the electrician is done."

"Electrician? Oh, yes, the electrician. Bound to be."

She placed her arms on his shoulders, reached up and gently, softly pecked his cheek. The she was gone.

He stood in the centre of the living room, empty wine glass twirling in his fingers, the place where she had placed her lips still radiating pleasure. He felt two powerful poles ripping him apart.

'Deaths of Maestros a Worrying Trend' read Stan Ward in his *Toronto Star* while enjoying a slow Saturday morning cup of tea with his wife Sandra at the breakfast table. He subscribed to a wide range of newspapers—some of which were spread out on the table in front of him—because he wanted his news from as many perspectives as possible. Even the most right-wing news sheets were useful; it's always good to get an inside look at the enemy's thinking. He enhanced this old fashioned way of keeping up to date with global events by surfing the news on the Web; so he felt he had it covered.

The dining room in the Ward's house in the Toronto Beach area faced east in an extension they had built onto the back of the 1930s structure. The house had been built when this area was really on the outskirts of the town, and they had bought it back in the 1970s when such places could be afforded on university salaries. Their son had long since flown, so they had room and to spare for pastime activities if only there was time to pursue them. There were windows on three sides of the dining room, so the small but carefully planted backyard, half fruit and vegetables and half flowers, made a panoramic backdrop to a slow morning. Striped shades above the windows kept the room relatively cool as the sun climbed to its summer maximum.

It seemed that, sifting through the journalistic hyperbole of this article, maestros were dying at the podium in numbers that challenged statistics. Local colour was provided by reporting the death of a local orchestra leader about a year ago. The term 'local' is very contextual; East Gladstone was about two hours north of Toronto and therefore virtually in its backyard. The newspaper had printed a picture of the maestro standing in front of his orchestra, and it was only by coincidence (although Stan detested ascribing coincidence to turning points in history, which retrospect would assign to this moment) that he noticed a face among the musicians; a fortyish looking feller with an oboe. Where have I seen that guy before? What's ringing a bell with me here? The wide-sweeping searchlight that his brain employed had picked up a shadow out at sea.

"Look at this, Sandra," he said to his wife as he passed the newspaper over.

"What, maestros dying? Should have thought there were plenty of them!" she replied.

She still had the gentle accent of the Hebrides, where she grown up before her family had moved to Canada in her teens;

not the strong accent of the populated strip between Glasgow, Edinburgh and Dundee, but one with a lilt and sibilance. Sandra Ward was a no-nonsense academic with a thin but well modeled face and, like her husband, an intriguing glint in her eye. Her fair hair, now graying to silver, was cut short, and she sported very little make-up. She focused on the newspaper through her bifocals and scanned the text.

"No, me dear," he replied. "I'm not talking about the global supply of the commodity. It's this guy here. Where have I seen him before?"

"Doesn't strike a chord with me. Perhaps a student?" she said, studying the grainy face in the picture.

"You're right! Got it! My goodness, what a fine brain I have!"

Sandra sniffed and returned her attention to her *Globe and Mail.*

"Rycroft! Jonathan Rycroft. That's the feller. He was a brilliant sciences student. So brilliant that I thought he'd make a damn fine physiologist. But he had other ideas; went on to do physics. And now he's a musician... How very interesting."

"Interesting, how? Do pour me another cup; I don't know why you insist on keeping the pot down at your end."

"It's this business I have with the anomalous results," he replied as he poured her tea and added just the right amount of milk.

He discussed his experimental work with his wife as a routine of long standing. It is surprising to some people how discussing even abstruse concepts with an outsider to the field can clarify and focus thought. She did the same with him in her profession of anthropology. She was aware of the intriguing results his team had come across, and was also appraised of the lack of enthusiasm his colleagues had about Stan's pursuit of the phenomena.

"Well," he continued. "You know, since finding this thing I've felt the need for someone who wasn't just a musician, but also had a fine scientific mind. I think I may have found my boy!"

"Boy? He's forty if he's a day!"

"He was one of my students, my dear. He will always be a boy."

"Why him? Why not just have someone play the music, like the Irish guy? My God, he was fun, wasn't he?"

"I don't know. But if this thing is real—and I'm damned convinced it is—I'd want someone whose brain I could use. It's that intuition thing with me, although I detest the glib way it's used to explain or justify pure guesses."

"Yes, I know you do, dear." She was all too aware of his views on intuition.

"But, you know how a thing irritates you, and can't put your finger on why? Well, the irritation has evaporated, so I know I'm on the right track."

"So, get in touch with him," she replied and applied herself to a rapidly cooling cup of English Breakfast.

So Stan sat down at the computer and did a Google search for the East Gladstone Symphony Orchestra. Up popped the index web page with the same photo he had seen in the *Star*. There were hot buttons for sections on the history of the orchestra, their calendar of concerts for the year, a flamboyant spread on their maestro, and even a discography. There was no list of contacts for the orchestra members—he hardly expected one—but there was a Contact Us link, which he clicked. He found he could book tickets through the link, but naught else. What to do? He Googled Jonathan Rycroft and found there were a great many of them, one of whom had published several works on microwave energy transmission. That might be his boy, but it hardly helped; it was a link to an on-line physics journal that carried the texts of his publications. Then he tried Jonathan Rycroft plus East Gladstone, and bingo! One single entry. It was Rycroft's blog, for the most part containing discussions about reed-making, oboe literature, and concert experiences. There was, however, a contact e-mail.

'Hello. I'm a researcher in physiology at U of T. I would very much like to contact you. Might I have your phone number? Stan Ward.'

He clicked send and went back to his newspapers.

The reply with a mobile phone number but no other text came back the following day.

It was a break in rehearsal and Kate was chatting with Liz Straker, one of the cellists she often practiced with. Liz was a few years older than Kate; they had known each other before East Gladstone and they often played together, either at Kate's place or her house around the lake. She and Kate had become close confidants. Kate knew more about Liz's love life than the bounds of friendship normally demand, although she herself had few secrets that she really wanted to share.

Liz had her cello across her lap and was peering into the F-holes and gently tapping the top with her knuckles.

"It's got a slight buzz. Listen." She swung the cello easily between her splayed knees and bowed a few notes.

Kate leaned forward. "Again?" She played a couple of random measures.

"Yes, I can hear it. It's very faint and intermittent, but it's there."

"Oh, my poor old cello," lamented Liz. "It'll have to go in for check-up."

"I think you've got a slightly loose glue joint somewhere. Bass bar maybe?"

"Guess so. I'll have to send it to Toronto. My boyfriend can take it on the bus; he's going down tomorrow night." She paused and eyed Kate mischievously. "He went down last night too!"

"What, to Toronto?"

"No, silly... Anyway, I'll have to use my back-up for the concert tonight."

"Think our fearless leader will mind?" Their control freak of a maestro had once discovered one of his musicians playing upon what he considered to be an inferior instrument, and had gone ape shit.

"It's none of his darned business. Anyway, why would I tell him?" She laid the cello down, straightened her skirt and gently pushed a strand of hair out of her eyes. "Another one yesterday. Did you see it on the news?"

"Yes. They're speculating it's some sort of Unabomber who's targeting maestros."

"Well, what other explanation *could* there be? But it's worldwide and random. Doesn't make sense." Their eyes met and each knew what the other was thinking: it could happen here.

"Your guy seemed pretty touchy about it the other day," volunteered Liz. They had been sitting around their usual table at a lunch break and speculating on the spate of deaths.

"He's not 'my guy'!" retorted Kate. "We just talk, that's all."

"Oh, right... Just talk... Anyway, he got pretty wound up about it. You know, when he told them all to shut up and talk about something else?"

"I know. There's a lot of stuff he doesn't talk to me about."

"Well, what *does* he talk to you about?" She leaned forward, face taut in anticipation.

"Nothing of any consequence," replied Kate, hiding some pain behind her eyes. "Nothing much at all really."

It was the day after Kate's visit to Jonathan's apartment, around eight thirty in the morning. When he poked his head out of the door there was a hint of rain in the air; he was damned if he was going to bother with a jacket, but as he watched it became more than just a hint. He had decided to do without breakfast as he planned to stop in at Second Cup, so he walked swiftly in the direction of downtown. The rehearsal was at ten, so plenty of time for a large dark roast and one of those nice muffins with all that stuff in them. The phone rang in his pocket as he strode down the tree-lined street. He hauled it out, saw the number was not one he recognized, and slapped it on his ear.

"Hell-o?"

"Is that... is that Jonathan Rycroft?"

"It is."

"This is Stan Ward. I e-mailed you."

"Sure. What can I do for you?"

Jonathan had agonized over that e-mail. Before responding he had decided to look up this Stan Ward on the web and was surprised to find that he knew him. He had taken an undergraduate class with Professor Ward and remembered him trying to promote the joys of a career in physiological research. Perhaps, thought Jonathan, there's a blissful parallel universe where I took his advice. But it isn't this one. He resented this message from the past opening up old memories, so he was reluctant to do anything. In the end he decided that the contact was benign enough, and it had piqued his curiosity.

"Well, look," said Ward, "this is all out of the blue, I'm sure, but you can always Google my name..."

"I already did. And I remember you from 'way back."

"Oh, that's excellent, excellent. It's... it's rather difficult to describe, so let me give you some background. You see..."

"Tell you what," interrupted Jonathan. "I'm just now walking down the street in the rain, so it might be better if you called tonight. I'll be in, and even if I'm not, I'll have the phone with me. Would that be okay?"

"So be it. I will call later, then. Thank you." And he hung up.

This will buy me a little more time, thought Jonathan; he consciously repelled a dark shadow from his previous life. And he might be a nutcase, of course.

At the end of a long and frustrating orchestral day—with the *Haffner Serenade* falling in ruins beneath the baton of their beloved Maestro, and with all the miscommunication, backtracking and imprecations to read the damned music—Jonathan let himself into the apartment and threw himself down on the chesterfield. It was nice to just stop and do nothing for a few minutes. After a while he rose to his feet, took off his jacket and shoes and mooched into the tiny kitchen.

He found some Chinese food in the fridge that he had quite forgotten, and sniffed it to be sure it was safe. He had a pretty good nose for the taint of rottenness, a legacy of bachelor days in university... and here now, of course. He fancied he could detect various aldehydes, ketones and mercaptans, and those molecules with hideous names like cadaverine and putrescine, down to at least parts per million. Better than a gas chromatograph. He had survived this far through some pretty horrendous culinary situations with no hint of food poisoning.

This stuff was still good, no question; probably loaded with preservatives anyway. He slopped it into a bowl and put it into the toaster oven. He didn't have a microwave; loathed them in fact. The toaster oven took longer and you had to keep stirring the stuff with a fork, but that was all right. Where was it he had read that archaeologists doing a social sciences excavation in a garbage dump had found intact wieners in the deepest levels, hardly decayed at all? Maybe an urban legend, but one of those stories that really should be true. Wonder if they tried them, he thought, as he stirred the Orient's legacy to the idle bachelors of the West.

He picked up a wine glass that was upside down in the draining rack, poured a glass of red wine from a half bottle on the kitchen counter, and applied his finely tuned nose to detect hints of acidity. There were some trace acetic radicals resulting from hydrolysis of the alcohol; just enough to bring the wine down to the gustatory level of the entrée.

He brought the meal to the chesterfield in the living room, and was halfway through fine dining Rycroft style when the phone rang. He put down his fork and picked up the phone from the table where he had left it.

"It's Stan Ward from U of T. Do you have some time?"

Jonathan eyed the cooling shrimp and water chestnuts.

"Sure."

"As I said earlier, I know it's out of the blue, but the research I am engaged in is to do with the energy consumption of human physiology."

"Yes, I got as much from the website I Googled, but what's this to do with me?" He took a swig of wine.

"Well, you see, I recognized your face in an article about the dreadful deaths of these maestros."

"No, wait a minute," interrupted Jonathan. "It was nearly a year ago and the poor guy just died of a heart attack. The worst kind of journalism..."

"No, no, I'm sorry. It's got nothing to do with that! Please... it's just that I recognized your face in the picture and thought: that's the man I need."

"Need? Why? What for?" Jonathan was on the point of ending the conversation, but intrigued enough to let the caller have his say. After all, he didn't need to commit to anything.

"You see, we've done work with athletes and have got fantastic results. On an impulse I tested our system on a musician, and the results were... well... equivocal. I thought to repeat the tests on the same subject, but then seeing your picture in the paper led me to thinking that a musician with a fine analytical mind would far better."

"And you don't have access to such generously endowed individuals in the big city?" asked Jonathan with an irony bordering on sarcasm.

"I... I suppose there are, if I only knew how to find them. But, look, without trying to flatter you, I really think you'll be a great asset. I remember you well from your undergraduate time here at U of T."

"So, getting down to details," replied Jonathan, "what exactly are you proposing? After all, I am employed full-time here with the orchestra. I can't entertain any contracts or anything like that."

"Hmm, well, you see, it's more on a volunteer basis. There is a small stipend..."

Ah ha, a drain on my time without recompense, he thought. But still, the idea of engaging in research again was beguiling, as long as it had nothing whatever to do with micro-fucking-waves, of course. The fact was, though his escape into music was deeply necessary—even adding the manic Maestro into the mix—he did miss the days of bending his mind to physical problems.

"So, not just as an experimental subject, then?" he asked.

"No. A musician with an analytical mind; that's what I seek," replied Professor Ward. "There's this anomaly in the data, and I really have to pin it down!"

Jonathan had one day free next week; no rehearsal, no concert and, of course, no social engagements. The remainder of the phone call dealt with times and meeting places.

He was intrigued and also a little frightened.

Oboe Concerto in C Major

Jonathan strode quickly downtown to the East Gladstone bus station, just at the far end of Main Street, carrying his oboe case and a small overnight bag. Bus was the only means of travel for him; he didn't own a car as there was no need in such a small town, and he never visited anybody anywhere else. He remembered the days of Voyageur, the Canadian-owned company that has segued into Grey Line and was subsequently gobbled up by Greyhound, the US-based super company. There was really no difference. It was still the cheapest way to travel across the hugeness of this country, while the rail lines concentrated on inter-city travel, serving fewer and fewer of the outlying areas. East Gladstone had once had a Canadian Pacific station back in the steam days, and trains to Toronto and places further a field had departed on a regular basis. The station building was now an art gallery—thankfully it had survived demolition—and the tracks were just a faint ghost in the tarmac where they had once crossed Main Street. Part of his regular walking route around the edge of the lake was upon the old rail bed. Without the almost complete dissolution of the rail network, he thought, the Trans Canada Trail would still be a twinkle in some visionary's eye.

Buses left for Toronto every two hours. There was an express, which made the trip in a little over two hours and stopped (if he remembered correctly) just once, and the milk-run, which took much longer and wove its way into every small sized town on the route. If you were in no hurry and fancied a look at the inside of small-town Ontario, this would be the way to go. He bought a ticket for the 11:30 A.M. express, hauled out a book and sat down on a bench to wait. He was in the middle of Vikram Seth's *An Equal Music*, and enjoying it immensely, marveling as an insider on the subtlety and nuance of the depiction. He nearly missed the bus.

The bus trip took quite a bit more that two hours. There had been an accident on Highway 400 and traffic had crawled for quite a few kilometers. From the Toronto bus station Jonathan took the subway north to Bloor and Yonge, then eastbound to Main Street where Professor Ward was waiting to meet him. It had been nearly twenty years but neither of them had changed appreciably. Or, at least, so they told themselves. They shook hands slowly, appraising each other.

"We'll walk from here if that's all right with you. It's a bit of a way; twenty minutes or so. The area's called The Beach; you probably know it. Sandra will have lunch ready."

While they walked Jonathan brought Stan Ward up to date on his 'life after science', although he edited it heavily. There were things that he simply didn't wish to share with anybody. There were things that would never go away.

"So, totally turned your back on science, eh?"

"I needed a profound change, that's all." From working on tools that can kill remained unspoken.

"You were damned promising," Ward continued, "when you took my introductory course as an undergrad. You'll remember I tried to lure you into physiology."

"I remember, and I recall being flattered at the time. There I was, in general sciences, not sure where to go, and an eminent researcher was wooing me. But in the end the physical sciences won the tug-o'-war."

"But you could have stayed in sciences, damn it! You were—still are, probably—quite brilliant. I don't understand why you threw it all in."

"Oh, it's... you know... lots of water under the bridge."

Stan Ward knew not to probe more deeply, especially on such slight and recent acquaintance. There was something here that was the lad's business, and no one else's.

"So you took up music? My, you must be one talented cove."

"Didn't really take it up. Never put it down, actually."

"No, I mean professionally. I knew you were a musician back then, of course. You probably won't remember a dance at the Faculty Club where you played the oboe. Hoo, that's a long time ago! But that's how I recognized you from the picture in *The Star*, although it took a bit of brain-hammering to place you."

"I don't remember that gig particularly; there were so many. I always played during my university and post-doc years; pubs, pick-up jazz bands, a few classical gigs if I got really lucky. So, it was a smooth segue."

"But surely, you'd have to be damned good to get a job in a symphony orchestra?"

"I'll tell you, Professor Ward..."

"Oh, for God's sake! My name's Stan."

"Okay... Stan... the audition is a fearful thing. Many applicants fail at auditions, not because they're not good enough, but because of a combination of nerves, luck and their place in the schedule. How much real discrimination do you think the auditors have when they've heard the same damned pieces over and over again all day? So, first off, you get lucky with an early slot. But not too early, because they're dead scared of forming impressions too soon. Secondly, the competition; that's where more luck comes in. Who are you up against? What nervous condition are they in? How prepped are they? Then, I had an edge on the competition because I've been around. Music students often get special coaching on auditions; calming exercises, yoga, meditation, drugs, you name it. Me, I don't suffer from that kind of thing, and it comes out loud and clear when I play."

"Drugs? They take drugs for *auditions*?"

"Not just for auditions; some orchestra players'll pop beta blockers when they're on for big solos. It's very common."

"You're joking!"

"No, not at all. Inderol's the favoured one. If we were athletes half of us'd be banned from competition. More maybe."

"So you pop pills to suppress your adrenalin response? No fight or flight?"

"Well, I don't, but lots do. I can see where they're coming from. You do what you have to do."

"I'll be damned. Learn something new every day." He paused for a few paces. "Still, I suppose all that playing on the side, as it were, kept you in good shape. I mean mentally as well. Gave you confidence?"

"Absolutely! And the final thing, of course: the East Gladstone Symphony Orchestra ain't exactly the New York Philharmonic!"

They laughed as they turned a corner, opened a gate and ascended some steps to the Ward domicile. It was a nice old house in a very comfortable part of town. Jonathan reckoned Stan was sitting on about a million bucks worth of real estate. Stan took his coat to the hall closet and showed him into the living room.

"Here we are my dear; Jonathan here's Sandra. Have a seat here."

"It's nice to meet you," she said, shaking his hand. "Stan speaks highly of you."

Now he remembered that gig. He had met her then, and it was nice to see her and Professor Ward—Stan—together; a side of him that had been utterly hidden. He remembered now, she was also an academic; a few years younger than Stan, with a high position in the Department of Anthropology. He couldn't recall her specialty, if he had ever known it.

He looked around the room. Tall bookshelves dominated the better part of two walls; they were completely full and, at intervals, there were books lying horizontally across the tops of the rows, evidence that alphabetical order was being maintained, but space was at a premium. What wall space was left by the bookcases was hung with oil paintings depicting scenes of water, islands and mountains. The centre of the room was dominated by a gorgeous low table about four feet across, made from a two-inch thick slice of an entire tree trunk, and thickly varnished to bring out the ring structure. Jonathan guessed it was elm, and probably a victim of the Dutch Elm Disease that had transformed so many Ontario towns. Very comfortable easy chairs of an old pattern and a chaise longue completed the furniture.

"Those are nice paintings," he observed. "Are they by a local artist?"

Sandra glowed. "Yes, I suppose so; they're mine. We vacation in the Scottish Isles. Well, they're done from photos, you know; I project the picture onto the canvas and work from there. Cheating a bit, really."

"Not at all," he replied. "Artists have been using the *camera lucida* for centuries. Legitimate way of forming the image, I'd say. But it's what you do with it that counts. And these are excellent!"

She smiled. "You are very kind. There are lots more around the house, and few in the attic. It's a bit of an obsession..."

Lunch was a simple affair; cheese, meats, salads, tea and wide-ranging conversation. Over their tea they talked of the upcoming experiment. It was clear than Stan had no secrets from Sandra. His experimental work and the strange phenomenon he appeared to have discovered intrigued her mightily. Nevertheless, it was Stan who did the lion's share of the talking.

"The reason we're going in during the evening," explained Stan, "is that my colleagues are always re-running what they call the *bona fide* tests of the equipment during the day. They're also busy with writing up the results so far. There's a huge publication in the works."

"So, you run tests on people and get some sort of result, but musicians give you something different? Have I got that right?"

"Yes. There's an anomaly in the data that we—or, perhaps I should say, I—cannot explain."

"So, what I am wondering is, why ever has this anomaly not

been noticed before? Let alone its cause," he added.

"Three reasons: firstly, whoever would think of looking? Aside from me of course," Stan added smugly, ticking that one off on his finger. "Secondly," grabbing another digit, "it's only in the last few years that our recording instrumentation has been sensitive enough, and our computer programs sophisticated enough, to model this behavior. It's a very subtle set of measurements, and a great deal of mathematical computation. We're looking at fractions of a nanojoule of energy. Our lab team at Medical Sciences is leading the world in this field. And, thirdly... Well, you tell me: upon what subjects are such physiological tests conducted?"

"Athletes?"

"Exactly. Athletes. A pure physical equation where energy stored and energy expended can be measured to a nicety. One would hardly expect discrepancies and, of course, none are seen. Why ever would a university lab use music students as guinea pigs? And the very idea of having them playing the fiddle while wired up is ludicrous!"

"So, what brought you to this conclusion?"

"Lateral thinking, my boy. Lateral thinking."

"Thinking outside the box?"

"For God's sake don't use that dreadful hackneyed term, Jonathan! But, yes, the idea is sound. There's too much compartmentalization in science. Too many people working in constrained models and failing to see the bigger picture. And, in particular, there's a clear schism between the sciences and the arts."

"Oh, I can appreciate that. Working on a PhD in electrical engineering while playing the oboe in nightclubs for money. My student friends never could work it out. You're not supposed to be able to do two totally different things well."

"Jack-of-all-trades, master of none," Sandra agreed sipping her tea. "And from elementary school onwards students are streamed using a very simplistic formula: can you or can you not do sums? Doors start closing before they're even into high school, for God's sake."

"Well, educators are coming round to the view that math can be made accessible to all, not just to those to whom it come easily. Look at the Ontario *Scientists in School* program."

"Too late for a whole generation or more who never had that chance," said Stan across steepled fingers.

"Ideally, science and art should be complimentary," said Jonathan. "I used to point out that Einstein was a fine violinist, but my classmates always said 'yeah, but don't forget, he was a genius'."

Stan produced a rare, full-bodied laugh.

"But, it's all very well to talk about lateral thinking," continued Jonathan. "You need some evidence first, surely, and you're not going to get it from hockey players wired up in the lab. How did you first notice this... anomaly?"

"It happened by pure luck really. Well, perhaps not pure luck; *carpe diem* and all that. Y'see, we were in this Irish pub in town —Paddy O'Leary's low down on Spadina, wasn't it my love?— enjoying a Guinness and a lemonade shandy respectively, as is our wont, and they had this extraordinary fiddler. The man used the most phenomenal amount of energy. One doesn't think of musicians expending a great deal of energy, although of course they do."

"Damn right they do!" Memories of many concerts where he had finished wet with sweat and wiped out with exhaustion attested to that.

"Yes. Well, I asked him if he would mind participating in a little experiment back at the lab, and once I had assured him a small stipend was available—a *pourboire* he called it, only in Gaelic I think—he consented."

"*Séisín* is the Gaelic word," put in Sandra.

Jonathan tried to visualize this Gaelic folk fiddler, totally out of his element and playing jigs and reels in a room full of wires, oscilloscopes and computers. The dispassionately viewed absurdity of some scientific endeavour. He stifled a laugh.

"And you know the result," continued Stan. "The music was wonderful—entertained the whole Department of Physiology—but the numbers didn't match up. Not grossly; just very, very marginally. I think, in retrospect, that if the numbers were wildly inaccurate, my colleagues would have sat up and taken notice."

"So, they dismissed these results?"

"Yes and no. Khan—that's the guy who runs the electronics—did some further checks. He thought his gear might be picking up acoustic signals. There was the possible issue of placing screening around induction coils. He enclosed and grounded all the components he considered suspect, but it came to nothing. Still missing energy."

"So they, or I should say all of you, went ahead and prepared to publish?"

"Absolutely. Y'see, there was nothing wrong with the set of

data they used, so the publication was—is, I should say—perfectly valid. I thought it rather foolish and not very scientific not to probe a little further. There are too many experiments conducted in order to validate preconceptions. The data don't fit; throw out the data. So, no musicians anymore. They went back to their reliable Varsity Blues hockey players. But I still use the equipment, and I am determined to try some more music; hence my request to you. I'm not done yet, but the other five think I've shaken a few marbles loose."

"But, again, why me? It seems like a strange impulse."

Stan Ward took a deep breath, appearing to be considering the question carefully and formulating his answer with equal care. He steepled his fingers.

"Well, as I told you, I saw your photograph in the paper, and I remembered you as a fine enquiring mind. And there you were; a musician as well. It just seemed the logical thing to do."

Jonathan felt that this was not a complete answer, but he let it pass.

"But surely, if this anomaly of yours is evidence of *something*, it's potentially enormous!"

"It takes an Alexander Fleming to notice a clear patch on an agar plate, my boy. Nobody had ever measured the energy output of musicians during the creative act to see if there is any net loss of energy. Well, who would? And, before the development of our instrumentation, it just wasn't possible to the required precision anyway." He paused in thought. "You see, it's not the observation, Jonathan, it's what you read into it. What they see and still dismiss an instrumental artifact is what I am taking and extrapolating."

"Well, I'm quite excited to be involved in this!"

"Hold your horses just a little," cautioned Stan. "We don't have enough data yet, and I would hate to get all keyed up for nothing. Slow and steady wins the race."

So the topic was left until their evening visit to the Physiology Lab at U of T.

They entered the Medical Sciences Building at a little after six. That would give them a full two hours before the security system was armed and the guards closed the facility for the night. They ascended to the third floor and entered Stan Ward's lab. A figure in a white lab coat was just leaving.

"Oh, Makharam, you still here?" Stan performed the introductions. "This is Jonathan Rycroft. Jonathan: Makharam Khan, our electronics wizard."

"Just on the way out. Stan's got some more music up his sleeve, eh?" replied Khan, noticing Jonathan's oboe case and surprising him with a west coast US accent at odds with his appearance. "He better be careful he doesn't throw a wrench in the works! Eh, Stan?"

"Just tying up the loose ends, dammit."

Khan eyed him speculatively and bade them both goodnight.

"Bit of an unknown factor," observed Stan. "I wonder about him; quite where his thinking is going..." He shrugged.

It would have been a strange set-up to eyes unfamiliar with sensitive electronic recording, because the whole room was dominated by a large electrostatic cage; basically, an angle iron structure covered in wire mesh—walls, floor and ceiling—which was connected to a secure electrical ground. A door, also of angle iron and wire mesh, opened outwards. All the monitoring and recording equipment was inside the cage, either on tall racks or on a desk-cum-table at the rear. Thus, the entire experimental area was screened from any electromagnetic radiation from the outside.

"This is where we do our work," Stan beamed proudly. "The best equipment that grant money can buy. 'State-of-the-art', to use that vulgar and misleading expression my colleagues are so fond of. Of course, if we had a new building, the electrostatic screening would be built into the walls. Still, can't complain."

Stan began flipping switches, booting up programs and tapping keys. On the rear table were several very large flat-screen monitors on which charts and diagrams appeared in many colours. In the centre of the cage was an exercise bicycle of the kind seen in gyms and spas around the world.

"Come in here," said Stan leaving the cage and leading him to a small office adjacent to the lab, which was almost filled with a desk and two chairs. "You can put your stuff down there."

He took a seat behind the desk, and steepled his fingers in a gesture that Jonathan was becoming very familiar with. Out of nowhere, he had a sudden stab of warmth for the old man as he saw him there, in his milieu, eyes twinkling in anticipation.

"So! In a moment, we're going to wire you up to the machinery and run a test. Takes about fifteen or twenty minutes to gather the data we need. Quite painless; no worry there."

Jonathan took out his oboe, inserted a reed from the little screw-top case, and moistened it with his lips. He had a ritual before playing that never varied, and he needed a few minutes in the office to warm up. He had a new reed, one he had made the day before, but he thought he would feel better if he was ready just to pick up and play when the time came. Talk about feeling weird! No gig he had ever played matched this one for strangeness. A few minutes of scales and both he and the oboe were ready to go.

Stan led Jonathan back into the lab.

"Now just sit yourself down here on the saddle. I want you on the bike so I can check the parameters during normal light exercise. Won't need to exert yourself."

He sat Jonathan on the bike, helped him insert his shoes into the pedal straps, and then had him stand on the pedals while he adjusted the seat column.

"There. Now, I have to hook up all the monitoring equipment. As I said, none of this is painful, none of it's invasive. It's just a lot of electrodes and sensors for all the bodily functions. It's amazing how far remote sensing has come," he continued as he puttered with leads and connections, attaching pads, clips and little self-adhesive metal disks to Jonathan's bared arms.

Even though Jonathan had done his post-Doctoral work in physics, he was still ignorant of the exact functions of most of what he saw. Physiological apparatus was far removed from his sphere of knowledge. He recognized amplifiers and oscilloscopes, and an ink jet printer, of course, and the instruments in vertical racks were obviously powerful computers. Clearly, a wide range of parameters was to be measured and fed into a computer program. The software and computing power, so Stan had told him, were such that an incredibly detailed and accurate figure would be produced of every nano-Joule of energy he expended.

"All right," said Stan Ward as he completed the wiring and began tapping on one of several keyboards. "Here's your basal rate with regular respiration, heart rate and so on. Let's have you pedal for a bit, just to see that every smidgen of energy you consume is measured and accounted for."

Stan came over to the bike and adjusted the pedal pressure to a moderate setting, and Jonathan pedaled for a minute or so.

"There we go! Perfect symmetry. All present and accounted for," he announced from behind the console of monitors. "Y'see, when we've got it right we get this level here with no spikes or glitches." From where he sat on the bike Jonathan couldn't see the screens and probably would have failed to understand an explanation even if given one. He stopped pedaling and awaited instructions.

"Now," said Stan as he came out from behind the monitors, "here's your oboe. Let's have you play something nice and have a look at what comes up on the screen. Anything you fancy."

Jonathan took the oboe in his hands, moistened the reed in his mouth, and began to play the first thing that came into his head, the opening allegro of Mozart's C major concerto, K 314. He had cut his teeth on this one away back and he never tired of it. As he played he tried to exclude the ridiculous image of himself conjured in his mind's eye, sitting on a gym bike, surrounded by gadgets and gizmos, and tootling away. What in hell would Mozart have thought?

He was only a few minutes in when muttered curses came from behind the rack of monitors.

"Damnation! Why am I not seeing it? It's completely bloody balanced!"

Jonathan played on a little longer, constructing in his mind the dialogue with the horns and the counterpoint from the second oboe, when Stan called out.

"Stop, stop! There's something out of whack here. Just give me a minute..."

I suppose it's not unusual to come across glitches when the set-up's this complicated, he thought. I remember some of those microwave rig-ups that were downright infuriating. There were often weeks of checking and trouble-shooting with the technicians and engineers, tempers getting more ragged by the day, before the set-up was ready to do what it was supposed to do. He slammed a mental door; the past was coming too close. Playing with science was bringing it all back.

"Now, everything's re-set. We'll start up again, a-a-nd... now!" And Jonathan began playing again from the top.

"Blast, sod, two damns and a bugger! What *is* going on?"

"What's up?" asked Jonathan, oboe poised in his hands.

"I'm not seeing it. I'm not seeing the discrepancy. It's just not there! You might as well be a bloody hockey player for all the difference it makes! Let's run it again."

They continued to run playing and monitoring sessions—the Mozart was getting a workout—until the door to the lab swung open and a portly security guard indicated that time was up. Stan

Ward was silent and withdrawn in the elevator, out onto the steps and the down to the diagonal path to College Street, but Jonathan could see the thoughts passing through his mind clearly writ on his face. His silence broke as they approached the entrance to the Queen's Park subway.

"Look," he said gripping Jonathan's arm just above the elbow, as they paused by the subway stairs. "I do apologize for all this. It's all so embarrassing. I just... I just cannot understand what's wrong..." A sudden thought crossed his mind. "Good God, you're not on those bloody beta blockers, are you?"

"No. No, of course not."

"Alright. Not sure there'd be an effect anyway... Oh dear, I am so terribly sorry to have wasted your time."

"It's okay," replied Jonathan. "I'm sorry too, and especially sorry that this has ended on such a flat note."

In truth, he was sympathetic to Stan's embarrassment but also irritated at the waste of time and money this had caused. But he was too polite and sensitive to let any of his annoyance show. The warm feeling towards Stan that he had felt in the lab office returned briefly, tinged with sympathy.

"It's just that the results from Subject 27 were so clear! So clear! I really thought there was something there. But, you know, irreproducible results are no results at all. I am so terribly sorry... Waste of your time and money..."

"Really. It's fine. The money's not an issue and, on a positive note, it's been just great to see you again—and Sandra too—after all these years. That's something to be happy about, surely?"

"You are very kind. Look, can I do anything else for you?"

"No, it's fine, really. I'll just walk down to Edward Street and see what the bus schedules look like. Might even get home before I have to get up and go to work!"

"Well, goodbye then, and please do keep in touch." A small sparkle returned to his eye and he smiled slightly. "I'm not finished with this yet; there's still some life in this old devil."

And with that he was down the stairs and gone.

Jonathan walked fairly briskly down University Avenue, fearful of the chance of just missing a bus and having to wait in the terminal. Transport facilities—train stations, bus stations, airports—seemed to him to be places where anxiety, desperation and boredom tainted and clogged the very air you breathed.

It was a blissful Sunday morning two days after his return from Toronto, no cloud of a rehearsal on the horizon, and Jonathan was spending a relaxing couple of hours with his reed-making tools. He had awoken late and had a simple breakfast followed by a small cup of strong, dark Turkish coffee flavoured with cardamom. Now, all was well with the world. He was sitting at the side table on a wooden chair, starting to tie a reed onto a staple, a small sheet brass cone about two inches long and about a quarter of an inch wide at its largest. He had just picked up the thread to begin winding when the doorbell rang. He rose impatiently and went to the door.

"Hello, it's me!" smiled Kate looking gorgeous. "Aren't you going to invite me in? Just thought I'd drop in as I was just passing by."

He smiled too, concealing his mixed reaction. 'Just passing by' where? Sure she's great company; sure I want to invite her in, but... He swung the door wide and welcomed her in with a sweep of his hand.

"Look, it's great to see you, but I'm just in the middle of making some reeds, and I can't really stop. If you wanna make yourself a coffee you can find where the stuff is. Do one for me too, will you?"

Like I need a good buzz right now.

"I would have called you," she sang from the kitchen, "but I'm having a hell of time with my cell phone. Keep dropping the signal and there's a tower right on the hill above town. Doesn't make sense."

He had got the folded-over reed attached to the staple and tied off, so he laid it down and stepped into the kitchen. It was small space and they were close to each other.

"It's not the closeness of the tower; it's the way the dishes are pointed. You see, the dishes are highly directional because at the frequencies they use there's not much spill-over. I'll bet they're angled to cover Highway 12. And I don't think we have too many micro- or pico-cells in the centre of town, so your phone's offset signal preference won't pick up the slight bit loss... and... well..." He reddened and looked away. "Milk's in the fridge. And... and sugar over there if you need it."

She looked back at him, steaming bodum poised, an endearingly quizzical expression on her face.

"It's nothing. Just something I picked up somewhere," he said offhand. "Why don't you just pour the coffee?"

"I just mentioned my cell phone, that's all; you're the one who volunteered the technical info," she replied. "Most of which goes right over my head anyway!"

"Just like your cell phone signal?" He smiled, she laughed. A chill left the air. "Bring the coffee in here and pull up a chair. I have to finish this."

He made his own reeds, as did all oboists. Each player has unique chops, and a reed made by one will feel unfamiliar to another. So, because of the idiosyncratic nature of their anatomy and playing style, reed-making was a craft that was essential to learn.

"You make your own reeds?" asked Kate mystified as to why this would be necessary. It was like hairing your own bow.

"Sure. You have to. No two sets of lips, teeth and tongue are the same."

"What's this made of?" asked Kate leaning forward. Her perfume moved forward with her.

"It's a cane. It's grown in the south of France; *arundo donax*."

"*Arundo donax*," she whispered, rolling the words around on her tongue, a faraway expression in her eyes.

"What?" he looked over at her quizzically. "What?"

"Some words are just magic. They take you places. *Arundo donax*! Like the Arabian Nights..."

"It's just a Latin name for a reed. See, you fold it over and tie it with fine thread like so."

He held up the one he had just attached. "I'll do another; show you how it goes."

Kate loved watching him work with his hands—the deft, economical way he had—and he found he enjoyed her watching him. She imagined those fine fingers caressing the keys of his oboe... or finding her intimate places.

There was quite an array of tools; little knives and scrapers, a tiny pair of pliers, scissors. A heavily grooved block of softwood served as a cutting surface.

"Where do you get the little metal thingy from?" she asked.

"The staple. They're handmade for me by a guy and his wife in Indiana. Usually they come with the cork already on, but I make that as well. I don't know what it is about these. Sure, you could mass produce them in a Chinese slave factory at a tenth the price, and they'd all be identical, but there's something about these that I like. It's the feel of the thing; nothing I can define."

"Sure. Same with bows. I test maybe ten supposedly identical bows until I find the one that just... works."

"Yep. These sorts of feelings about your equipment are beyond ordinary description. It simply isn't that *kind* of information, is it? Maybe it's just because I know the staples are handmade one by one. Anyway, whatever it is, I swear by them."

He finished tying the folded reed onto the staple and set it aside. He then took a nearly finished reed from a pile and sat back rotating it between his fingers, for all the world like a connoisseur admiring a well made cigar. He then placed his mouth over it, closing his lips on the string binding over the staple, and made it squawk.

"Needs some more scraping. I want a nice string of Cs," he muttered cryptically as he set it aside.

"So, that's a finished one?"

"Nearly. Needs tweaking." He picked up the reed he had just tied. "You have to split the reed and shape the sides and then, once it's folded, tied and cut, you gently shave and scrape here and here," he indicated the areas with his finger. "You give it its first squawk and then it gets tricky. Having present company I'll leave that 'til later."

"So!" she said, sitting back. "Microwaves."

Microwaves; a sick feeling washed over him. Look at her, he thought, sitting there in her lovely dress, knees together, with her hands so sweetly in her lap! Look at the expression on her face! God damn it, what is she? Some sort of beautiful Lorelei who's going to lure me back... I should never have spoken to her in the first place... Stan Ward's sucking me back into the other world, and now she's set to try as well. He sighed. He would have to shut her down.

"It's a previous life, a previous career," he said in a tired, somewhat chilly voice. "I was not always as you see me now," he proclaimed self-mockingly, arms spread wide, trying to break the solemnity. "If you must know—and I really don't see *why* you must know—I spent my university years studying physics and was employed on microwave research as a post-grad."

And, damn it, that was *all* she was going to get out of him.

"Wow! Post-grad? So, you're a doctor?"

"Yup. Doctor Jonathan Rycroft. BSc, MSc *and* PhD, all from U of T."

He bowed ironically from the waist.

"But however did you get into music? You can't just chuck one thing and pick up another!"

"I was always a musician. In high school I could have gone in either direction, but I chose sciences and played music on the side. I got lucky with the audition for the EGO. And that is all I want to tell you, Kate Heinrichs. Have another cup of this excellent coffee."

And keep your distance, thought Kate. Well, that's a small thin wedge of the mystery, but it doesn't go nearly far enough. There's enough pain in him to float an iceberg.

She stayed for a little while longer and they chatted about this and that. Sensing they had come to stasis with imaginary lines drawn, she stood up to leave.

"Look," he said as he opened the door for her, "I don't want you talking about any of this—about me—to the others. It's my business and nobody else's."

She put a vertical finger briefly to her lips and, just like the time before, tiptoed and gave him a little-sister peck on the cheek.

He returned to the side table with his reed-making tools and sat in thought. Stupid! Stupid to let her in! He picked up the knife and plunged it into the cutting block. A video of the past that Kate had evoked played across his mind.

It was just a chicken. Colonel Sanders had dispatched millions of them less humanely. It was just an organic object, almost brainless, bred purely to be killed. It didn't suspect a thing; there was no anticipation, no feeling, and surely no pain. Death was close to instantaneous. But it wasn't the chicken at all—the way it had literally detonated, a cloud of smoking shreds flopping to the sand in a wide circle—it was his research colleagues, who had cheered, high-fived and whooped like hockey fans. He had looked into their faces—their *eyes*—as they shook hands and slapped each other on the back, their test triumphantly concluded, and he hated what he saw.

Then there was the accident... No, no, no! Push it back; push it back! Repel the black wave.

Research into the science of killing had not been on Jonathan Rycroft's agenda when he took the post-grad job. How naïve must I have been, he thought, not to realize that the stuff I was working on was as applicable to dealing death as it was to transmitting energy for the good of Mankind? Take a beam of microwave energy, tuned to a certain frequency and focused to a certain distance, and whatever it impinged upon would be vastly energized. In his dreams, away back in undergraduate, he had visualized a series of geosynchronous satellites equipped with huge arrays of solar cells, beaming energy to receivers on Earth that would convert it into liberal electricity. He dreamed of his research forging a way forward, battling Humankind's addiction to fossil fuels.

He had been recruited on patriotic grounds—the Chinese are working on this, and so are the Russians—it's a question of who gets there first. Death-dealing in portable form; your latter day Samuel Colt. Was I so young then that I still believed in country, flag and good old Western democracy? No, never did; took the job out of pure vanity. But he remembered how he had eased his cognitive dissonance back then by telling himself this was just a brief excursion, and that he would be back on track as soon as an opportunity presented itself. Besides, the salary was more than generous and would pay back his student debts far ahead of his even most liberal projections. There were no parents to foot his bills, and no legacy from them either; he was on his own.

One exploding chicken had changed everything. There was no going back. From that point onwards he knew it could only be bent to the bad. His dream had become ashes.

Thank God for music; whatever would I have done if I couldn't have escaped into music? As it turned out, a few club and pub gigs in Toronto, the audition for East Gladstone, and hey presto! a new life made to order.

He went back to his reeds, but the desire had vanished.

Jonathan arrived fairly early at the concert hall the following day and found Kate there before him. She was sitting at her assigned place, music stand in front of her, and working on one of the pieces they would go through today. He had vowed to keep his distance—her increasing closeness disturbed him, and he felt guilty that he had encouraged it—but as soon as she saw him she got up from her chair, put her fiddle down on it, and sauntered over.

"Hi, what's new and exciting?" she asked.

Seeking some neutral subject he started in to tell her about his work with Stan Ward at U of T, and how exciting he found it. She laughed beautifully at the image of Jonathan festooned in wires and whatnot playing Mozart on the oboe to an audience of one professor and several computers.

"Problem is," he concluded, "the results we were looking for didn't show up, so the session was a bit of a downer. Still, he vowed to continue, so perhaps I'll be down there again for more."

"How did you meet this guy? What was his name again?"

"Stan. Professor Stanley Ward, Department of Physiology. I knew him when I was in undergraduate. He tried to woo me into his field, but I went the other way."

"Ye-es, *Doctor* Jonathan..."

"Remember what I told you," he warned, irritated. "Not here!"

"Mum's the word," she replied with a finger across her lips as she returned to her chair.

He damned himself for somehow leaving an opening for her to winkle her way back in. But I can't just cut her dead...

Other musicians began to filter in and sit at their usual places. There were folders of scores already placed on the music stands by Mr Gropius and his assistants, each folder containing the parts for the material to be worked on that day. As she sat down again and opened the folder containing the first piece of the day, Kate recalled that horrendous occasion when she had taken some parts home to work on and had forgotten to bring them back in the morning. Never again! There had been some frantic activity with the cooperation of a second-violin colleague and the concert hall office photocopier, all under the indulgent smile of an admin assistant who had probably seen it all before.

There was much chattering back and forth before the players settled in and began to get focused on the job in hand, taking up their places and warming up themselves and their instruments. Some few of the more gregarious players had arrived quite early and had spent a good time shooting the breeze before reluctantly sitting down to work. As usual, the trombone section were practicing with much more gusto than the others considered quite necessary. Berlioz's *Symphonie Fantastique* wasn't for a few weeks yet, so why blat out the 'March to the Scaffold' now?

Once the Maestro strode in with his scores tucked under his arm they all stowed their individuality away in some safe place, the better to become mere tools under the command of his baton.

Another long day had begun.

They had played to a full house at the opening of the Summer Series, and although it was the usual old chestnuts—kick-off with

Beethoven, then a bit of Dvorak to lighten things up, and finally some Brahms to serenade them out—the reception was tremendous. Even the Maestro seemed in a genuinely good mood, bowing to the thunderous applause then turning with the smile still plastered across his face, arms raised to acknowledge his musicians. He gave special attention to his concertmaster, indicating him with a wide swinging arm as he stood and bowed for the ovation, and even when he strode off the stage he was beaming to himself.

Jonathan felt more musically satisfied than usual. He hadn't been singled out in rehearsal—well, nobody had really—and the Maestro seemed unusually content with the level of performance. Perhaps he was mellowing out. More likely going fucking deaf. Whatever the cause, there was a sense of fulfillment in playing music, a sense that had been lacking for a while.

Back in the dressing room below the stage Jonathan had his oboe disassembled at the joints and was cleaning the bores through with a brush. The instrument needed to be dried out inside before it was put away. He had noticed a slight sticking in one of the keys, hardly perceptible but probably a harbinger of problems. He resolved to do some servicing when he had a free hour or two. Many players took their instruments to a technician for even minor problems. If it was major work, like replacing paddings and corks, he would take it for service to Toronto and use his back-up, but minor things like this were much easier and more convenient to do yourself. It might be as simple as cleaning away a little fluff and relubricating.

The chatter all around him focused on the growing number of deaths among the world's maestros. He simply didn't want to listen. The more he read and the more he heard, the more horrified and downright frightened he became. He knew exactly how such deaths could be engineered...

He was just packing the instrument away in its plush-lined case when his phone rang. It was Stan Ward in Toronto.

"Hello Jonathan? It's me, Stan. Do you have a minute?"

"Look, I'm just packing up to go home. Do you have a Skype account?"

"Well, of course I do! Just because I'm a stickler for decent English doesn't mean I live in the Middle Ages!"

"Here's my Skype address; got a pen there?" He dictated the address and repeated it to be sure. "Call me in about two hours, okay? I'll have the laptop booted up."

He ambled slowly into the centre of East Gladstone and found a café along the main drag. It was a little after six and although he was hungry he just didn't fancy another evening at home with the leftovers, or phoning in for something either. Eating alone was such a drag. He knew Kate would jump at any invitation like a shot, but he just didn't want that. She was so damned appealing, so bright, so youthful... Well, she'd better back off before it gets really painful...

He plumped himself down at the nearest table and stared moodily at the menu, not really seeing the offerings. Damn, where did the elation over today's rehearsal go? The waiter approached.

"Just bring me a large coffee, will you? Yeah, café Americano. Thanks."

The coffee was good and it lightened his mood. He thought of the project with Stan Ward and wondered what the old guy wanted. Probably to resume the tests, do it again and see if the anomaly would show its head. It was so disappointing that nothing had happened, but he suspected he hadn't seen the end of it yet.

He picked up a Twix at the counter, paid for his coffee and headed slowly home munching his supper. There were a few passages he wanted to go over, so as soon as he got in he placed the laptop on the table in the living room, flipped it open and called up some printed music saved on the hard drive. He had a cupboard in the bedroom full of sheet music, but he found this way a lot easier; single click to turn the page, built-in music stand, nice clear script.

He had decided to work over a tricky part from *Le Tombeau de Couperin*. In his sensitivity to the players, Maurice Ravel had written these two measures in the prelude for first oboe, but had assigned the central phrase in each measure to the second oboe, because it was so difficult for a single player to carry the whole line. But, just occasionally, some mendacious little bastard on the podium, disliking the slightly different voices of the two oboes, would 'ask' first oboe to take the whole thing. It was a great exercise, and good insurance, so for a half hour or so he was totally absorbed in his work.

The Skype icon in the corner of the screen blinked an incoming call, so he put the oboe down, minimized the sheet music, clicked on Skype and sat front and centre. There sat Stan, apparently in his upstairs office, framed certificates and family photos in the background, and in his paw a large glass of red wine. Seeing it made Jonathan wish he had one of his own.

"Jonathan, it's good to see you. Isn't technology marvelous? I'm old enough to remember smoked paper... well, never mind. Do you have a minute?"

"Sure. I was just practicing."

"Look, I want you back here in Toronto as soon as possible, but that's not what I'm calling about. Or maybe it is..."

"It's pretty busy around here, and every time I miss a concert I have to pay the sub out of my own pocket. But anyway, what is it? Not the anomaly this time?"

"Well, yes and no. It's about these dying maestros..."

"No, no, that's... that's not..." He started to feel cold and sick.

"What! What is it?"

"Nothing! It has absolutely no relevance to... to... Just... just leave it, okay?"

"Could I just say a word or two. Please?"

Jonathan ran his hands over his face and rubbed his eyes. He could swear that if this was a phone call he would have hung up, but having Stan Ward sitting there on the screen made it seem somehow impossibly rude. 'Isn't technology marvelous' indeed.

"All right, what about it then?" He felt unreal; he felt resentful. He was being dragged somewhere—some *when*—against his will.

"I have read that it's generally agreed that they are being targeted." This was Jonathan's nightmare; he could visualize the mechanism but, like everybody else, couldn't fathom the motive.

"Yes." He drew a deep long breath. "Parallels have been drawn with the Unabomber."

"The what?"

"Unabomber. He was this nutcase who posted letter bombs to university profs."

"Yes, yes, I heard you. *Una*bomber!? Is that because he targeted *Una*versities?"

"Una, uni? Never thought of it before." Where was this going? Away from him, at least.

"Exactly! Never thought of it. Nor did the journalist who coined this ignorant term! Or anyone—anyone at all—in the entire English-speaking world who could correct this abortion of our lovely language!"

Ward took a deep breath and a large draft of wine, and his eyes showed that he was far from finished. Jonathan realized he had touched a sore spot, but didn't mind the diversion.

"It's these bloody Americans! They can't even speak the language, yet they take it over and do what they damned well please with it! What about 'laptop'? You have a lap top?"

"Everyone does these days, if they don't have a tablet. I'm sitting in front of mine!"

"No, no, no! I said *lap top*, not laptop."

The mystified expression on Jonathan's face said it all. How much of that wine had the old boy already taken in?

"When you sit," Professor Ward continued, in a manner more suited to addressing a slow student, "you have a lap. Should you wish to place your computer on that surface, you would then have a *lap* computer, would you not?"

"Well, yes..."

"So why laptop? Laps don't have *bottoms*! At least none that I've seen do!"

"But, the language has to adapt and change with the times."

"That I will grant you. But why must it change through ignorance and stupidity? Damn it, there should be a bloody *Academie Anglaise* to oversee the language and tell these ignorant bastards in no uncertain terms 'No, we will not allow you to send our language down the Thomas Crapper!' They have hot-wired our beloved language—the finest and most versatile form of human communication on Earth—hijacked it, and left it in a ditch with its windows smashed and its tires slashed!"

"Hot-wired?" murmured Jonathan, waving a red flag. "That sounds awfully like an Americanism."

"I didn't say all changes were bad! It's a usage that has some utility. Even Americans can sometimes coin a phrase." He sat fuming for a few seconds while Jonathan waited, on edge, for the conversation to resume. "ISBN *numbers*, ATM *machines*, PIN *numbers*, God help us..."

"Stan," interrupted Jonathan, becoming a little irritated and trying to bring him back to earth. "I really think I should get back to my oboe."

"I'm sorry, sorry. Quite carried away. Yes, yes." He took another good swig at his wine. "Look Jonathan, I don't know how, but I feel that this spate of deaths has some sort of relationship with our research."

"No, no! Drop it! Leave it! I can't..." He felt weak and sick again. "It has nothing to do with me, with us..."

That great red flood washed suddenly before Jonathan's eyes

again; his heart pounded and his vision blurred. The flood of associations, images and memories was overwhelming him once more. This was impossible! This simply could not be happening. He held his head in his hands and closed his eyes tightly. In a few moments he regained a little composure and saw that Stan Ward was sitting looking at him with a shocked expression.

Jonathan calmed himself further, rubbed his hands over his face and took a few deep, rather shaky breaths.

"I'm sorry," he said in a tired and wobbly voice. "I do apologize. It's just that this subject has got everybody rattled. We're all on edge. And I simply cannot deal with it right now. Okay?"

"No problem, no problem. Let's just leave it there shall we? I honestly didn't mean to..."

"Okay. It's fine. Really."

"I'll... I'll be in touch about another test, shall I?" asked Stan, from the expression on the screen clearly worried that he had lost his collaborator.

"Sure. Call me next week. Sorry to tear you off."

The first thing he did after closing Skype was to go to the kitchen and fish out a bottle of wine. A glass and a bit later the world's gloss was a little restored. His heart rate was back to normal and he felt calmer. Jesus, where was this going? What the hell nonsense *was* this, and what the hell was Stan Ward getting at? It's in the past and I want it left there...

He maximized the music on the screen again, picked up his oboe and resumed where he had left off, glass and bottle beside him on the table. He surprised himself how easily he slipped back into the music; a shit storm like that usually meant a total lack of concentration followed by a sleepless night. He wondered as he played whether there was some research to be done on the efficacy of Pinot Noir and music on mental stability and wellbeing. Somebody should put together a grant proposal.

But, thank God for music, because without it, it would be all Pinot Noir.

"Creativity," announced Stan Ward as he put down his dessert fork and wiped his mouth on the napkin. "It's the unique human faculty."

"Sure, we're agreed on that," replied Sandra. "Remember what a fuss I made about that TV program where they were going on about animals painting pictures?"

"Elephants with paintbrushes held in their trunks, monkeys daubing paint on canvases!" Stan laughed. "And the ludicrous argument that their work was the equal of Jackson Pollock at his best!"

"More fool the millionaires who have more money than sense," she replied. "Or, I should say, aesthetic discrimination."

"Big bucks for a painting that is no work of art at all."

"There is absolutely no evidence that I know of," she replied, "to suggest that what they are doing is creative. It's classic anthropomorphism."

"I agree. Yet, plausible for all that."

"Plausible only if you fail to differentiate play from creation."

"Of course. Even the lowliest of animals knows how to play. It's clearly a phase in the process of learning. And it seems to have nothing to do with either feeding or procreation, the chief traditional drivers of the animal kingdom. And us, of course."

"That was funny, wasn't it?" said Sandra. "The YouTube video of the snow-boarding crow?"

The video had gone viral some time ago; it showed a crow picking up a jar lid in its beak, jumping aboard and sliding down a snow-covered rooftop. As if the crow wished to demonstrate that this was no coincidence, it did it again and again.

"It was pure play," she observed rising from her chair. "Let's move into the other room; the dishes can wait."

They picked up their glasses and the bottle from the debris of the table and moved to more comfortable quarters.

"Yup, pure play," said Stan as he eased down into his favorite chair. "And it shows that crows are mighty clever for their brain size."

"Among the cleverest of the birds, but still not creative."

"Then there have been arguments for self-awareness as a faculty unique to humans," he observed. "But that doesn't wash either."

"No, there's a lot of evidence that some higher animals have a degree of self-awareness."

"So, we agree," said Stan returning to his opening thrust, "that creativity is the one unique faculty of us humans. Shared by no other organism on the planet."

"There was a point somewhere in human development," observed Sandra, "perhaps as far back as a million years ago, when creativity emerged."

"But the evidence is nowhere near that old, is it?"

"No; we have to extrapolate, of course," she replied. "The earliest clear example of human creativity is the famous Hohle Fels Venus; the chubby little ivory carving of a woman."

"That pre-dates cave painting, does it not?"

"By a few thousand years. She's about 35,000 years old, whereas the earliest cave paintings are only about 32,000; the Aurignacian culture. But this is sophisticated work, especially the painting, so it must have developed over a very long period. There just isn't a lot in the archaeological record."

"And they had music too, didn't they, around that time?" asked Stan.

"Sure did. Very near the same location as the Venus of Hohle Fels they found a five-hole flute made from the wing bone of a bird. Five holes; that's pretty sophisticated music-making, and that didn't emerge overnight. There is a much earlier one, from Slovenia, but there's a lot of debate over that. It's a fragment; it might not have been deliberately carved at all. Similar issue with finds in Alaska and the Yukon, fueling the debates over when exactly the Bering Strait was crossed; are the pieces they've found manmade or natural?"

"Making music, painting pictures, carving sculpture," mused Stan, fingers steepled and resting lightly on his upper lip. "It all emerged as part of our developing, growing brain. But I'll bet that, of all of them, music came first. I'll bet it's deeply embedded in our wiring and all the other arts are comparatively recent cultural accretions."

"Yes, but where are you going with this?" She was well familiar with the paths that his thinking took, and she knew that this was the groundwork for some speculation, and it certainly concerned his 'anomaly'. That was all he thought about these days.

"The creative practice of music," he announced, "is all tied up with this missing energy."

"Oooh, that's heavy!" she cried. "Pour me some more will you, this needs thought!" He topped up the glasses, and she took a long and thoughtful drink. "Stan, my dear, I thought I had been married all these years to a physiologist. When did the philosopher sneak into the picture?"

"It's quite simple. Well," he corrected himself, "it's not; it's actually bloody complex. But, if you have an anomalous result that doesn't make sense according to your regular, linear scientific lines of reasoning, then you have to cast the net wider. So, I thought to myself: where is this extra energy going? It can't be lost because basic thermodynamics doesn't work that way. So where is it *going*?"

"And now you know?"

He laughed. "Oh, I do so wish! No, no, my dear, I'm no nearer than I was before. But I do believe that it's being stored... somewhere..."

"I know you haven't read much science fiction lately..."

They had a long shelf above the headboard of their bed that stretched its entire width, loaded with ancient SF paperbacks. Although they hadn't been there recently, there was a bookshop on Queen Street West that had an extraordinary second-hand selection of all the old stuff. It used to be their bedtime reading at that time of the day when you want to put your mind in neutral and let someone with wild imagination do the driving.

"Ah, no my dear; not since the good old days of Brunner, Clarke and Asimov, eh? But remember, what was once science fiction eventually becomes science fact. But, no, I haven't thought it all through, and even if I had, I think until I establish the reality of the anomaly, I'll keep it to me-self."

"There's a drop left in the bottle," she observed, and he held out his glass.

Symphony No. 8 in B Minor

"I've got a great idea!" announced Kate after a particularly strenuous rehearsal. "We've got Saturday afternoon off. Let's put together a picnic and take it to the lake. There's that great spot up past the windmill, where there's that little beach."

The city had graciously accepted the donation of a working windmill from the Dutch government as thanks for the efforts of Canadian troops in the liberation of the Netherlands at the close of the Second World War. It was a beautiful addition to the scenery, located on a point of land jutting into the lake.

"Great idea!" replied Jonathan. "We could invite Stephanie—you know Stephanie, she teaches music in the high school; great oboe player, subs at second when either of us is away—and anyone else you get along with in the orchestra. What about Liz? And maybe Steve? I know he's a trombonist, but he's always good for a party."

"No, that's not quite what I meant," she answered quietly. "I meant just us. You and me."

"Well, yeah... that would be great too."

"Meet at eleven? By the windmill?"

"Sure."

"I'll bring the food. You do the booze. What can't you eat?"

"Bring anything but chicken."

"Hmm! Well eggs, cheese or maybe ham would fit the bill. Okay?"

"Sure. See you there with bells on!" he cried, hoping it didn't come out as false as it felt. He was feeling the pincers tightening upon him again. She's a lovely woman, and I would love to get closer; she knows that. But I can't. I just can't. Shit! Why couldn't I just say no?

The weather on Saturday was fabulous. There had been rain storms on and off during the week, but today was warm and dry. Most of the town's population appeared to have had the same idea as Kate, and the beach she had planned for their little tête-à-tête would be crowded. They met by the windmill, he with a bottle bag from the LCBO and she with a lunch cooler, and walked side by side up the beach, close but not touching. She wore a light, pale blue dress to mid thigh and, as always, had a matching head band. He thought she looked absolutely gorgeous and knew that if she so much as touched him he was lost.

With a bit of walking they soon got clear of the majority and found a nice patch of springy grass at the edge of the beach with a fine view of the upper reaches of the lake, and the windmill back the way they had come. It was only eleven thirty but Kate had been up early, and it seemed such a long time since she had last eaten, so she opened the cooler and started to distribute the goodies. She was a generous packer, so while the egg salad and ham sandwiches, pickles, chips and apples came out, he uncorked the bottle.

"Cheers!" they toasted each other with a Johannisberg Riesling, still cool from the liquor store fridge, and went at their lunch with a will. Jonathan thanked God she had asked him what he wanted; he loathed chicken.

Lunch finished, and another glass dealt with, Kate sighed and laid back on the grass, eyes raised to the blue of the sky. He sat beside her, hands around one knee and looked out across the lake. Nothing was said, but it was a nothing that lay heavily between them. Presently, she sat up, moved alongside him and placed one hand gently on his arm, just as she had at the party. The soft touch—so slight, so feather-weighted—made him tense and stiffen. He looked around him, up and down the beach, almost desperately. They were alone. Just the distant voices of children at play far beyond the windmill.

"Tell me about it," she said quietly. She thought he hadn't heard so absent was any reaction. "Tell me about it."

He leaped quickly to his feet, pushing her hand away, and strode down to the water's edge. As she saw him standing there with his back straight and looking pointedly away into the distance, her heart contracted. She stood slowly and walked towards him, arriving gently at his side but keeping space between them.

"I'm sorry. Please forgive me."

He nodded, lips pinched between his teeth, and remained staring out into the lake, with back straight, arms folded. Time had almost stopped.

"I didn't mean to... I'm a pushy little nuisance, aren't I?"

He nodded again. They stayed so for a long while, following the progress of a small boat across the lake with their eyes, thoughts elsewhere. After a time, he sighed and shifted. There were tears on his cheeks.

"It's... I... I need space. You... you crowd me. I can't breathe."

She pulled gently away then, doubling the distance between

them, hurt and confused.

"No problem," she replied quietly past the lump in her throat. "If you need me, you know where I am."

"Good!" He shook off his mood, wiped quickly at his face with a hand, and walked rapidly back to their picnic things. "I guess we should head back. This has been nice, but I have a bunch of things I need to do this afternoon."

They walked back the way they had come, Jonathan setting the pace and hardly speaking at all, until they reached the road into town where they would part company.

"See you soon, then," she said, almost as a question.

"Sure. Big rehearsal tomorrow. Schubert." And with a wave he was gone.

Kate walked slowly back to her apartment with her heart in ruins. Oh, what a mess I'm making. What can I do? Oh, what *can* I do?

Jonathan had played the orchestral concert repertoire for years, first as a student and amateur and now as a professional, but now, with the East Gladstone Symphony Orchestra, he had never before had his feelings for the works so violated. And he knew the others in the orchestra felt the same. Damn it, anybody with a modicum of sensitivity to this music must see that the Maestro's readings were pure schmaltz. How could he be so wrong about the composers' intentions? Or were the composers' intentions of no interest to this prancing mountebank? God almighty, André Rieu did it better! Last week's joy had totally evaporated.

They were on the stage of the East Gladstone Centennial Centre rehearsing Schubert's Eighth Symphony in B minor, the so-called *Unfinished*. It has just the two movements; the third had only been sketched out for piano and remained incomplete, and it is unknown if a fourth was planned. Several musicologists have 'completed' the symphony, but none of their renditions are part of the major concert repertoire. Write your owned damned music was the general opinion. Quite why Schubert never finished the symphony may well remain mysterious, but it is among his most loved, and frequently played, pieces. There are gorgeous parts for the oboe, especially in the second movement, the *andante con moto*.

So, Jonathan played his oboe the way he felt deeply in his

heart it ought to be. He was not one to compromise, and this lack of flexibility—or intransigence to his critics—had been his downfall on many previous occasions. Several times during the second movement, after the clarinet had passed the melodic line to him, the Maestro stopped the show and made pointed comments. Jonathan glared back but bit his tongue, and in order not to delay the rehearsal any more and get everyone's knickers in a twist, he complied with the clown's wishes.

After the rehearsal he left the stage, and was halfway down the stairs to the dressing room below the auditorium, oboe tucked under his arm, when the Maestro caught up with him.

"Hey, you! Mr Rycroft!" he shouted in his slightly accented Italian with shades of Brooklyn. "What did you think you were doing back there?"

"Playing the music. Reading the score."

"Look, we had this out just now. I'm the maestro. You play it the way I tell you to, not some fancy way you've invented."

"Invented!" By Christ, he was stung. "Talk about the pot and the kettle! I'm playing what's written on the damned page. I'm playing what Schubert wrote."

"You're not employed by EGSO to imagine what Schubert wrote! You'll play it the way I tell you to play it! It's my reading that counts, not some damned oboe at the back. This is an orchestra, not a God-damned debating society."

"You've said it; it's all about you, isn't it? Bugger the composer, bugger the musicians!"

"Now listen here! You better start coming round to my view, or you're out of here!"

"Don't you threaten me..."

"You'll play it my way tonight, God damn you, or you'll have your marching papers!"

And he turned on his heel and strutted off in swirl of tuxedo tails and expensive deodorant.

Now here was a facer. Who wins this little battle? Jonathan, Stalwart Defender of Musical Purity or Carlo the Conducting Coxcomb? One thing was for sure, if he stood by his principles and played it *his* way—the way Schubert must surely have heard it—he could start looking for a job in the morning.

Why does it always have to be this way? Is the purity of the music that God-damned important? If he were ever to look deeply into himself he would see that it had nothing to do with Schubert or Beethoven or any of that crowd. It had nothing to do with music at all.

Kicking against the pricks had never seemed so appropriate.

And the biggest prick of all held Jonathan's future in his manicured hands.

The *Unfinished Symphony* was first on the program. No matter how many times this had happened before, or how many times they would have it again before they retired from public life, the musicians all felt that thrill as the lights dimmed and the auditorium hushed in anticipation. The coughers finished their coughing, program rustlers were stilled; the concertmaster strode in, fiddle neck clutched in one hand, bow in the other, and gave the nod to first oboe. It was Jonathan's job to give the orchestra its pitch. Of all the instruments in the symphony orchestra, the oboe is the least tunable, and so the tradition has arisen that the other instruments take their pitch from it. Jonathan sounded the A above middle C for the woodwinds and brasses, then another for the strings. The tuning ritual completed, the musicians sat in the still silence and waited.

The Maestro timed his appearance nicely, making them hang in anticipation of his entrance, before swanning in; playing the audience like the true egomaniac he was. From his low, slow bow he turned smoothly to face the orchestra, tapped his evocative baton on the music stand before him, and... they were away!

Though he played in his usual state of concentration, a part of Jonathan's mind was still ticking and clicking; weighing the pros and cons of doing what mature and sensible adulthood would suggest, or doing what his heart desired. Swallow your pride, turn Schubert into kitsch and keep your job, or stare the bugger down and win by losing?

The second movement began with low strings, with trumpets, horns and high strings playing in counterpoint. Jonathan felt a slight pressure at his temples—the sort of feeling you get before a thunderstorm—but he put it down to the tension of his indecision. Where had he felt this before? The second theme appeared in the part for the solo clarinet. Jonathan raised his reed to his lips as the clarinet passed the line to him, and began to play.

His decision was never made. No sooner had the first sweet notes sung from his instrument, than the Maestro emitted a piercing yell, flung his baton high in spinning circles into the auditorium, clutched his chest as if to tear his ribcage apart, crashed down from the podium in a welter of flailing arms and legs, and tangled himself with the concertmaster. The orchestra wailed down into silence, several oblivious instruments persisting for a bar or two. The crunching of antique Cremona wood, and the click, tick, bounce of the baton into the stalls, could be heard clearly in the vacuum quiet that followed his fall.

Audience members rose from their seats for a better look, offering the first standing ovation the Maestro truly merited. The house lights came up, Gropius the theatre manager stepped quickly out from the wings to calm the mob, and emergency medical staff appeared as if from nowhere. Nothing could be done to save the great man. The lifeless body of Carlo Mascagni was covered with a theatre drop sheet, the auditorium emptied in buzzing conversation, and the musicians filtered slowly away in shocked silence. First Trumpet glanced briefly at Jonathan. Their eyes met and slipped away, and Jonathan knew that never again would anyone call him Jonah... to his face.

That night the *Unfinished Symphony* was even more unfinished than usual.

Jonathan quickly stowed his instrument, threw his coat on and left the concert hall. He wanted to be far, far away and as quickly as possible, but no matter how hard he strode the scene burned into his eyes followed him. It was madness! Madness! This couldn't be happening.

Although headed home, he took a long, roundabout route, striding through a thin, warm, penetrating rain, oboe case tucked under his arm. It wasn't far to his apartment in the lower end of town—nothing was far in East Gladstone—but he took the route on the bike paths by the lake to be alone with his turbulent thoughts.

Why was this happening? Why? It must be just coincidence. It *must* be! Two of them felled before his eyes. Microwaves...?

A horrible buried demon whispered in his ear: you wanted him out of your life and hey-presto! He can't sack you now!

No, no, never like that! I never wished him *dead*! Not like that! His past reared up like a dark spectre and he crushed down hard on an almost overwhelming image of death.

Breathing deeply, screwing down the mental C-clamps, he strode the paths in a fog. Not death, even wished! He walked and walked in the darkening evening, oblivious of the light, invasive rain. As he neared home he allowed his mental pressure to ease, but the horror of the evening came flooding back yet again. Not dead! I would never wish that. It couldn't be happening. It couldn't!

He arrived at his front door with the turmoil still in his mind, not quite sure how he had got there. He was soaking wet, water dripping off his inadequate coat. Thankfully, the oboe case was the waterproof clamshell kind, because he had even forgotten he was carrying it. As he was shoving his key into the lock he saw the note, half in the letterbox, the exposed triangle damp from the rain.

'Came by to see you. Didn't wait 'cos didn't know how long you'd be. Turn phone on, Kate.'

Shit, shit, shit and shit!

Oh, leave me alone! Please! She's *got* to leave me alone! I can't have her in my life! I can't! Why am I drawn to her when I want to be left alone? That first day I saw her...she looked so much like... I should never have even *spoken* to her.

The phone stays turned off.

It was business as usual with the EGSO the day after the disaster; even the death of a maestro could not derail the performance schedule. They met, as usual, at ten in the morning. If anyone could have wished their dear departed leader dead it would have been Stefan Kulikofski. As concertmaster he was obliged to take over as conductor until a replacement could be found, and it was a duty he performed with ill-concealed pleasure. This meant that the strata of the violins underwent an upheaval; one lucky first violin became acting concertmaster, while a second violin (not Kate) graduated to the front row. The show must go on.

The body of Carlo Mascagni was to be returned to his native soil later that day, so the exequies normally attendant on such a prominent demise were curtailed in favour of a brief eulogy delivered by Kulikofski, and a minute's silence before the rehearsal began. These formalities were unfortunately overshadowed by the huge buzz that was on everyone's lips. Nobody was sure of the truth, but it seemed that the Maestro's death was being investigated by the police. What everyone thought was a heart attack now took on sinister overtones. No one knew what evidence there could possibly be, but opinions flew like lake-effect snow.

So, instead of buckling down to their first rehearsal of Hector Berlioz's *Symphonie Fantastique*, which was a tricky one as few of them had played it more than once before, the concertmaster had to content himself with delays as each musician was called out by the police to be interviewed. The rehearsal hobbled along in this way, with constant interruptions that threatened to make the Kulikofski tear out what remained of his hair. They would limp along for a while missing one first violin, then out would come the cops from the little off-stage storage room where they had set up their inquisition chamber, and a trumpet or an oboe or another fiddle would get extracted for five or ten minutes. Doing the whole orchestra in this way took most of the day, and by the time it was all done tempers were far too ragged and Berlioz had to be set aside for a calmer occasion.

Looking at the day's work, Kulikofski reckoned at least half what he had planned had failed to be accomplished, and as stand-in conductor until the Board could find a maestro, he hardly wanted his debut ruined. Pity they'd printed the damned brochures and flyers, because it would be just great to drop the *Symphonie Fantastique* altogether and go with something they could all play in their sleep; Beethoven's Fifth or the damned *1812 Overture* maybe. Save some money on all the contracts for the extra musicians, too. Having a tuba drive all the way up from Toronto for just a few notes in the *dies irae* was plain silly when they could have pulled in one of the local guys to play the bass trombone. Of course, Mascagni had insisted on the tuba; God knows why, as everybody knew it was originally scored for a bass ophicleide. And you won't find one of those clattering garbage bins within a day's drive of this place. Or a serpent either, if it came to that. Still, nothing to be done about all that; just soldier on.

He was mourning the damage to his violin; Mascagni's last selfish act. It was a Bergonzi that he had managed to buy, with help from a very supportive family friend, long before these instruments became the sole property of millionaires. He'd had it for most of his playing life, and although he could probably retire a rich man if he sold it, it would be like carving away a part of his soul. It was at the moment under restoration in Montreal with a firm he trusted utterly. Word was that it would be back as good as new—or even better than new, actually—within a few weeks. It was wonderful what they could do.

Secretly, Kulikofski wished the Board would have some trouble finding a new maestro; it would be very interesting to see how well they would do without one—well enough he guessed—and his new role up at the front was rather beguiling. Too much of a break with tradition to be tenable, unfortunately.

Jonathan's turn to be interviewed came towards lunchtime. There were two plainclothes policemen from the local cop shop, an older and more experienced looking one, and a clear junior being shown the ropes. It didn't look to him as if this whole thing was being taken very seriously.

They showed him into the storage room and sat him down on a folding chair extracted from a pile of them on a trolley. They perched on two others, surrounded by notice boards, music stands, posters, boxes of crockery, a broken coffee urn and other concert hall bric-a-brac and cast-offs. It's not much fun being a cop he thought as he looked around, and imagined them doing this routine over and over again the whole day in this welcoming ambience.

"So, let's get to it," said the older one as the young policeman folded over a new sheet of paper on his notepad. "Could you tell us what you saw please?"

"Well, it's not all that easy because most of the time you're not watching the conductor—or maestro, I should say—because your eyes are on your score, or taking in your immediate colleagues."

What he didn't point out was the dislike he felt at looking at the bastard when he absolutely didn't have to.

"Hmm, yes, we're hearing this a lot."

"So, I heard him yell, then I saw him pitching into the front row of violins. It was horrible."

The video started playing again in Jonathan's mind. He went clammy and shivery, and felt quite unwell for a minute or so.

"Nothing else you can tell us? You saw no symptoms, nothing previous to when he fell?"

Jonathan remembered an ominous feeling he had, like an impending thunderstorm, but that surely came from within. He had been under stress during the concert—albeit self-imposed—but when the Maestro fell, it *was* like the relief of an enormous pressure. He hated to think of it that way.

"No. Really. I'm sorry. It's hit us all rather badly."

"No problem. Thanks for your time. Let's get the next one in here..."

And that was it.

Kate got him alone later in the neutral space of the dressing room below the auditorium. They compared notes on a light, superficial level, his distance stoically maintained. Her interview had been just about the same as his, and even though she was much closer to the 'action' there was little more she could contribute. Just glad it wasn't her violin that got crushed; there are benefits to being in the back row. She thought it would be unwise to ask him if the subject of his argument with the Maestro had come up. Some things are better left undisturbed. Most of us, she thought, are getting over the shock, and some are even opening out a little, but Jonathan seems to be stewing on it. Hope he's not feeling guilty. After all, it's almost like wish-fulfillment; a major source of irritation suddenly wiped from the slate. And a huge argument could lead to a heart attack, couldn't it?

She ached to discuss this with him, but she knew it would be disastrous. The Berlin wall was still intact.

Two evenings after the police interview Jonathan was surprised by a ringing on his doorbell. Nobody came visiting, unless perhaps it was neighbour or the same Jehovah's Witnesses he sent packing last week. As he rose from his chair another thought struck him; he wondered if he would see Kate standing there, wearing one of her lovely headbands, waiting to be asked in. He couldn't even think of seeing her right now. Things were just too complicated.

He swung the door back to find two gentlemen he had never seen before. It was like the cops all over again, he thought, only these two looked hard somehow; an older one with a face that said absolutely nothing, and a younger one with cold eyes. They showed him identification cards with their mugshots on and invited themselves in. The cards said CSIS, Canadian Security Intelligence Service. He turned cold and sick. What could they want with him?

He sat them down on the chesterfield in his small sitting room, still in their coats, and brought the wooden chair from the kitchen for himself. He gripped his hands on his knees to ease their shaking and took a slow breath or two to calm himself.

"How can I help you?"

There was a disconcerting silence that lasted 30 seconds or so while both of them looked at him. Not a particularly aggressive stare; just an incurious examination that made him at least as uncomfortable as if they had shown outright aggression.

"So. Carlo Mascagni, your maestro," began the older one. "Didn't like him, did you?"

"No, I didn't." No point in lying thought Jonathan; it was so bloody obvious. "Actually, to be quite honest with you, I loathed the bastard. Then again, most of the orchestra did."

"Heart attack," continued the older one. "Do you believe that?"

"Everybody said it was a heart attack."

"That's not what I asked you. I asked you if you believe that maestro Carlo Mascagni suffered from a fatal heart attack, did I not? Yes or no?"

What possessed Jonathan he could not afterwards recall, but before he could stop himself he blurted out "No!"

"No? No heart attack?" Now they were both sitting forward, losing the detached air that they had so far cultivated.

"No. He couldn't have had a heart attack. He didn't have one." He regretted this as soon as it was out of his mouth.

"Har, har. Very funny. Quite the little comedian, aren't you. I don't suppose I need to tell you that murder is serious business."

"Murder? *Murder*!"

"Yes, we believe so."

"No, no, I can't believe that! How?"

"It was an electric shock that killed him. Huge voltage."

He felt all cold and sick again. Both men kept their eyes on him, gauging his reaction. Terrible images were looming in his mind. He sat a moment trying to organize his thoughts, trying to calm himself. Their stares blew his efforts away.

"You... you... This isn't... Why? Why are you telling me this?"

"Because we're investigating a death through suspicious circumstances, that's why, and we're interested in knowing what you know."

"But I don't *know* anything! I was told—we *all* were—that he had a heart attack! How could it be anything else?"

"Burns on the fingers and palm of his right hand—his baton hand—soles of his shoes melted." The younger agent spelled off their findings on his fingers. "No sign of any electrical equipment that could account for it. The desk lamp on the music lectern checked out just fine. Besides, that's only one-ten AC. We found his baton; halfway up the stalls, under a seat. Singed cork handle, and the paint was melted."

"But what's all this got to do with me?"

"You had a blazing row with him that day, didn't you," stated the older agent. No question at all.

"What are you implying? What the hell are you talking about?"

Somebody must have blabbed this to the local police, and these guys had picked it up. Could have been anybody; there were enough petty backstabbers in the orchestra. First Trumpet maybe? Jonah...

"And you had a blazing row with the previous... er... maestro as well. Isn't that right? Same day he died. Heart attack."

Jonathan's balance wobbled. He could hardly credit what he was hearing. It was almost as if his raging thoughts that awful night were taking concrete form. These men were trying to force coincidence into a shape he never saw in his wildest imaginings. He tried desperately to calm himself and think clearly. He took a long, slow breath.

"Look," he replied, in a less than steady voice. "I don't like what you're implying; I think you should just get out of here. You're trying to make me guilty of something I had nothing to do with. Just go away and leave me alone! If you want to come back with a proper warrant and question me properly, then I'll contact my lawyer."

He got up and stepped towards the door.

"You did government work as an electrical engineer, did you not?" shot back the older one, still resolutely seated. "Microwave transmission systems, wasn't it?"

A great red flood washed suddenly before Jonathan's eyes, his heart pounded, his vision blurred, and he would have fallen over had he not grabbed the doorframe. His past life was flooding in, a great chaotic tsunami of associations, images and memories. This was impossible! This couldn't be happening.

"No! No! This has got nothing to do with me! That was all a previous life. It's done; it's gone!"

"Previous life? We at CSIS think you only go round once."

"Yeah," piped up the younger one. "We don't believe in reincarnation. That's why we think suicide bombers are so stupid. 'Specially the young ones."

"You know some guy by the name of Khan?" asked the mature agent. Jonathan looked blank. "Makharam Khan?"

Khan! Of course he knew Khan; met him anyway. But what... *Jesus Christ*, these fuckers have been watching me! A *year* and they're still on my case! But the work at U of T has nothing to do with the Maestro, the orchestra, or anything else. What possible connection could there be? This was horrible! Now Jonathan became angry. He swung away from the doorframe in a rage and tore the door wide open.

"Get out! Get out of my house! I won't listen to this! Get out right now. If there's anything you want to ask me, you'll do it properly. I don't even believe you're who you say you are."

They steadfastly refused to rise. Jonathan stood at the door, hand on hips, looking down at them, panting and with racing heart.

"We are here simply to ask you a few questions," continued the older agent in a calming voice, which had the perfectly opposite effect. "We are, indeed, who we say we are, and you will do yourself no favours by antagonizing the authorities. If you wouldn't mind sitting down, we can conclude this quickly."

Jonathan slammed the door and returned to this chair, collapsed, deflated, defeated. It was all too much for him to understand. It was insane; he had been thrown into a mad world where logic and common sense simply didn't operate. He took a shuddering breath.

"You have a coincidence of two deaths in my presence," he tried to summarize. "You have a coincidence of some trivial arguments—everybody has those; you obviously don't know shit about an orchestra—and you have some idea that these deaths are connected with microwave radiation. Then you bring in some chance acquaintance by the name of Khan. What the hell kind of terrorist science fiction bullshit are you suggesting?"

"We are not suggesting anything. We are merely verifying some facts that have come to our notice. Getting all our ducks in a row."

"Okay, so you've verified them. The ducks are all in a fucking row! Now fuck off out of here and leave me alone!"

The older man rose to his feet with great gravity and the younger one followed as if choreographed.

"I hope you don't intend to travel anywhere any time soon," said the older one as he opened the street door.

"Yeah," said the younger one. "We'll need to know where you are. At all times."

"And I hope you're not forgetting your exit interview," put in the older one, halfway out of the door. "Remember? You're still covered by the Official Secrets Act, and will be for the rest of your life."

A brief swirl of wind, the slam of the door, and they were gone.

Jonathan Rycroft started to laugh. All the tension, fear and incomprehension of the last twenty minutes resolved themselves into manic laughter at the farcical nature of the whole scene. It cracked him up to think that he was now an Al Qaeda agent aiming Star Wars death rays at the maestros of the insignificant little orchestra of a nondescript town in southern Ontario. He laughed until it hurt.

He laughed until he was exhausted and then, revisiting the scene in his mind, the seriousness of this nonsense—if that wasn't a complete contradiction—reasserted itself. He had heard of Security Certificates, and the cavalier way the government had flouted the very essence of democracy in its secrecy, false accusation and knee-jerk reaction to perceived threats. He had heard of people falsely accused, completely exonerated, yet still under continual suspicion. He had heard of people spending hundreds of thousands of dollars on legal services in vain attempts to establish their own innocence. He heard of people whose names had been erroneously placed on no-fly lists, and even with proof positive of mistaken identity, they were still restricted prisoners in their own country.

He realized that, laughable as all this was, he was in serious trouble. And why zero in on Makharam Khan? Is it just crude racial profiling, or do they know something that I don't...?

After the death at the podium Jonathan withdrew into music, plunging himself into hard playing, distancing himself from everything but his chosen craft by working at it all his waking hours. It was the only way he knew how to cope. He scarcely checked his e-mail, refused to answer the phone, and was aloof and distant with all around him. His psyche had taken a hammering but at least he could get lost as long as the music played. In the space of a less than a week his carefully constructed East Gladstone world was cracking apart. The half beguiling, half frightening near-breach of his defences at the picnic had left him fragile, and the second death at the podium had come at him hard and blind-sided him. Now, to be singled out and suspected of some sort of crime, at first laughable, was weighing upon him as well.

One morning several days later, he was working over the third movement of Vaughan Williams Concerto for Oboe in A minor. Not that he believed the EGO would ever come anywhere near offering it in one of their programs; he was working on it just because it was bloody difficult. The writing for oboe was one thing, but the parts for strings were downright wicked; a definite no-go for the EGO. He had wrestled the oboe part down some years ago—that is, found his way through it without missing any notes—and now he was in the second phase, trying to make it sound like a piece of music. This was therapy.

His phone had rung repeatedly this morning (should have turned the damn' thing off) and now, halfway through the third movement, it was going again. Shit! The tangible world reasserted itself, and he knew that sooner or later he would have to come up for air. It might as well be now. He stopped in mid measure, laid down the oboe, marched over to the coat rack behind the door, and hauled the shrilling thing out of a pocket.

"Yes!"

"Jonathan, Jonathan, is that you?"

"Well, of course it is. Think it was Sun Yat-sen? Oh... Stan?"

"Yes. Listen, listen. When you were here you played the same piece for all the sessions, right?"

"Sure. The Mozart concerto."

"I thought so! Idiots! Idiots! You'll have to come back again. We've got to do this again, change the parameters."

"Stan! Stan! What the hell is going on?"

"I really can't explain. It's too... it's just too... well, theoretical. I can't say anything until we do it again. Can you come? Soon?"

He sighed. The last little excursion had cost him money, not just in the travel but also paying for Stephanie to sub while he missed a rehearsal *and* a performance. Not only that, you keep absenting yourself and hiring subs, they get the impression you're replaceable. Graham, the second oboe, might start getting ideas above his station. You can't afford to keep skipping out if you value your job; the concertmaster was being more than flexible, but there are limits.

"Look, I really can't get away just now, Stan. Truth is, we've had a death here."

"I know, I know! Your poor conductor. My God! I've been trying to call."

"Yes, and I've been trying not to answer," he replied rudely.

"I am so sorry... I didn't mean to..."

"No, no, it's okay. I shouldn't have been so rude, but we're all in total shock. It's happening everywhere and nobody knows what's going on, and now it's come right here to us."

He thought chaotically of microwaves and chickens and the men from CSIS.

"I am so sorry to hear this. It's somehow... No." He paused and Jonathan thought for a second he'd dropped the call. "Look," he resumed, "I really *must* see you Jonathan. It really is of the greatest urgency. It's all tied together somehow."

"What do you mean 'tied together'?" The sick feeling washed over him again.

"No, no, I can't get into it now, on the phone. I need you here."

"Can't you get someone local to help you out? What about your Irish fiddler. A little more Gaelic *pourboire*?"

"No, it's you I need. I can't explain. I'll try when I see you."

"Well, look, let me see if and when I can get away. I'll have to check the schedule."

He hated being worn down but he just didn't have the energy to argue. Why in hell did he pick up the phone?

"All right. Please," begged Stan, "please phone me as soon as you can. Bye for now."

Jonathan slapped the phone shut, cursing under his breath. What in hell was this all about? His schedule was not the issue; he knew there was one day available, early next week, but he needed time to think this through. I've got Kate Heinrichs breaking in, and that's all my stupid fault. I've got the death of the Maestro and goddamned CSIS making my life miserable, and now I've got this fucking nutcase Stan Ward. Why won't they just leave me alone? I'm being pulled to bits here!

He picked up the oboe again, but it was pointless. He began to feel cornered and frightened.

Oboe Concerto in A Minor

As Jonathan walked he stewed things over. He had abandoned his practice session with Ralph Vaughan Williams, thrown a light jacket over his tee shirt, and headed for his favorite paths by the lake. His mind was whirling and his past kept tapping him on the shoulder. The things that had happened in the last few years, the decisions he had made, the choices that he had forced upon himself, came up one after the other and jeered at him. The island he had created for himself in East Gladstone simple wasn't sustainable, but you can't go back in time. She was back there... Oh, to be able to erase the tape that tried to play over and over again in his mind, night and day.

Lunchtime came and went as he walked, and finally hungry and tired he plumped himself down at an outdoor café table in the old town centre. He ordered a coffee and some sort of fig bar and stared unseeing across the street. Finally he took a long swig of his coffee, realizing how good it was and how hungry he felt. The fig thing disappeared and he pushed his chair back slightly and stretched his arms. The food and drink had helped him to focus.

He wasn't going to run away again, but he sure as hell needed some breathing space. What if he faced Stan Ward and his project head-on? Or would it be out of the frying pan...? It would take some courage, because he was frightened by hints he had picked up, but it could be therapeutic. So, why not drop down to T-O again; this time stay overnight and chill out a bit? Maybe Stefan Kulikofski would cut him a bit of slack. Decision made, he pulled his phone out of his pocket.

"Hey Graham, would you mind taking over my chair tomorrow night? I could ask Stephanie to sub for you."

"Ah, come on, Jonathan, that's really short notice." Graham Swann never refused the opportunity to play first oboe, but he made a principle of complaining about it.

"Well, I suppose I could ask Stefan to let Stephanie sub for me instead. She could always use the extra money. Remember, I have to pay her." This was a red flag; no contract player would ever be allowed to sub at first, and Jonathan knew that. Second always moved up to first when there was an absence.

"Okay, okay, there's no need to be shitty about it. I'm gonna be doing it. You know I am."

"Thanks Graham. You're a real pal."

"Up yours!" Click.

"I'll call Steph..." but he was already gone. Graham had an agèd mum in Pickering who he was often obliged to see at the drop of a hat, and Jonathan always took on the job of making the arrangements with Stephanie, ensuring she had access to the scores in good time, and so on. He always felt that such gracious behaviour could be better rewarded—Stephanie was always effusive in her thanks—but Mr Swann didn't have it in him to overcome his primary grievance. Well, fuck you and the horse you rode in on.

Now his decision was made he felt a bit more able to deal with things. The police business was frightening but he held fast to his belief that the two deaths were pure coincidence. Any other explanation was madness. And Kate... well, he would just have to distance himself from her, although he knew she would be hurt. It hurt him to hurt her, and it was all his fault... Why the hell did he... Oh, don't start the cycle all over again, please!

Jonathan got home around six, surprised to realize he had been out half the morning and the whole afternoon. His feet were tired and he was hungry and thirsty, so the first thing he did after kicking off his sneakers was to pour a large glass of Smithwick's and carry it over to the chesterfield. His mind ranged over the contents of his fridge and found nothing in his memory that he remotely wished to eat, so he settled on something available by phone. Damn it, he thought, I'm going to be a modern, sophisticated, technocratic man and call for food without getting up out of this seat. He flipped his phone open, speed-dialed PizzaPizza and sat back to enjoy the rest of his beer.

Later in the evening with the pizza gone, and another beer sent the same way as the first, he phoned Stan Ward. The phone was picked up on the first ring, sure sign that he'd kept the old boy in suspense.

"Stan. It's Jonathan... Yeah, yeah... Look, I can come down to Toronto tomorrow. I was thinking of staying overnight... No, really, I can stay somewhere downtown. Yes, I'm quite sure, really... So, see you at the bus station around three? Okay. Bye."

He logged on to the web and booked a hotel room in downtown Toronto, not far from the bus station. Done. Now let's see what curve balls life's going to pitch at me.

As the bus thrummed through the flat rural landscape, away from the granite and sandstone and into the fertile plain left by the retreating ice sheet, Jonathan half dozed and let his mind wander. When you make a complete break with an earlier life it's like looking back at a stranger. He'd heard immigrants relate this; the life they had led in another country was akin to the activities of a different person. To emigrate, even today with easy access to global travel, was still a huge break, a fault-line in a life, although still tangible. But, when you tried to invent a new life without having that real, tangible division, the old life kept reappearing, almost as if it were alongside you, instead of in the past. The mental effort of keeping the past distant, the continual wakefulness, was enervating, and the stranger who used to be you was always there. And no matter how much effort you expended in maintaining the barrier, it kept breaking down. One little hint—just the word 'microwave'—and it all slips, exposing raw areas. And during the night, of course, the defences were totally down.

And Kate Heinrichs... I can't go there... She's trying to take me where I simply cannot go.

Oh, the exhausting stupidity of moving along yet still being stuck with the past! The aching hole that won't mend.

This was no way to run a life. Maybe, he mused, I'm one of those who just aren't suitable for life; it just doesn't fit properly. Trouble is, there ain't nothin' else. Like the man said: We at CSIS think you only go round once.

He hoped that Toronto would give him some sort of... escape, if nothing else. It would actually throw him headlong into a furnace.

"Look," said Stan Ward to Sandra as they sat over the remains of their lunch. "I'm going to the lab for a meeting with the team, then off to pick up Rycroft at the bus station at about three. We'll get a meal somewhere, then do our evening session."

"So, he's booked a hotel then?" She finished her tea and started to pour another.

"Yes. Somewhere just off University Avenue. I suppose he could have stayed here but in retrospect he'd probably like a little distance."

"I could've had Peter's old room ready. Still, it's better this way. Funny, he's an outgoing type, but you feel a... what is it? An emotional barrier of some kind?"

"Yes," agreed Stan. "I found him very evasive about his past. I wanted to talk to him about these deaths, but he closed up tight. He actually appeared quite frightened."

"I feel there's some deep damage there, Stan, but it's none of our business."

"No. No, it isn't I suppose. But I need him fully informed; *you* know!"

"Yes, you and your impossible theories. Anomalies and dying maestros!"

He had shared much of his thinking with her over the years, and while it stayed in the sphere of physiology she could remain comfortably in her role as a neutral sounding board, but recently his ideas had become a little fantastic.

"I sometimes wonder, my dear," she continued, "if you've not started an early decline into senility."

"Humbug!" He rubbed his hands together. "So, I'll take him back to the lab, let him meet the others. I want his involvement to be legitimate, if you see what I mean."

"I'm sure they still think you're crazy. Especially Livermore. I know I do."

"Well, I did have to tell him that the tests Jonathan and I had done yielded nothing. And y'know, I think he was almost relieved!"

"Until you told him you weren't finished," she laughed.

"But it's fine with him, and the others, if I continue on this track, as long as I continue to get no results. But, what if...? Eh? What if?"

"What *will* you do if you get something? Tonight?"

"Then," my dear, he paused dramatically, "a whole new universe opens up before us!"

"Oh, go away you melodramatic old bugger! Go play with your science toys."

"You'll see. You'll see."

He put on his shoes and coat, checked his wallet for transit tokens for his guest, and opened the street door.

"Good luck!" she called.

"I'm going to need it! See you later tonight."

Stan had to wait more than twenty minutes in the bus terminal, a horrible echoing space that stank of burnt diesel fuel and fatty fast food. He sat on a hard moulded fiberglass bench that fitted no backside in all humanity, and watched the constant stream of people with cases, backpacks, bags and hold-alls and wondered where they were all going and why. Bus stations, airports, train stations; people continually on the move. It has never been so easy to travel, and the world has never been so small. Several buses rounded the corner into the enclosed bus bay before the one from East Gladstone came in sight.

Stan spotted Jonathan first, rose from his seat and walked over. They shook hands appraising each other all over again.

"Well, here we are again. I'd like to take you to the lab to meet some of the team, but do you want to drop by your hotel first?"

"Sure. Be nice to drop off my bag and check in."

"Good. Off we go then. It's on our way. I hope you don't mind a walk?" It seemed to be the old boy's chief form of local transportation. "I've got some transit tokens for you, so you won't have to walk back!"

"Now," he continued, after a block or so had been covered. "This afternoon they'll be running some tests—a few little bugs to be seen to, but nothing serious—so we won't get to our stuff until later, but I want you to meet the people and get an idea of them. Y'see, they think I'm some sort of crackpot, but I think it would be nice for them to meet you. Frankly, they're all rather keen that we find no results at all. Put their minds at rest."

"And if you do see results? What then?"

As Jonathan strode along Dundas Street, just keeping pace with Stan Ward, he realized that here was a fit, sprightly human being.

"I think we'll leave that bridge until it's ready to be crossed. As I said on the phone, it's all very difficult to explain. Even if I understood it myself," he added with a hint of doubt in his voice.

"And Mozart?" asked Jonathan. "You were all excited on the phone about Mozart. What was that all about?"

"Again, Jonathan, please let me be obscure. I should not have got so excited when we talked. I would hate to raise false expectations. If we see results tonight, then well and good. If not..."

They walked in silence for a minute.

"Ah, here's your *auberge*," indicated Stan, pointing to the entrance of a tall, nondescript high rise. He pushed the door open and walked in. "I'll wait here in the foyer for you. Take your time."

Jonathan checked in quickly and rode the elevator up to his room. He dropped his bag on a wooden rack near the door and quickly cased the room. The usual: huge double bed, easy chair, table with phone and TV, couch along one wall, crap Picasso knock-off prints on the walls. He was back down to the foyer in minutes.

They strode on, up a slight rise with the Ontario Legislature in Queen's Park Circle looming before them. It was a fine day and Jonathan found the walk refreshing; two and more hours in the bus had made stretching the legs a pleasure.

"Tell me," he asked breaking a long silence. "What exactly is it you are measuring? No, that's not quite what I meant. I've seen the set-up of course, but how can you be so sure that what you're seeing is the whole picture?"

"Well, there's a great deal of very abstruse biochemistry, the greater part of which I will not bother you with. Indeed," he observed with a raised eyebrow in Jonathan's direction, "since you went to the *other side* you might not be so well informed as to such biochemical functions as the Krebs Cycle, hmm? Vaguely? Huh! Only the most inspired piece of biochemical genius ever, that's all! Suffice it to say that the most reliable way of measuring energy consumption in organic systems is chemical. We can measure levels of adenosine triphosphate in the muscles, and its restoration during physical exercise by the creation of creatine phosphate. You've probably heard of CPK—creatine phosphokinase—which is used to measure muscle damage in heart attack patients. No? Well, it's one marker of physical activity in the muscles. Then there's anaerobic breakdown of glycogen, followed by aerobic utilization of glycogen, fats and proteins. Respiratory gas analysis is also an essential component, but that we can do remotely by monitoring levels in the blood. And, naturally, body temperature. And these things all interact in such a complex and dynamic way that modeling it has been the life's work of many a researcher. I think you get the picture."

"And you can be sure you're capturing a full picture? No loose ends?"

"We believe so," he replied. "We think it's a damned good model. And scientific reputations depend upon it. That's why the team is so very confident that this anomaly I have observed is indeed false. And we shan't know that until this evening, eh?"

"But aren't all your measurements based on muscular activity? What's it to do with the brain? That's where the creative process is working, surely?"

"Your thinking processes—creative and otherwise—are still driven by a system of energy supply and demand; basically highly sophisticated chemical reactions. Glucose plays a big part."

"So, a very mechanistic view of the living human machine, *n'est ce pas*?"

"Ah, now, now, don't drive me in the direction of theology! That way lies madness!" And with that he would say no more.

Five minutes of hard walking later they strode up the path from College Street, entered the Medical Sciences Building and made their way quickly to the third floor. Stan knocked on a door and ushered Jonathan into the office of Ken Livermore, the co-leader of the team.

"It's very good to meet you Mr Rycroft," began Livermore somewhat diffidently. "Please have a seat. Stan tells me you're here to help iron out a little bug in our system."

"I hope I can be of some help..." he replied feeling acutely ill at ease. He felt he had much less than Livermore's full attention.

"We'll run some tests this evening," Stan intervened quickly and rather too heartily, "and then we'll see what's what."

"Dr Khan—he's our electronics guy, Mr Rycroft—has gone over all the circuitry now, so I can't see there will be an issue. I just hope you won't think your time wasted. After all, last time you were here you found nothing, I understand."

"Double check," interrupted Stan. "Absolutely no sense in taking chances. Thank you Ken; I want to introduce Jonathan to the crew."

Livermore stood and shook hands coolly with Jonathan and returned to his chair. Stan led Jonathan along to the lab, and just outside the lab door he stopped and put a hand on Jonathan's sleeve.

"Look, Ken's under a lot of pressure with this thing, and he's actually shit scared that we might upset the apple cart. He would rather you weren't here at all, but I felt this was better than skulking around at night."

"Yeah, that was really uncomfortable. Are the rest of the team going to be like that?"

"We'll see," as he swung the lab door open, "but I very much doubt it."

A lab session was in full progress with a wired-up subject pedaling away on the exercise bike in the electrostatic cage, while three researchers watched progress on the computer screens. One of the researchers, a younger guy, noticed the visitors in the outer lab and came over to the door of the cage.

"Hi Stan," he greeted, peering through the mesh. "Won't be

long; just a couple of minutes left in this session and we can open the door."

The session came to an end, and on a signal from one of the researchers the sweating athlete stopped pedaling.

"Great, let's file that one and take a break," smiled the East Indian scientist over his shoulder as he opened the cage door and came forward to greet the guest.

"Makharam, here's Dr Jonathan Rycroft back for more." Stan placed a nice emphasis on the Doctor.

"Good to see you again," said Khan shaking hands. The CSIS agents had aroused Jonathan's suspicions, but this Khan seemed friendly enough.

"I know Stan's got this bug in his ear about this supposed anomaly..." continued Khan. He smiled at Stan, and Stan smiled back, "...but I've done thorough checks of the whole system and the last time you guys ran a test nothing showed up. Heck of a relief, that was!"

"As I said, Makharam, a final check to ease the last doubts in my mind." Turning to Jonathan and smiling sideways at Khan, he continued in a fake conspiratorial whisper, "Just to humour the old buzzard, y'know."

The other two emerged from the cage leaving their subject—still sitting on the bike and hooked up to the network of wires, sensors and monitors—to catch his breath and swig from a water bottle, presumably before the test session resumed.

"This is Robin, Robin Tokarek our post-doc student," Stan performed the introductions, "and here's Celia Wong our biochemist. John not here today?"

"No," replied Wong, briefly shaking Jonathan's hand. "He's got a consultation down at the Air Canada Centre. Doesn't really need to be here for this anyway."

"John Rolfe is our sports med guy," explained Stan. "Well, we'd better not hold you up. Jonathan here is just going to set my mind at rest regarding the anomaly." He chuckled. "I only really invited him down here, because I like to hear him play!"

"Oh sure!" replied Wong. "But if that's the case what's the matter with your Irish fiddler?"

"Oh, I think we need a higher class of music altogether," observed Tokarek with a smile. "In keeping with the elevated status of our work, don't you know."

They all laughed and Stan and Jonathan made to leave.

"Hey," called Celia Wong as they were at the door, "we'll be through in about a half hour. Why don't you come back at, say, five instead of your usual night owl routine?"

"Great idea," replied Stan as they left the lab. He turned to Jonathan. "I was going to suggest eating out somewhere then coming back to the lab, but we might as well wait. How about a coffee, then a stroll?"

They sat in the cafeteria downstairs drinking some lamentable coffee that came from a machine on the counter by the cashier's desk. God, thought Jonathan, imagine having the smell of that thing in your nostrils all day; put you off coffee for life. Their conversation stayed at a superficial level; neither wished to speculate on the up-coming test. It was almost as if they felt that the test results could be influenced by the very act of discussing them. Stan thought of Schrödinger's cat.

Once their refreshment was finished, Stan took Jonathan on his customary stroll around the campus. Just as they were passing the east door of University College Jonathan darted up the few steps and opened the door with Stan just behind him. He crossed a short foyer to stand at the foot of a staircase beside a coiled wooden dragon carved on the newel post. He gently stroked the worn serrations on the dragon's back, as had legions of students before him as they passed down this staircase.

"This is the most subtle patina any object can achieve," he observed. "A surface developed by generations of caresses."

Stan ran his hand down the silky wooden surface, achieving a new sense of oldness, tradition and the interactions of people with things. It gave him an insight into the relationship that musicians like Jonathan had with their instruments.

They returned to the lab at just after five, giving the team time to complete their work and pack up for the day. Jonathan sat in the little office, as before, and worked though a few exercises to loosen himself up and get the oboe ready. When he was all set they entered the cage, and Stan closed the door securely behind them.

"There's no need to sit on the bike," he said as Jonathan prepared to mount. "We'll just have you sit comfortably in a chair. We don't need to record physical exertion this time; we can use a resting baseline. Where's your music?"

Jonathan tapped his head. "In here."

"How do you *do* that?"

Jonathan shrugged. "It's just what we do..."

Stan brought a chair round from behind the table of monitors and computers, pushed the bike aside and positioned the chair in its place. Jonathan sat while Stan busied himself connecting all the sensors in place on the various parts of his anatomy.

"Right! Test of the system just to get a good baseline. Just sit there for a few minutes while I go through this."

Jonathan fingered his oboe, loosening his fingers, and sucked gently on the detached reed between his lips.

"Right," announced Stan after a short while, "we're stable and all balanced. Let's see what we can do. Why don't you play something a bit out of the ordinary? Something you don't hear very often; perhaps more recent."

Jonathan was more than intrigued. Stan had gone on about the Mozart, shouting idiots! idiots! down the phone, and now here was some more obfuscation. He was on the verge of asking him again what this was all about, but held it back and concentrated on the music. The Vaughn Williams seemed to fit the bill, but how well he could do this one from memory remained to be seen.

He had scarcely played the first few bars when Stan yelled, "Yes! Yes! No, no don't stop playing! Keep going, keep going. Yes, yes! Ha hah! It's there! It's there!"

Ralph Vaughn Williams will be rolling in his grave, thought Jonathan, as he soldiered on trying to concentrate on the flow of music in his head while the chortling and whooping continued from behind the monitors.

"That should do it. That should do it," called Stan as he clicked the mouse to save the recording. "It's most definitely there. Of course, I knew it would be. Hah! Now tell me about this piece you just played—lovely, by the way, simply lovely—what's its story?"

"It's the 'Minuet and Musette', the second movement of Vaughan Williams's Concerto in A minor, but I really wasn't doing it justice. It's very tricky."

"When was it written?"

Why in hell would he be interested in the date of composition, thought Jonathan.

"In 1944, while London was being bombed by the Luftwaffe."

"Excellent! Excellent! Now," announced Stan like an impresario introducing a death-defying high wire act, "I want you to play the Mozart again. Exactly like last time. All ready?"

Again he was on the edge of asking for some sort of explanation, but again the urgency of the moment drove him to continue playing. This one was easier, although again his concentration was shattered by yells of "Hah! Zero! Undetectable! I thought so! I thought so! What do you think of that then?"

They did several more runs, using various pieces of music from Jonathan's memory, but as the tests continued Stan's demeanor changed and the beaming, chuckling and rubbing together of hands turned into a quiet pensiveness.

They finally ran down to a stop at just before eight o'clock in the evening, after half a dozen test sessions, and Stan Ward strode out from behind the monitors.

"Now we see it! Now we see the anomaly in all its nakedness. And now, we open one awfully big can of worms, my boy. Awfully big. Pandora's box..."

"Stan! You absolutely *have* to tell me what the hell is going on!"

"Let's get you unhooked, and we'll go and sit in the office." He glanced at his watch. "Tell you what, you unhook these monitors while I pop down to the cafeteria and get us some coffee. It'll still be open." And with that he was gone.

Damn you, damn you, thought Jonathan as he tore off adhesive pads and unclipped sensors, you're bloody playing for time. The excitement and anticipation were sliding into anger and frustration. Something momentous had occurred and he needed desperately to know what. Why was Stan being so God-damned cagy? But the anger he felt was masking a cold fear.

Ward was back in five minutes with two tall paper cups of coffee, which he took straight into the office with Jonathan on his heels. The ride up from the cafeteria to the third floor had cooled the coffee enough for it to be drinkable.

"Now," said Stan after a long draught of coffee, "this is extremely complex but, more to the point, so incredible that you'll think I'm crazy." He took a deep breath, looked Jonathan in the eye, and took the plunge. "You have complained that I have been reticent, but when I have tried to broach the subject you have shut me down.

"It starts with the deaths of all these maestros and vast bolts of lethal energy..."

"No! No! No! I can't! I can't!"

The cold fear leapt forward. Suddenly the past and the present were simultaneously in Jonathan's mind. He cried out in an agony of spirit as the red wave rolled over him. The past rushed in; a huge overwhelming tide. He felt again in full measure the loathing, followed by the anger. He was in the car with *her* on that icy road—the scene that played out over and over again in his mind whenever he let the barrier down, day and waking night—the noise, the impact, the shower of glass in his face, the blood on his lips...

He had come here in the foolish hope of redemption; that the fearful spectre in his waking dreams could be laid to rest, but instead there was an explosion of the mind. Shaking and crying, with his head in his hands, he jumped up from the chair and ran out of the door, along the corridor, down the fire exit stairs and out into the world.

Horrified at what he had set in motion, Ward rushed after him calling out, but he was too far ahead. He stopped eventually on the diagonal path leading to College Street looking around him, but saw no sign of Jonathan.

My God, he thought, oh my God! What have I done? What *have* I done?

The triumphant results of the experiment had turned to ashes.

It was a very woebegone and tired Stan Ward who let himself into the house, sat on the stairs in the hall, and slowly removed his shoes. He placed Jonathan's oboe case on the shoe rack beside the door.

Sandra appeared at the top of the stairs and leant over the banister. She noted the droop of his shoulders and the slow, methodical way he removed his shoes, and her heart went out to him.

"So, no luck then? I am so sorry, Stan."

She knew how much confidence he had pinned on a positive outcome, and knew how confused and depressed he would be. He was still physically as active as ever, she thought, but perhaps he was getting too old for this sort of roller-coaster emotional ride. He ought to start acting like a real Emeritus.

"The contrary," he replied quietly. "Results, results and more results."

She came halfway down the stairs, perplexed. "What?" Then she saw the oboe case. "His instrument? Stan, what's happened?"

"I tried to explain..." he began, then appeared to catch himself and backtrack. "The results were there. They were *there*! We sat in the office afterwards—he was all impatient, angry almost, probably because I was being so reticent—and I tried to explain about the deaths and the energy. Well, I knew there was some sensitivity; we talked about it, eh? That Skype call, when he acted really strangely?"

"Yes, yes, but what happened?"

"He went absolutely crazy, stormed out of the building, and now he's God knows where! If he comes to harm I'll blame myself for ever."

She came down to the last stair and held both his hands in hers. He was shaking.

"So, you don't know where he went?"

"No. I hope, back to his hotel."

"Well, then, give him a call. Right now."

They went and sat in the living room. He picked up the phone from the side table, dialed and waited but it went straight to voicemail. "Jonathan, it's me, Stan. I'm really sorry. Please, please call me back."

He looked up the hotel in the telephone directory, dialed and was put through to Jonathan's room, but it rang and rang.

"Hmm, PTSD perhaps?" she observed.

"Bloody acronyms..."

"Post traumatic stress disorder," she spelt out, "common among soldiers, firemen, EMTs..."

"Yes, yes, I know. I just didn't catch the acronym, that's all."

"Poor guy. I wonder if he's been in a war zone."

"No mention of it, at least to me. Far as I know he worked in physics then transferred rather abruptly to music."

"Perhaps none of our business, but it's a worry."

"We'll just have to be patient, damn it."

They spent the rest of the evening quietly, while Stan tried twice more to contact Jonathan by phone. There was nothing much else they could do. Should he go to the hotel, he wondered, but then decided against it. He'd just continue to be patient.

Sandra brought a large tome in from her bag in the hall, the spiral binding very reminiscent of an academic work in draft. He asked her what it was.

"It's a bloody PhD thesis the Dean asked me to read," she replied, "and it's absolutely shocking."

Excellent! This was just the distraction Stan needed.

"The usual tack, eh, 'using the English language to render his meaning obscure'?"

"Right on. Listen to this: 'a further systematic examination and rationalization of the existing metadata in the context of the newly-formulated paradigm outlined in section seven might be seen to yield the potential for future exploration of both the information in its raw form and its subsequent extrapolation, retrieval and analysis'."

"What the fuck, if you'll excuse my Romantic poetic language, does that mean?"

"I think it means 'please renew my research grant for another year'." She paused, shaking her head slowly from side to side. "I remember, a couple of years back—maybe I didn't mention it to you at the time—I had this student who produced just such a line of tripe. I said to him: What in God's name does this mean? Give it to me in simple words. So then he explains it to me in language I can understand. So I said: *write down* what you just said to me!"

"But you know the problem with that, of course," he observed. "Put it in sensible, understandable language and it ain't a dissertation of a hundred thousand words any more!"

"You got it in one!" she replied, laying the great tome down upon her lap with a finger inserted to keep her place.

"I do wish they'd teach kids to write," he complained. "I mean, how hard can it be? They did it to us, and we're not damaged, are we? How's *your* self-esteem?"

"Well, it's a new educational paradigm these days," she replied with a laugh, emphasizing the word paradigm because it was the word on everyone's lips and she new it would get a rise out of him.

"Yes, and one that abhors the practice of critical thought. There's a lovely quote from Richard Mitchell—my goodness I love that man!—who said, more or less: 'Thinking is done in language, and understanding, a result of thinking, is expressed in language, but, when we simply adopt and recite what has been expressed, we have committed neither thinking nor understanding'. Perfect, eh?"

"That's what this great work of fiction is all about," she complained. "Or, at least, I think it is... We'll never get a generation of incisive thinkers if we don't get them young, and lay the groundwork in the heads."

She shoved the dissertation onto the table in front of her. "I can't work through this bullshit any more tonight. Have a look yourself, see how I suffer."

He smiled, and reached for the great tome to see for himself. It really was a good distraction from his guilty thoughts.

The good thing about rehearsals was you could dress casual; even in the Maestro era the dress code had been relaxed. Kate wore tight blue jeans and a loose pale green shirt, buttoned up the front, with long sleeves, but not loose enough to mess with her bowing arm; she found that distracting. Her headband was silk and matched the shirt.

Jonathan had told the group he would be away in Toronto and wouldn't be back until about eleven, but when he didn't show up for the afternoon rehearsal, Graham Swann cornered Kate in the passageway leading to the stage during a brief break.

"Where's Jonathan?" he asked, buying the orchestra scuttle-butt that he and she were an item. "If he's not going to be here, he always calls. Has to get Stephanie set up to sub. No idea? Shit, that's inconvenient."

This surprised Kate; it really was unlike him to be absent without notice. "No, he never said anything to me. He was down in Toronto; due back this morning."

"Okay, I'll sort it out," he replied with ill grace, and headed off to the dressing room. "Phone her myself I 'spose..." he called over his shoulder.

Kate was worried. She knew he had been down to Toronto, working with that professor what's-his-name, but he should have been back this morning. All afternoon her mind wasn't fully on the music before her, and she had experienced a glare or two from first violin. She felt bad for her colleagues because, although Kulikofski couldn't tell who was fluffing, he knew it was somebody in her section. She'd have to apologize to them later, and then of course they would have heard about Jonathan's AWOL stint, and... Oh, damn, things do get so complicated.

During the mid-afternoon break she went outside to the rear patio that fronted the lake, flipped open her phone and nearly cried with relief when she saw that it was picking up signal. His phone was off, so she left the briefest of messages and went back to her seat on the stage.

What more could she do? There must be something wrong with him; he was the most regular, most predictable member of the orchestra practically. Where could he be? Perhaps if he had problems in Toronto professor what's-his-name would know? Oh God, what *was* his name? Think, girl, think! Stan! Stanley Ward, physiology, U of T. She opened her laptop, right there beside her chair, and Googled his name. After a short search she located him; there was an e-mail address but no phone number, so in an agony of impatience she composed a quick message saying who she was, and included the number of her mobile. The concertmaster looked pointedly in her direction, probably fuming about the addiction of the young to technology, and called the players to order. She closed the laptop, noting that the battery-low flag was showing.

The resumed rehearsal was absolute torture, and as soon as they finished for the day she rushed to the women's washroom for privacy, plugged her laptop into the sockets at the counter beside the sinks, and switched on her phone. She was frantic. There was a brief voicemail from Stan Ward—thank God, thank God—and he had also e-mailed his phone number. A couple of players entered the washroom chatting, glanced quickly at her, opened adjacent cubicles, and continued a conversation on one particularly challenging cello passage while their clothing rustled down. Kate decided to seek further privacy, unplugged the laptop, and went outside to the rear patio again.

She flipped open her phone and dialed. "Professor Ward? My name's Kate, Kate Heinrichs. I'm trying contact Jonathan... He *was* there...?" A long stretch as she nodded several times and tears started in her eyes. "Oh no! But... Where was he staying? Okay, Dundas at University... No, I think it might be better if I went... As soon as I know... Bye."

Oh, my God, she thought, something went badly wrong. I have to go down to Toronto; go to the hotel. What if he isn't there? The police...? A wave of panic overtook her and she sat down on a low stone wall beside the patio unable to think. After a few minutes she breathed deeply, wiped her face with a tissue from her pocket, and began putting her thoughts together. First thing, go find Liz and hope to God she hasn't gone home yet. It was gone six.

She entered the cafeteria by the patio doors and spotted Liz Straker, deep in conversation at one of the tables.

"Liz, could I have a word?" Liz saw from Kate's face that there was big trouble, excused herself and walked with her towards the doors.

"What is it? What the heck's wrong?" She placed an arm softly around her shoulder.

"Jonathan has gone missing. He's in Toronto and I have to go find him." The tears started again. "Look, do you have your car here?"

"Yes, yes I do, but you can't just take off..."

"I have to! I *have* to! Please, *please* let me borrow your car!"

"Boy, you are serious!" Liz thought for a moment. She always drove to the concert hall as she lived with her boyfriend in a small cottage a long way round the lake. "Okay, no problem, I can get a lift home. Here's the keys. But, are you sure...?"

"Yes. I *have* to be there. Look, could you clear this with old Kulikofski for tomorrow? The sooner I can go the better."

Liz moved her arm right around Kate's shoulders and drew her close. "Okay, I'll fix everything at this end. There's clearly a lot more to you and him than you let on."

"Thanks, Liz! Thanks," said Kate as she broke away and made for the door, "you're... you're the best. I owe you one!"

Kate found the car in parking lot, fumbled with the keys in her haste, and had to grope beside the car to retrieve them. They were lying a couple of inches from a sewer grate. She plumped herself down thankfully behind the wheel and familiarized herself with the layout. She had a driver's licence but hadn't owned a car since coming to East Gladstone; in such a small town there was really no need. On the infrequent occasions when she needed a car she would take a rental from an outfit down by the bus station.

She started up and drove out of the lot. As she headed for Highway 11 she recalled Liz's parting words, 'There's clearly a lot more to you and him than you let on', and only wished it were true. After that day at the picnic she wasn't sure of anything anymore. She used to think heartache was just a turn of phrase, but it wasn't; it really did *hurt*! What if he didn't want to see her? What if he wasn't there? What if...? No, no, that was impossible to think about.

So Kate, with phone, laptop, handbag and nothing else, pointed the borrowed car south and hit the gas.

Highway 400 had never felt so long as she sped along praying that there was no police radar on the prowl; whether she would be able to weep her way out of a ticket was a moot point. Once into Toronto she swung east onto Highway 401 and prayed again that traffic flow would be easy. Mercifully, both the express and feeder lanes were moving well and it wasn't long before she was fuming at the southbound stop-start traffic down Avenue Road. She pulled into the hotel's underground parking lot in the early evening, scarcely an hour and half after leaving East Gladstone, and made her way directly to the reception desk.

There was only one person looking after the desk, infuriatingly answering tourist questions of an elderly couple who were clearly either mentally retarded or deeply mired in senile dementia. Kate danced and fumed in impatience before the old couple toddled off muttering about the CN Tower while trying to fold a tourist map the wrong way, and the receptionist finally turned to her. He was a slim, thin-faced young man with a carefully nurtured three-day growth of beard and one gold earring.

"I would like to speak with one of your guests please. Doctor Jonathan Rycroft. Could you please give me his room number?"

"I'm sorry, but it's hotel policy to respect the privacy of our guests and not reveal room numbers."

"Well, could I at least talk to him? Couldn't you phone the room?"

He checked the register on his monitor, dialed a number on the house phone at the desk below counter level, checked that it was ringing, and wordlessly handed her the receiver. It rang and rang and rang.

"Perhaps he's not in his room?" suggested the young man. "Although his key's out. He may have taken it with him, of course. Wanna leave him a message?"

"Look," Kate pleaded, "I need the room number. I absolutely *have* to speak to him. This is terribly urgent!"

"I'm sorry, but it's hotel policy..."

"Listen!" she interrupted leaning forward over the counter with her jaw clenched. The frustration and fear of the last six hours poured out. "If you want a whole load of police to show up outside your God-damned hotel with sirens and lights flashing I can call 'em *right now*!" She flipped her phone open and poised a finger above the keypad. "So, do you want a shit storm right here in the foyer, or do I get the fucking room number?"

"Okay, okay! Room fourteen-twelve. The elevator's over..." but she was punching the 'up' button before he finished speaking. "You'll get me fired..." he called to the closed doors.

Kate fumed up to the fourteenth floor, pacing the tiny elevator car like a cat in a cage, and burst out before the door had finished opening. She looked wildly for the room number signs, turned the wrong way, backtracked, found the door of room twelve and began pounding on it with her fist.

Kate thought the door would never open. If he wasn't in there, then where was he? How could she ever find him? What if he *was* in there, but...

The latch clicked; the door swung slightly open. He was a horrible sight, but the flood of relief that tore through her buckled her knees and drove her sobbing and clutching onto him. He led her into the room, moving like a wooden doll and let her down onto the edge of the bed. He stood over her for minutes, a look of incomprehension on his face, until suddenly the incomprehension was replaced with anguish. Pure anguish racked him and he collapsed onto the bed beside her, sitting with his face in his hands, elbows on knees, and wept. Their roles were reversed; she regained her composure as he lost his. He cried and cried, until she thought he would never stop.

It must have been a quarter of an hour before she was able to place her hand gently on his arm. He shuddered but didn't pull away. Eventually, his weeping spent, he raised his head from his hands and stared out of the window, across rooftops and neon signs and streets where people were happily leading their little lives.

She moved her hand to his shoulder; still he made no move.

"I... it's... you're..." She kept deathly still, fearful of breaking the spell. He couldn't continue.

There was a long silence while they looked out of the window together. In the distance, on the far skyline, the white light on the top of the CN Tower flashed regularly, a metronome for their thoughts.

"You're... too much like her," he finally sighed. "If you were... different, it wouldn't be so bad. As soon as I saw you. First time I saw you. I should never have... You are too alike. And, and..."

"Go on," she murmured softly. "It's just little Kate from the old EGO. Just us chickens."

She felt his back tense into rigidity and only slowly relax.

"It's another world, and you close doors." He turned to her with wild eyes. "You start again and you don't want to go back. But, things don't stay back there, do they? They come with you. And then I find someone like you and..." he shuddered.

"And it all comes back?"

"Yes, it all comes back. It's out and I can't put it back."

"It'll always be there, that's the truth, but it can be softened with time. I can help it soften... if you will let me."

He nodded. Tears ran down his face again and a terrible pain was in his eyes. He sat quite still and stared unseeing out into world. That touch; one slight hand on his sleeve and then his shoulder had undone him. He was lost and he knew he would never get back.

"Did she die?" she asked, scarcely in a whisper lest he close up again.

He nodded, eyes closed, lips between clenched teeth.

She leaned further forward and put her arms around his shoulders, one across his back the other over his chest. Her scent was in his nose, her warmth upon him, her hair teasing his ear, her breasts pressing upon his arm. He neither moved away nor came closer. They sat, locked like a statue of star-crossed lovers, for a long, drawn out moment.

Presently, he moved closer to her and rested his head upon her shoulder. He sighed and, for the first time, placed his arm about her.

"Yes," he said quietly. "I killed her..." He tightened his arm upon her as if willing her to stay with him. She held still, suspended.

"It was... I..." but he couldn't continue.

"Start from the beginning. We have all the time in the world."

"I was so angry. So *angry*. The machine worked, but the look in their eyes, the way they rejoiced... I couldn't stand it. It was all wrong."

He stopped speaking and looked far away, out into the past. Kate waited silent, again willing the spell to remain unbroken.

"I collected her at the club, and we drove... I drove... It was cold, dark, icy. I was so angry and we argued. Why?" he pleaded with Kate. "Why would we argue? Then, I hit this ice... That's what they said afterwards," he assured her. "They said it was an accident. She... I... I looked. When the car had stopped. And, and..."

He broke down again in tears, and this time Kate took him in her arms and hugged and hugged.

"The whole side of the car gone... She was dead and I wasn't even injured! She used to call me Jon..."

"Oh, my poor darling," murmured Kate, gently stroking his hair. "No wonder, no wonder. I'm here and I'm not going anywhere."

"Never told anyone before..." and the tears continued.

Some minutes later he stretched himself, easing Kate's hold.

She was relieved. Oh this is so ridiculous, she thought, a critical tipping point in my entire life, and I'm dying for a pee; don't remember when I last used the bathroom.

"Back in a sec," she said as she withdrew from him and stepped into the bathroom. While she sat on the toilet she pulled the phone out of her jeans pocket and quickly texted Professor Ward: "Im with him now all ok kate".

When she returned he was standing at the window, back to the room, not watching the activity in the city beyond the window. She came slowly up to him, placed her arms around his waist and pressed her cheek between his shoulder blades.

"I thought it was Stan, phoning," he said slowly. With her ear to his back the resonance of his voice was magic. "Didn't answer... Then you thumped on the door. Saw you in the peephole... I knew you weren't going away... camp out there, you would. I don't know why you came; the crap treatment I've given you."

"It's because I love you, you stupid idiot," she whispered into his back. "Ever since we first saw each other."

He stiffened against her arms. She led him gently by the hand back to the bed and they sat.

"What happened? Yesterday. Can you tell me?"

She held his hands and looked into his eyes. His gaze stayed with her.

"He... We got the results he wanted, but he... I thought he was playing with me. Wouldn't come out and say; delaying. I got angry, then he started talking about deaths and... energy, and it all came back again." He gripped her hands and there were tears again. "It all came back, and I had to get away."

He gulped and paused for a few minutes while Kate waited, hanging on his silence.

"I walked and walked. Nearly all night. I don't know where I was... I was on this bridge over a ravine, and I looked down at the pavement below... I thought... I said... it can all end right now. Just climb onto the railing. But," he looked down at her hands and his grip tightened, "I just didn't have the guts. Just couldn't do it."

"You *did* have the guts! You *did*! That's why you're here now!" Again they fell together, arms around each other, and stayed so.

Practical Kate Heinrichs emerged from their embrace, and a spell of some kind was broken.

"Look at the time! It's nearly half nine," she announced, "I don't know when you last ate, but I'm starving."

"Yeah, it's been a while." He rose slowly to his feet.

"And I bet those are yesterday's clothes. Why don't you take a shower and change? If you could just see yourself! I'll get on to room service and order some grub. Hope they're still open, 'cos I don't fancy wandering around Dundas at this time of the evening."

He made a weak smile. "No, don't want you doing that." He headed for the bathroom and she got on the phone.

"Anything you fancy?" she called just before the water started running.

"Anything but chicken," came a muffled reply. She ordered sandwiches and a large pot of coffee. Decaf? they asked. Are you kidding!

As she waited for him, she sat in the chair by the phone and a deep uncertainty settled over her. Oh my God, she thought, what have I got myself into? What's all this about a 'machine that worked' and the look in their eyes? And the accident; he's carrying all that guilt. And now, instead of relief that I've finally broken through to him, I'm frightened. Will he hate me because I've come too close? Will it be worse now, not better? There's still a huge shadow over him, and he might yet hide behind it; there's a dead woman tapping him on the shoulder; a dead woman who I'll never replace. Oh God, where the hell am I going?

Then the resolve returned. Pain or misery, likely both, but I'm in it for the long haul; I can't give him up now, it'll destroy me and maybe him too. There's a point in life—one glance when eyes meet—and your whole world changes. It can plunge you into misery if you let it, but I'm damned if I will! I've sure chosen one long and tough row to plough, she thought, harking back to her days on dad's tractor on the Kindersley farm, but we're not done yet.

The bathroom door swung open.

"My God! What a transformation! You look almost human. Food's on the way."

She came over to him and hugged him, and was moved again to tears. He returned the hug, but it was as if he was holding something fragile and strange.

"I know you're good to me, but..." he began as a rapping started on the door.

She swung away from him reluctantly, opened the door and brought the tray in. She placed it on the table beside the phone and began unwrapping packages and spreading out the feast. She sat in the chair by the phone, he on the edge of the bed. He poured coffee, adding a little milk but no sugar just as she liked it. There were no words between them now. Nothing needed to be said, or could be said.

Once the meal was finished and a second cup of coffee had been poured, she took his hands across the table, looked him in the eyes and said, "So now, we go forward."

"Yes, we go forward," he replied, and inside him for the first time since... then... he felt a blending of that past life and this one. It was tentative and fragile, but it would grow. They sat for a while, facing each other, each with their own thoughts. He watched her face and read the thoughts that crossed it. Then, as if a profound decision had been made, her face suddenly brightened.

"Let's have a wee drink, shall we?" she proposed as she jumped out of her chair and knelt down in front of the mini-bar. "Good God, you've really been through this, haven't you? And you didn't even check off what you took on the sheet. They charge an arm and a leg in these places. There's nothing left here!"

At this he was able to smile, and chuckle a little. "You really are something else, aren't you, Kate Heinrichs?" He shook his head. "You really are something else."

Even with the coffee on board, the tiredness born of anguish, fear, worry and catharsis began to set in. They yawned almost simultaneously, caught themselves at it, and exchanged thoughts by pure telepathy.

"I've got a car downstairs—it's Liz's—but neither of us is in any state to travel," she answered his thoughts. "So why don't we catch a few hours sleep and then see what tomorrow brings? I can stretch out on the chesterfield. Is there a spare blanket in the cupboard?"

There was, so after a quick trip to the bathroom she stretched out on the chesterfield and pulled the blanket over her. Once covered, she unzipped her jeans and struggled out of them. The top was just too much hassle so she left it on. It was early but she was exhausted, and with the lights out and snuggled beneath the cover, she quickly fell into a deep sleep.

He stood for a while looking down at her, reached over and gently pulled the cover across her shoulder. He washed his face quickly at the sink and attended to hydraulics; he tried desperately to flush quietly—a clear impossibility—then returned to the room and lay down on the bed. A curious peace came over him; he couldn't remember the last time that the tiny, inch-high mile-wide space between waking and sleeping had been so calmly unpopulated. He slept.

It is often said that today is the first day of the rest of your life, and it could not have been truer for them that morning. They had been so tired they had forgotten to draw the blinds before falling asleep, so the sun slanted in from the east over the tops of the buildings and made their alarm clock.

Kate stirred first as the sunlight slid across her face. She stretched, wondered and then woke with her heart thumping. She felt foul. She slid silently off the couch, in hopes he would stay sleeping, and slipped quietly into the bathroom, jeans in her hand. Relief and a quick shower helped, but she had to put yesterday's clothes back on, which appealed not at all. She left her hair loose about her shoulders.

When she returned to the room she saw that her stirring had woken him. He sat up on the bed, swinging his feet to the floor and rubbing the sleep from his face. He avoided looking into her eyes. He didn't say anything; there were no words he could say, but she felt an understanding that transcended speech. She nodded, perhaps agreeing to his thoughts. He broke a long silence.

"Look. You've been wonderful... It isn't easy, and I need time. I can't just... pick up and carry on. Go forward. I can't."

"You don't want to talk some more?"

"No, no! I can't. Don't... just... just..."

She seized his hands. "Okay, okay. Listen, this is the practical Kate Heinrichs from good old East Gladstone talking. You have been through living hell. You tried to run away, but you can't run away from something you carry with you, can you? The pain will be there as long as you live—that's a fact of life—but I will always be here, and I will help you in any way I can."

He stood and clasped her shoulders but kept her at arms length. She tried to come closer but he maintained the distance. The touch was intimate but the distance was isolating. Presently he released her shoulders and dropped his arms.

"Nature calleth," he announced softly, "I would fain ignore her."

Kate sat on the edge of the bed while he was gone. She

thought again of how hard this was going to be. He's tender and vulnerable; is he pulling away? She tried to look into the future but that was hopeless; there was nothing visible there. Well, this is the road I've chosen, misery or delight, but I wouldn't take any other.

"Hungry?" she asked as he emerged from the bathroom rubbing a still unshaven face.

"Yeah, let's eat in the hotel breakfast room and decide what we're going to do."

They picked up their meager belongings, turned off the lights and headed for the elevator. He was very quiet and withdrawn—embarrassed, vulnerable and raw—and scarcely said a word until they had nearly finished their meal. Kate hoped in her heart that this silence was different from the one she had encountered after that terrible picnic. Was this the silence of acceptance; a silence that spoke of closeness not distance, or a silence of hurt and withdrawal? She didn't know.

He finally broke his silence over his second coffee. "Stan has my best oboe—I left it there—but I can't bring myself to contact him. Not yet."

"Can you do without it for now?" she asked finishing her grapefruit juice.

"Sure. The back-up's okay. Maybe I should just send him a short text? I know it sounds cowardly, but I just can't face talking to him."

"Sure, why not."

So he fished out his phone and tapped out the briefest of messages, assuring Stan he would be in touch soon.

"Let's check out and hit the road," she said as he signed and wrote his room number on the restaurant bill.

They had made a fine couple as they walked up to the reception desk, he unshaven and gaunt and she with hair loose, no make-up and clothes that desperately needed to see an iron. Behind the counter was a young woman in her twenties with dark hair and high, Slavic cheekbones. She knew exactly what they had been doing up in their room, or thought she did.

"Thank you," she smiled in an east European accent as she acknowledged the breakfast charge that would not have made it into her database yet. "I do hoop you had a pleasant stay vith us, and vill come again soon!"

"Oh, yes," answered Jonathan. "It was absolutely wonderful and we can't wait to come again."

Kate stifled a laugh and her heart swelled for him. They headed for the underground parking lot.

She didn't ask him if he wanted to drive.

The traffic up Avenue Road wasn't bad as they were driving against the rush hour, but until they got to Highway 401 it was tedious and required Kate's concentration. Again no words were exchanged.

"I know!" said Kate brightly as they sped up on the highway going west. "See if you can get Classic FM and we can play Spot the Composer."

He found the channel on the car radio. Invariably, when you turn on the radio you will join in the middle of the music and, unless it's one of the old chestnuts, it's a great guessing game. She had played this often in her teens during long drives with her parents, but it was new to Jonathan. He turned up the volume.

"So, what is it?" She glanced over at him as she drove; he was smiling gently.

"Baroque. Late baroque; well, *style gallant* really. In a minor key. Not really my forte," he replied. "But let me see... Definitely not Mozart, even the young Mozart."

"Of course, you can pick him up anytime, especially after Mannheim. Tipped them on their heads, he did."

"But it's German, isn't it?"

"Frankly, it's not my forte either. I don't recognize it. Could even be J.C. Bach."

"Hmm. Well, if it's German—and I'm sure it is—I don't think it's Telemann. You can tell him a mile away. It could be Haydn—one of his earlier works—but I'm going to opt for Stamitz."

"Carl Stamitz," she called out, the steering wobbling a little. "Any advance on Carl Stamitz?"

"Kate, for Christ's sake keep you eyes on the road!" He was frowning, thoughts racing behind his eyes.

"Sorry," she concentrated on her driving, passing two tractor/trailers and then finding a clear stretch of road. She peeped over at him, scared of a major setback, so to lighten the mood she said mischievously, "It could even be Dittersdorf."

"Hey," he cried, shaking it off and getting right back in the game. "That's cheating. Sowing doubt just when I've made my decision."

"Well, if you're sure, 'cos this is the rondo so it's going to end soon."

"Stamitz," he replied firmly slapping his hand on the arm rest.

The music came to a close and after a tasteful pause the female voice of the host said, "You have been listening to Toronto's Tafelmusik Baroque Orchestra playing Symphony in D minor, opus fifteen-three by Carl Stamitz."

"Yes!" he shouted making a fist. "Yes! Am I good or what?"

Then he became quiet and introspective, glancing over at her as she drove. What is it about this woman? She's seen me as raw as I could be, she's winkled stuff out of me that I would never tell anyone; she's got *inside* me for Christ's sake! And now she's got me laughing and playing silly games. She must be some kind of witch. I can't let her do this to me, I just can't. But how...?

He remained quiet all the way home to East Gladstone; they listened to more music with few words exchanged between them. She drove to his apartment and pulled up beside the house. He undid his seatbelt and made to get out of the car.

"Thanks Kate... It's..."

"No words," she replied placing her hand on his. "I know. I'll give you a call."

He took a deep breath. "I've got the schedule for this week. I'll be right back into it, no problem. Can't have Graham Swann lusting after first oboe!"

She laughed lightly, reached over to him, and gave him one of those little pecks on the cheek. He swung out of the car and she watched him get his key into the lock before pulling away.

There was a rehearsal that afternoon, and there was Jonathan Rycroft, cleanly shaven and bright eyed, sitting at his chair and going over a sheet of music with Graham Swann beside him. It was as if the last day had been a crazy nightmare, thought Kate, as she pulled her music stand closer, took out her rehearsal sheets and checked through today's work. She caught his eye and he nodded. That's all it took. Her heart glowed and she blinked her eyes before she thought anyone could see.

Liz Straker, behind and to one side with the cellos, caught her glance at Jonathan and his returned nod, placed her cello carefully on its side on the floor, and came over.

"Good to see you back so soon," she smiled. "And all looks well."

"Yes, yes it is," answered Kate. "I've got your keys here. I filled her up. Thanks a million, Liz. I owe you one. I don't know what I would have done. Honestly."

She delved into her bag and pressed the keys into Liz's hand.

"Well?" whispered Liz, leaning closer. "Did you sleep with him?"

"Yes," she replied quietly, with a secret smile. "Yes, I did."

The concertmaster-turned-maestro appeared with a sheaf of music under his arm and called for everyone's attention. It was funny, Kate thought, how quickly he had transformed from a nice old guy with a fiddle under his arm to a hard taskmaster with great visions. Guess the rarified atmosphere up there gets to all of them. Won't it be tough on him when the Board finds a new maestro and he gets busted back to the ranks?

"Today I want us all to concentrate on the Tchaikovsky. It's on the program in three days and I think you are all aware that it still needs work. And if we have time—and that is entirely up to you—we can make some inroads into the Mahler."

Kate knew which part of the Tchaikovsky in particular needed work. Oh God, she thought, if I didn't have to play pizzicato ever again I'd be a happy woman. It was the third movement, scherzo, of Tchaikovsky's Fourth Symphony, and it called for pizzicato *ostinato*, or in plain words, fucking plucking all the way through. It was hellish.

The conductor led them off and all went well for while. She tried to concentrate on the job at hand, but little glances across at Jonathan (to see, perhaps, if he really did exist) made the effort lapse. Fortunately, there were enough issues with other members of the orchestra that hers seem to fly under the radar. She hugged herself with glee when Second Oboe was given a roasting; just didn't like him, that's all. However, her turn came not long after.

"Stop, stop, stop. Second violins: turn back a page, measure 43. Now, look at the phrase in measures 46 to 48. See the crescendo? It's marked *mezzo* forte, but I'm not hearing a difference between it and the following phrases. When you get to measures 49 to 52 it's piano to forte, and in the third phrase, 53 to 56, I want piano to fortissimo. So, I don't want you big on that first phrase. I want three crescendi in a row, building as they go. See?"

Well, thought Kate, that's not what's written here: they are not 'building as they go'; it says *p* to *mf* in the first phrase, but the other two are both marked *p* to *f*. However, I'm not Jonathan, so I'll do it the way he wants; it's trifling. She took her propelling pencil from the music stand and wrote in an extra *f*.

"Now," tapping the baton on the music stand, "from 43..."

And so it went all afternoon, swinging along in fine style, then suddenly the stop, reverse and start again. Perhaps he didn't realize that if you have too many stops and starts the musicians' concentration gets shot to hell; it's a slippery slope. They never did get to the Mahler. The afternoon finally wound down, and in the refuge of the dressing rooms below the auditorium the musicians cleaned and stowed their instruments, wound themselves down and generally chewed the fat.

Kate was desperate to know how Jonathan had managed to weather the day, and wondered if that heroic persona he had dressed himself in had stayed intact. She admired his courage in resuming where he had left off, and this gave her an insight into the strength of will he must have shown for over a year.

She followed the sound of squawking to an adjacent room and found him, reed in mouth, blowing away. They were alone.

"How are you?" she asked a little tentatively because she felt their new-found closeness to be yet fragile.

"Great!" he replied too brightly, but she could see the strain in his eyes and the slight slope of his shoulders. "Bearing up just great. Boy, that was a hard session playing Spot the Composer all afternoon. Tchaikovsky would be mortified."

"Ah, it wasn't all that bad, even the loathsome scherzo," she laughed. She plucked up a little courage. "What are you doing tonight?"

He glanced quickly towards the door.

"Kate, Kate, I need to be alone, okay? I can't *do* this! You have to understand."

She nodded through the lump in her throat. "Yes, yes, I do understand, I do," she whispered.

No, she didn't; didn't want to. Not at all.

"Let me try to explain..."

"No, you really don't have to..."

"But I *do* have to," he interrupted, standing up and facing her. "Look. When I'm by myself, maybe walking on the paths down by the lake—and often just after I've seen you, spoken to you—I have these dialogues in my mind. I'm discussing music, maybe... And it's with *you*. But it's also with Julie. She's still *there*, and..." He shook his head in frustration. "Oh, Jesus! I can't explain... I want to, but I just can't."

She nodded by way of saying: I'm with you.

Julie, she thought; a name. Progress...

"Look," he continued after a moment, "there can't be two of you. There just *can't*. It's just not *sane*. It's not..." He covered his face with his hands in frustration.

"I understand; I do understand. It's you must call the shots."

"The best way to help me right now is to stop trying to help me. It's that simple."

And with this he stepped back. She nodded, the lump in her throat preventing speech.

They parted company outside the concert hall, and as she walked back along the familiar streets with tears in her eyes she thought back to that day of the picnic. Her heart ached for him, but surely things were now different. Surely, she was closer to him; she so wanted to believe it was true. Stop trying to help... But, for how long? Oh, God, for how long?

A hard road for sure, but I'm already a-ways along it.

Musikalische Exequien

When Kate's text came in late on the second evening, Stan Ward was immensely relieved. He had been unable to think of anything else, and kept playing Jonathan's dramatic departure over and over again in his mind. He had not slept well the night before, and had been distracted all day. When Kate phoned him from East Gladstone asking Jonathan's whereabouts he had only then realized the seriousness of the situation. His concern had turned to downright worry. He kicked himself for an insensitive old fool. He and Sandra had talked about the pain they could sense in the boy, and he should have taken things more carefully. Then again, the positive side argued, had he not been diffident enough; had he not slowly and reluctantly raised the issue that was on his mind? But there was something in Jonathan's past that he had opened, raw and painful.

They were sitting as usual reading and half listening to music; a CD of piano sonatas put on by Stan as a distraction, and simply not working. An early bedtime seemed on the cards. He seized the phone on the first ring, read the text and sat for a while breathing slowly with his eyes closed.

"Good news?" Sandra asked.

"Yes, thank God. It's his young lady, Kate. She's with him and things seem okay."

Sandra sighed in relief. This last twenty-four hours had been hard on him, and she thought again of reminding him he wasn't as young as he used to be. She resolved to arrange some sort of vacation, and soon.

"What did she say?"

Now, with the immense relief of finding the lad safe, the old Stan Ward emerged.

"Hard to say. Look at this," and he showed her the text.

"How difficult is to use punctuation and uppercase letters?" she asked. "I do hope she isn't one of those illiterates who say 'like' about twice every sentence."

Had they known the circumstances of the texting they probably would have cut her a little slack.

"Sounded fine on the phone. Panicky of course, but nicely spoken, I thought."

"Well, if he's attracted to her, she must be mature and sensible," she observed. "From what little you have seen of him, do think he would go around with a juvenile ignoramus?"

He laughed. "No, no, I guess not. Let's away to bed; I am absolutely exhausted, and I will sleep like the dead."

He took the CD carefully out of the player, apologizing under his breath to Robert Schumann for interrupting him in mid-phrase, and began turning off the lights.

As he left the darkened living room Sandra met him in the hall. He squeezed her hand.

"You're my rock."

"Aye, well," she returned the squeeze, her mind's eye away out in the Minch beyond the harbour of Stornoway. "You'll be my lighthouse then."

She went to the kitchen to prepare their tray of tea, which they had every morning before getting out of bed. He went slowly up the stairs while she was getting the cups out, and she heard the bathwater running. All was well with their little world. She wasn't one for prayer, but she did say a few silent words to whoever might be up there listening.

It was a couple of days before Jonathan could bring himself to contact Stan Ward. Stan had not tried to contact him, God bless his tact, because if he had it would not have gone well. Embarrassment was at war with intrigue, but more than anything else he desperately wanted his best oboe back. The spare he was using was okay, and he could hack along with it just fine, but it just wasn't as comfortable. He decided not to Skype; this was a situation for something not as immediate as face-to-face, yet not as impersonal as text. He flipped open his phone and speed dialed Ward.

"Stan, it's Jonathan. You have a minute? No, no really, you have nothing to apologize about... Yes, yes, much better. It's really fine... No, *really*... Look, I do want to come down to T-O again and... Oh, you brought it home with you? Good. And those results... Absolutely, I really want to. So, look, I've got a heavy load this weekend; concerts Friday, Saturday and Sunday, but I'm off on Monday if that would be okay? Great. Around eleven? No, no, I'll find my way on the subway. Bye."

Well, he thought, that's a relief, but I still have the face-to-face to deal with. Still, Monday's a long way away; there's a great big lump of Mahler and Tchaikovsky to negotiate first.

The following three days saw Jonathan throwing himself back into his work with a passion. The three big concerts went off beautifully, and he felt he had never played so well. This was how he had handled it at the beginning, just after... And this was how he stabilized his life now; he plunged in.

He thought often of Kate, and replayed that scene in his mind where he had told her that the best help she could give was none at all. The more he thought of it, the shittier he felt, but it was a hell of a tightrope. He needed her, yet he resented the need. He couldn't let her crowd him, but he still needed to let her feel they were in some way 'going forward'. He should have been kinder, and kicked himself for being such a total asshole. So he repaired the damage as best he could with smiles and exchanged glances, and he hoped that by this strategy he wasn't causing her pain. He just needed time and a total immersion in the music he loved.

Good Lord, he thought as he climbed on the bus yet again—his beloved music once more on the back burner—Greyhound are making a fortune out of me, but it's the only way to go; he would never drive a car again. He made for a seat near the back and hoped the bus would be empty enough that no one would sit beside him. He was lucky. During the trip, stretched out sideways over two seats, he mused upon the results Stan and he had achieved, and wondered again in pure perplexity about this thing with Mozart. Why in hell would Wolfgang Amadeus produce no response, yet Ralph Vaughn W. did? And then there was the frightening cloud of death and energy. Stan had tried to discuss this with him, and he was hurt and embarrassed that it had set off such a reaction. Again, what in God's name did any of that have to do with the experiments? It made no sense at all.

As the bus approached the outskirts of Toronto Jonathan came to a decision; he would tell Stan the more complete story of his research work. Kate had opened up a raw hole, but she had shown him that exposure might be preferable to concealment. Perhaps opening up to Stan would help; he would give it a shot.

So, it was with some trepidation that Jonathan found himself ringing on the doorbell of the Wards' house in the Toronto Beach. The bus had been slow and it was nearer to eleven-thirty than eleven, and he could bet that Stan Ward was pacing and worrying.

"Come in, come in!" cried Stan ushering him into the house, shaking his hand and failing to let go. "It is so good to see you. So good! I felt so awful..."

"It's fine," interrupted Jonathan, still being shaken. "Really! As I told you on the phone, you have nothing to worry yourself about." He extricated his hand.

Stan ushered him into the living room and sat him down in an easy chair. His beloved oboe was on the table in front of him, and he quickly opened the case and fondled it, playing casually with the keys.

"Sandra's at the university at the moment; she has to earn a living, unlike we emeriti! Let me get you some tea, or would you like coffee?"

"Tea's fine," he replied, realizing how keyed-up the old boy was.

While Stan bustled off to the kitchen and was soon clattering with cups and saucers, Jonathan fondled the oboe and sat in thought. Once the tea was poured and cooling Stan sat forward on his chair, and Jonathan knew that it was crunch time.

"Now, the hypothesis that I have been working on," began Stan, "is so crazy that I wonder if... Well, whatever. Sandra is half convinced I've lost me marbles, and there are times when I can almost agree. When I raised the issue with you of the lost energy and the deaths of maestros I was making a very wide and tenuous connection between quite disparate events..."

Jonathan knew a rehearsed speech when he heard one, and realized that poor Professor Ward was terrified of a bad reaction, so he took his courage into his hands and interrupted the discourse.

"Stan, I want to tell you a story."

This speech would be equally rehearsed; he had composed it in his last half hour as a guest of Greyhound, and had refined it while riding with the Toronto Transit Commission. This was going to be tough.

"As you know, before I became a professional musician I was employed as a physicist. It was in microwave research and the outfit I was working for—I can't tell you a thing about it because I am still covered by the Official Secrets Act—was developing a method of killing people. It's that simple. It has all sorts of lovely euphemisms attached to it, so as to keep the employees sane, and it's trumpeted as patriotism, the good old flag, keeping the enemies of freedom at bay, whatever. But the bottom line is, I was a key member of a team that developed what the popular press would, I am certain, call a death ray."

"Good God! I think I *must* have opened a 'can of worms'," declared Stan, applying verbal quotation marks; clearly uncomfortable with the vernacular description.

"That's not the half of it!" he continued. And the greater part of it, he said to himself, I will not, *can not* tell you. "I quit the job under a cloud; I was suddenly repelled and disgusted. We were killing chickens—blasting them to bits—and I wondered how long it would be before we started on Afghans, or Iranians, or any other flavour-of-the-month enemies our elected representatives didn't happen to like. This was far, far from the career in science I had dreamed of, and I am ashamed that I took the job in the first place, ashamed that I used my training and intelligence for such a purpose. I make no excuse for myself, you understand. That's in the past."

"Aye," observed Stan. "The moving finger writes; and having writ,/ Moves on: nor all thy Piety or Wit/ Shall lure it back to cancel half a Line,/ nor all they Tears wash out a Word of it."

"Oh my Lord, I love Fitzgerald's translation of the Rubaiyat. I'm pleased you know it."

Nor all thy tears wash out...

"Ah, no," replied Stan self deprecatingly. "It's a very popular passage." Although he may not have realized it, the Professor Emeritus was making Jonathan's task a little easier. "Sorry, an aside."

"So, I broke completely with science and, by just plain good luck, made a smoothish transition into music."

He paused for a while; the rehearsal had gone well on the subway, but this was still proving painful. Stan Ward sat silent, sensing how hard this was for him and understanding, to the level of his knowledge, the anguish the poor boy had been carrying with him.

"Anyway," said Jonathan loudly, slapping the arm of the chair, "my life has not—if you will excuse me—been a Harlequin fucking Romance."

"No, it hasn't. I find myself privileged that you are sharing it with me."

"Stan, music has been my life raft. Frankly, I don't think I would have remained sane without it. And the world I had slipped into would have unfolded very nicely for me, except for what followed. Only a few weeks after my arrival with the EGO—oh, I'm sorry, the East Gladstone Symphony Orchestra—I had a big fight with the conductor. Fine, this happens. I know now that I was carrying a lot of anger, and I am also a musical perfectionist. However, the very next day this conductor collapsed of a heart attack and died."

"Oh, good God, Jonathan. A perfect storm!"

"A perfect storm. But utterly coincidental, I am convinced. You see, musicians argue with conductors all the time. No conductor, no matter how good he is, can presume to know how to play every instrument. Sometimes the musician happens to be right. But that's what happened. That's the stuff you read in the *Toronto Star* the day you saw my picture."

"Oh, no! Oh, no! Then your second maestro died! Oh my God! I had no idea that my talk of energy would hit such a sensitive spot. I am so thoughtless. I really do apologize!"

The poor man looked mortified. Jonathan felt deep sympathy.

"You have no need to; I told you. You could not possibly have known!" He took a sip of almost-cold tea and placed the cup carefully back on the tray.

"Yes, then it started to get complicated." He laughed without humour. "A couple of days after the latest death I was visited by two 'gentlemen' who said they were from CSIS. As far as I know, they really were; their IDs looked genuine anyway. They told me that the maestro did not die of a heart attack; he was killed by what looked like very high tension electricity!"

Stan Ward was breathing deeply and visibly shaking. He rose quickly from his chair and started busying himself with the tea tray.

"Pop in there and put the kettle on again; can't have tea getting cold."

The cups on the tray chittered together as he carried it to the kitchen.

Jonathan stretched and rubbed his hands hard across cheeks, eyes and forehead. He thanked God that Kate had run him through the furnace that night in the hotel. It was like being ground into hamburger, but it made possible what he was doing now. Really, Stan was doing for him what Kate had done, but without Kate he would never have been able to compose his thoughts on the bus, let alone sit and pour them out to a comparative newcomer in his life.

This was progress. This was therapy.

"There, more tea. Do let's drink it while it's hot this time."

Stan placed the tray down on the glorious elm-slice table, swirled the pot to aid brewing, and fiddled with the milk jug.

"Jonathan, this business with CSIS," he began tentatively. "Should you be telling me...?"

"No, most certainly not. As I said, I am covered by the Official Secrets Act until I die—and probably even after that, knowing those buggers—so what I have just told you would certainly land me in the slammer. And if I gave you details of the device, they'd probably reinstate the death penalty 'specially for me."

"Safe with me. So now," he took a deep breath, rubbed his chin under his beard with a forefinger, and took a few moments to compose himself. "We come to the crunch. Let's talk about music, energy and Mozart. And let me say, right off, that what I tell you will do two things," he marked them off on his fingers. "One: it will assure you that the deaths of the maestros have nothing whatsoever to do with your secret weapon. Two: it will test your credulity to the maximum."

"Well, yes, the idea of some maniac targeting maestros is just too ludicrous to be taken seriously," replied Jonathan. "But there was a perfect storm of coincidences and no clear mechanism..." Even so, he felt an immense weight shifting from him.

"Right. You can set your mind at rest. Now, here was my thinking: Once you eliminate the impossible, whatever remains..."

"Yes, I know the quote," interrupted Jonathan. "...no matter how improbable, must be the truth. Good old Sherlock Holmes."

"Quite. So here's the hypothesis: imagine, if you will, that each piece of music ever written has assigned to it a 'file'. It helps to think of computer storage folders, but the analogy won't hold I'm afraid. Imagine, then, that these files..."

"Sorry, I'm not with you. What files? Where are these files?" Perplexity was writ large upon his face.

"This is so hard to explain. I went over it with Sandra and she seriously wonders if I haven't got a screw loose. You see, they're not really anywhere that we can perceive. I call the place where they 'are' the Music Continuum," he emphasized the 'are' with two curling index fingers. "It could be that the Music Continuum is all around us, or in us. It's... I can't say *where* it is, and it might be that we cannot ever know."

Holy shit, thought Jonathan, what have we here? "I see. That makes it a bit awkward, doesn't it? From a scientific perspective, I mean. There is, after all, the burden of proof." He couldn't avoid a note of sarcasm.

"Bear with me here. We are seeing energy disappearing from a human body, and it has to go somewhere..."

"But, surely, there are all kinds of ways in which leakage could occur?"

"We work in an electrostatic cage, remember. There's nowhere it *can* go."

"Okay, so energy is disappearing into—somewhere—and you are trying to account for it how exactly?"

"Imagine then that Beethoven's Fifth Symphony, *Finlandia*, Handel's *Messiah*... all of them—every piece of musical creation *ever*—has a unique 'file' in which creative energy is stored. And it's not just the act of creation that adds energy; the playing of the work also adds energy. And that's what we're seeing in the lab."

"Let me get this straight. You're saying that the act of creation itself contributes energy to the files in this continuum thingy, but that playing the music contributes more again."

"Yes, yes, because when you play the music you are involved in a creative act. Would you agree that playing music *must* be creative?"

"Absolutely! That's why I keep getting into arguments with these baton-wavers who know so much more about it than I do. But I still don't know where the hell this is going. And what the hell has it do with Wolfgang Amadeus bloody Mozart?"

"The files, Jonathan," replied Stan, in didactic and measured tones, "are of limited size—perhaps they are elastic, how can we ever know?—but at some point they must get full. And when they get full, they overflow!"

Jonathan felt a spark of comprehension, followed by the misgiving that he might actually start believing this nonsense.

"The Mozart! Its file's full because it's been played many, many times over 200 years!"

"And the Vaughn Williams is more recent and has not been played so much! I believe, Jonathan, that as the flow into the Music Continuum continues, it becomes slower and slower, stops, then reverses. Perhaps it can remain stretched for a long time. I don't know..."

"So that would explain why you got no results when I played the Mozart?"

"Exactly! Exactly! The flow must have been almost at zero."

Jonathan's head reeled. This can't be true, he thought, this can't be true. This is mad; completely barking crazy. He put his elbows on his knees, rested his face in hands and rocked backwards and forwards gently for half a minute. Stan Ward sat, leaning forward, his entire hypothesis hinging upon what Jonathan would say next.

"So, it all comes spewing out? A great big acid belch? Like from anchovies and green peppers?"

"Yes, yes! A reflux if you like!" He chuckled.

"But why just the maestros?" Here was a fly in the ointment. "Shouldn't the whole damned orchestra get hit? Why just the guy with the stick?"

"Jonathan," replied Professor Ward in a serious and sober tone, steepling his fingers, "I think the maestro must somehow be the focus. It's probably only coincidence that he is also called *the conductor*."

This last statement pushed Jonathan over the edge. He didn't know whether it was his disappointment with this mad hypothesis after such a long build-up, or the serious way in which it was couched, but it suddenly struck him as richly comical. He burst out with roaring laughter; a cathartic laughter that had been bottled up inside him for one long year. Poor Professor Ward sat still in his chair looking shocked, shrunken and dismayed, while Jonathan laughed himself into tears and coughing.

"It's incredible," he spluttered when the first wave had passed. "It's like a dream come true! These prancing fops, these arrogant sons-of-bitches, are the architects of their own destruction. It's like Zeus is up there on Mount Olympus and he looks down and he goes: You down there! You with the baton! Enough with the fuckin' Mozart! Take that you bastard! Boom!"

The second wave of laughter overcame him while Stan sat mute, small and very unhappy. Perhaps I am losing the old faculties, he thought, perhaps I should quit this stupid game, or leave it the younger generation. A wave of sadness passed over him.

"I'm sorry, Stan, I'm sorry," Jonathan gasped when he had got his breath back. "But if you knew how many people in my orchestra would crack up over this..." He thought of what Steve Mah would make of it. "It's the old one of the bull and the orchestra."

Stan's incomprehension was clear on his face.

"Oh, sorry Stan," he chuckled. "Look; what's the difference between a bull and an orchestra?"

"I have absolutely no clue."

"Simple. The bull has the horns at the front and the asshole at the back!" Another wave of laughter and a slight smile from Stan. Then Jonathan thought of the lifeless body of Carlo Mascagni, and he shrunk from within. My God, you don't wish that on anybody.

Stan looked so tired and forlorn that Jonathan felt immediately contrite. An awkward silence ensued.

"Look, Jonathan," sighed Stan at length. "It's useless making tea; this second pot has gone cold, for Christ's sake. Let me get the Lagavulin out."

He opened a cabinet door in a lower bookcase, removed a bottle and two glasses and, with hands shaking, poured a generous dollop of the Creature into each.

He sat again in his chair and they raised their glasses. "Here's tae us!" The whisky did its job. They sat in thought for some minutes while the warmth spread.

"I must say," began Stan, "I was hoping you would be a little more receptive of my hypothesis, but when I think about it..."

"Sorry I laughed, but it's a hard sell, Stan. It's so impossibly off the wall."

"But, *do* remember Sherlock Holmes. Yes, it's improbable, but do you have a better hypothesis?" he was almost pleading.

"Well, no. I mean, it's so irrational, so random..."

"Quite. Let me propose this then: we have a cause that is evident in my physiology lab, and we have an effect that is visible in the outside world. Let us accept those two phenomena as valid, and not concern ourselves with what strands of logic or reasoning might lie between these two. Let us go forward and try to find some way of turning hypothesis into theory. Is that fair enough?"

"It's a huge leap of faith. Why would these two disparate phenomena be connected in any way at all? Really Stan, I've done my bit with playing the music for you. I don't know how I can help any more."

Stan Ward sat in thought for a long time, and as Jonathan regarded him over the rim of his glass he realized that, for all his energy, wit and intelligence, the Professor Ward he had known in undergrad wasn't really there anymore. He was no longer even middle-aged, his colleagues at the lab regarded him as a harmless eccentric (when Jonathan thought back to the meeting he had had with them he understood now why he had felt so uncomfortable) and he was out on a limb. And now, his one possible ally in unraveling this mystery had gone and found it laughable.

"But I think you *can* help some more," Ward mused, swishing his glass gently under his nose, breathing deeply, then taking a small sip. "It's difficult... if you had been just a musician, you might have better accepted the hypothesis. But as a scientist as well..."

"You mean I'm just too rational? Too analytical? That you'd be able to sell this to a mere musician?" He hadn't intended it to come out that way; it sounded harsh and crude, and he immediately regretted it. "I'm sorry, I didn't mean it like that..."

"No, no, no; I see your point, and I am the one in error. The problem is, I have landed you smack in the face with this, and it'll take time to... absorb, perhaps." He reflected for a few seconds then sighed. "Sandra's coming round to it, but even she has... reservations, shall we say?"

"Maybe you're right. I dunno. Look, I'll head back to the bus station now, and I'll give this a lot of thought, let it settle in. Perhaps I'll call in a day or two. Would that be okay?"

He finished his whisky and stood. They shook hands at the Ward front door, and he made his way up the hill to the subway station at Main Street, oboe case in one hand, travel bag in the other. He felt a little sad now, not just because his hopes for a rational answer to the experimental work were as far away as ever, but because he had disappointed Stan and made him look like a fool.

The bus trip was more purgatorial than usual; he had missed the three-fifteen bus by a matter of minutes and had to wait nearly a full hour in that smelly, resonating cavern, only to have some selfish swine pile his SUV into a tractor-trailer right at the intersection of 401 and 400. Why don't these people think about rush-hour before they decide to have their accidents? The more he sat, stop-starting forward by increments, the worse he felt about the meeting. He replayed the scenes at Chateau Ward in his mind and the more he reviewed them, the worse they looked. It was like having a bad trip on weed. Finally, he got his phone out, flipped it up and called Stan.

"Yes, it's me... Look, I feel really bad... No, really... It's been a very tough day for me, but I'm not making excuses... You do...? Well, that's very kind... Sure, in a few days... Okay, and thanks for your understanding. Bye."

That felt better. Poor guy, but really, his stuff is just too far off the wall. He tried to switch his thoughts somewhere else but Kate/Julie swam into view.

It was right back into the heavy rehearsal schedule the day after Jonathan's visit to Toronto. He had had very little time to think deeply of that crazy few hours when he had bared his soul and mocked Stan Ward, but he knew that a decision would have to made, and soon. He wondered whether it would be an idea to bounce some ideas off Kate. Their relationship was so strange now; can you be intimate and distant at the same time, he wondered. God bless her for biding her time and giving me space. I seem to have turned a corner; she's made me feel as if I can really mourn, and if I can mourn then surely I can heal. So, yes, talk to her about this, because now I think I can.

He came over to her table in the cafeteria during lunch break, where she was in a heads-together session with two other whispering violinists, but he didn't move to sit down. He had no lunch with him. She saw the serious expression on his face and felt a little shrinking at the base of her stomach.

"Sorry to disturb you ladies," he said, "but I would like to borrow Kate for a moment."

Kate stood up, leaving her lunch on the table, and followed him out. The two at the table watched the couple leave by the patio doors, walking out to the terrace side-by-side but not touching, then their heads were together again. It's funny, because Liz Straker told me...

"Kate, I need to talk to you. Since coming back from Toronto I've been doing a lot of thinking."

Her heart squeezed painfully and a rush of weakness rushed upwards. Oh, please, oh, please! Don't let this be happening! In this frozen moment everything was hyper-real; the dazzle on the water was brighter, the sky was bluer, and sounds seemed somehow magnified. She had gone quite pale, and seeing this he stepped quickly forward and took her hand.

"It's okay. It's okay. It's not about... us..." She breathed deeply and her colour returned. "I've just come back from Stan Ward's place and, well... could we... could we get together later? I have to talk through what he's told me."

I ought to be angry, she thought, being drawn into the role of his confidant and crying-shoulder, while not being offered anything but the slightest intimacy. But there's no one else he can use, and he's opened up so far to reliable old me that I can only set resentment aside and practice patience. He needs me. My

God, I'm sounding like Nancy in *Oliver Twist*!

She was so tempted to invite him to her place, but she knew he'd refuse. She was on a tightrope, but the other side of Niagara Gorge was visible and nearly tangible. Then again, she hadn't been to his place since Toronto, and so much had changed. Well, we move forward...

"I could drop over tonight, if that's okay," she replied. "Shall I bring a bottle, or is your wine cellar well stocked?"

"I think there's half a bottle of cooking sherry under the kitchen counter," he laughed, "just beside the garbage bin."

"So that's a yes or a no?"

"Just bring your... yourself. See you around seven? And I might even wash the glasses."

Her knock on the door came exactly at seven. He had just put some music on the MP3, so he crossed the room quickly and swung the door wide to welcome her in. She had changed; the rather severe straight skirt and blouse she had worn for the rehearsal had been replaced with jeans and a white T-shirt. The hair band was denim and matched the jeans.

"Ooh, that sounds lovely!" she cried as choral music arose from the MP3 speakers. "Baroque, but what is it?"

"Early Baroque, really. Schütz; the *Musikalische Exequien* of 1635. Stop, listen, listen to this..." He placed a hand gently on her wrist, and they paused in the entrance to the living room as the chorus 'Er spracht zu seinem lieben Sohn...' swelled out into the room.

"How?" she breathed when the last bar had died. "How could he *do* that? It's super-human."

"You know what? I think there are times when we're so damn involved in making the bloody music that we don't just sit back and *listen* to it."

"You're right. I can't listen to the music we play every day without criticizing it. I can't help it. It's not 'ooh what a lovely symphony', it's all 'what a fast tempo' or 'I wouldn't phrase it that way'. Know what I mean?"

"Oh, sure. It's our occupational hazard, isn't it? That's why I often listen to this stuff. It's because I will never, ever play it! Come in, sit down."

While she sat and listened—entranced because she was experiencing something as if for the first time—he made welcoming bottle and glass noises in the little kitchen. He appeared with two glasses of a deep red wine, and then again it was: "Wait, wait, listen. Listen to this bit," as he put the glasses on the mantel and cranked up the volume a little.

She stood up and seized a glass, sipping a little as the chorus 'Durch ihn ist uns vergeben...' drew them in. It was a glorious wall of homogenous sound, delicately ivied with harmonic intricacies. She had heard this music before, of course, but this was the first time she had *listened* to it. It blew her away. She resolved to listen to more.

"So, that's yer culture for the day," he said, turning Heinrich Schütz down and beginning to look very practical. "When I was down in T-O at Stan Ward's place he filled me in on his hypothesis. I don't know how much I've told you..."

He looked into her eyes and took a big gulp from his glass. He was thinking of exploding chickens again.

"Hmm, this is tough. Look, his team is measuring metabolism, finding where all the energy of the human body goes. Okay? That's me, festooned with wires and blatting away on the oboe. What happened was, he found that some energy was unaccountable when music was being played; the sums didn't add up. This is what he calls his anomaly."

"So, you play and some of your energy gets eaten up somewhere?"

"Exactly. Fractions of a nanojoule, but measurable."

"Nano what?"

"Nanojoule. Much, much less than the energy of a flea."

"And it's going where; this music energy?"

"Into someplace, somewhere. God knows, 'cos he doesn't."

"All music? For ever?"

"Yup. Since the first Cro-Magnons whacked a stick against a skull and started hollering, apparently."

"But that's..."

"...nuts," he finished. "Tell me about it. But listen; it gets worse. He starts telling me his hypothesis... This is where it gets really bizarre because he starts talking about the deaths of these maestros..."

"He *what*? What's *that* got to do with it?" Some wine slopped.

"I told you it gets bizarre. His argument is that the energy stored—God alone knows where; like I said, he doesn't—leaks out and kills these guys. I mean, it's completely whacko."

"Jesus, Jonathan, has he lost his marbles?"

"He seems perfectly rational. But I have to say, when he told me all this I nearly pissed myself laughing. I'm a bit ashamed now, although he's very forgiving. It was an impolite thing to do in someone else's house, but the thought of it... There was a lot of tension... I was expecting... well, I don't know what I was expecting, but not something as far off the wall as that."

"Well, did he back it up with anything? He's a scientist, after all."

"Yes, you see, there is a logic to it. When I played the Mozart on the first visit—I think I remember telling you—there were no results at all."

He spent the next ten minutes give her a condensed version of what had happened, while Heinrich Schütz played gently on.

"So, there you are. He quoted that famous Sherlock Holmes phrase... Have you read any Sherlock Holmes?"

"No, I know of him, of course, but that's not my kind of reading. More please?" as she held out her glass. He complied.

"Basically it's: eliminate the impossible and what is left, no matter how improbable, must be the truth."

"That's a bit simplistic, though, isn't it?"

"Yeah. Fine for detective fiction, but not such a great match for real life. Think of the wave/particle duality, for example..." she had never thought of it, and was not equipped to think about it now, but she forbore to interrupt, "...where you have two solutions, both of which are equally true." He outlined it to her and she nodded that she understood. "But, Kate, back to practicalities, what do you think I should do?

You are asking *me*, she thought. How can he balance this reliance upon me with the fact that we scarcely even touch? How can I be friend, confidant and advisor yet be barred from the real intimacy that should be the biggest part of the package?

She paused for a while, contemplating their weird relationship, and trying his request from all sorts of angles. One thing had become clear to her some time ago—with this project, away from East Gladstone, and away (she shrank to even think it) from her—he could find some sort of fulfillment and distraction. This would be extremely valuable. Sure, it sounded like the nuttiest of wild goose chases, but what the hell.

"Do it. What do you have to lose? A bit of time and some bus fares. Not a bad price to pay for a chance to get back to your science."

They toasted each other with glasses raised and their eyes met and held. Tears appeared in his but he made no move to prevent them flowing.

"Tears...?"

"Yeah... I'm sorry... Happens quite often... Since you..." He couldn't continue.

"Tears are good," she almost whispered. "She deserves your tears. Come here, let me hold you. I'll just hold you... if you want me to."

He sat beside her and she placed her arms around his shoulders, softly. His arms responded.

"You help me to... to..."

"And I will help you as long as you want me to."

And they sat as the '*Nunc dimitis*' played, arms around each other, gently together, gently apart...

...while out in the world beyond their walls maestros were still detonating.

Jonathan was at his usual evening practice session, starting with the oboe parts from Dvorak's *New World Symphony*. This perennial favorite was on the program soon and, although he knew the parts well and loved the piece dearly, familiarizing himself with it would do no harm. Practicing every day is a slog, so a little treat once in while helps the medicine go down. He just wished he could take the cor anglais solo from the second movement, but that task is always left to the second, so Graham Swann would have that joy. He sometimes wondered what it would have been like had Graham won the competition for first oboe. At least he would be happy playing the instrument he loved so much.

With the Dvorak out of the way, he worked over some other pieces he knew very well, interspersing these with newer material. He had got onto a website that boasted some of the hardest oboe writing ever, and he couldn't help but agree. For the latter part of his practice session he was reading the music right off the site on his laptop, when the Skype flag popped up in the corner. It was almost a relief to put the oboe down and minimize the music. It was Stan.

Since bending Kate's ear on the topic of the 'files', he had now come round to agreeing with her; he would offer to help Stan as much as his limited capacity as a musician would allow, and let the science come as it would.

"Hey, Stan!" The old professor had a glass in his hand and a twinkle in his eye. "Is that the Lagavulin?

"No, my boy, it's Laphroaig 18, so eat yer heart out."

"Boy, I can smell if from here!"

The image on the laptop swirled the glass, took a long sip and came to the point. "How are things in your belief department?"

"Good. Well, no, not exactly. But I think I would like to do some more work with you..."

"Excellent, excellent!" he interrupted. "I knew you would!"

"But, hold on. Listen. I can help you as a musician; beyond that, I don't know. I still think this whole thing is absolutely crazy, but I am prepared to cut you some slack."

"Cut me some slack? What the devil does that mean?" with a mock incomprehension.

"You know damned well what it means, you linguistic fraud."

"I am suitably chastened. Now here's my proposal; well, it's Sandra's actually. We'd like to visit you in East Gladstone and hear you play. Save you some bus fare too. What is the concert schedule like for the weekend? What's on the program?"

"Good timing. We've got Friday, Saturday and Sunday evenings. Start you off with the *Enigma Variations*, then a little Brahms—some of the *Hungarian Dances*; the usual ones—then blow you out with Dvorak's *New World*. You'll get to hear a few nice oboe solos; some of the loveliest writing."

"Dvorak's *New World*, eh? That's a dangerous one."

"*Dangerous*?"

"Well, yes. Its file could be almost full..."

"Oh, now come on! I said I'd cut you some slack but..."

"All right, all right, enough said." He held his palm up to the camera. "We'll take it slowly, shall we?"

"You do that. It'll be great to see you, so give me a call when you're booked. I can meet you at the bus station."

"No, no, we have a car. We keep it in a lock-up down the road. Don't use it much, but at weekends we'll go to Kleinburg or Sharon, places like that."

"I'm at 25 Sanders; you can check Google Maps."

"Excellent, although we prefer Map Quest. We've been on the web and found what looks like a nice little B-and-B; what was it...? Hmm, yes, Ivy Lea. We'll go ahead and book the room and some concert tickets. Now tell me, how will you be fixed for time? After all, don't you have to rest and prepare for these things?"

"I sometimes wonder why we couldn't just stick our instruments on the chairs and let them do the playing. They've done it so often. No, seriously, we have the morning and at least early afternoon on all three days, and there's also Thursday evening."

"Good. Now, another small issue. I spoke very briefly to your young lady on the phone that... that day... And Sandra says—well, I say as well, of course—that we'd very much like to meet her. Is that a possibility?"

My young lady? thought Jonathan, that tastes strangely on my tongue but, yes, I suppose she is. In most people's eyes we are already an item, and now we're developing a social circle. No, no, stop...

"Sure. I'll give her the word."

"Right. We should get to East Gladstone in the afternoon, so would seven on Thursday suit? If anything changes, I'll call. Goodbye for now." The screen went dark.

Jonathan looked around his bleak apartment and wondered what sort of entertaining this place could sustain. Maybe I can buy some stuff, make it look a little more homely. And Kate...? Yes, she would get on well with the Wards.

The rehearsals for the Elgar, Brahms and Dvorak concert at the weekend were the usual hard slog. Perhaps even more so. Most of the musicians had played these pieces often before, if not with East Gladstone, but there were still a great many issues to be resolved before the acting maestro was even halfway happy. To give him his due, Kulikofski was desperate to make a good impression on the Board. He had a strong financial argument: he figured that if he performed well in this job they might decide not to go looking for another high-priced stranger, but would give him the job and save a bundle of money. But money was only one issue; it really all hinged on the social aspect, and the music simply didn't enter into it. Would the East Gladstone arts scene be irreparably damaged without its flamboyant musical centerfold? Would they be content with an older and more experienced guy who just stood up night after night and did the job; a conductor rather than a maestro?

So, Kulikofski's ambition drove the rehearsals hard, and the musicians ended the days tired and frazzled. But, weary though they were, most of them noticed there was less anger, less polarization. And this was probably due to the fact that, although he was a violinist first and foremost, Kulikofski knew and respected the other players, was aware of the idiosyncrasies and foibles of their instruments, and had a clear idea of what could be reasonably asked of them. The segue from musician to conductor relies upon this wide vision of the whole ensemble, and a feeling for musical strategy, and occasionally a great musician makes a poor conductor.

As he slogged through the days Jonathan realized that if audiences only knew what damned hard work goes into every performance, they would have a completely new appreciation of the result. Wouldn't it be a novel idea to invite people—maybe season ticket holders—to attend a rehearsal or two? But, on the downside, you kind of wonder about the distraction, and there's occasionally some dirty laundry out there for all to see, although not quite as soiled as in the old days.

On Tuesday of that week Jonathan and Kate decided to take their lunch out onto the patio overlooking the water, and be damned to the wagging tongues. It was breezy day, but not uncomfortably cool, and the air played nicely with her hair. He had bought a sandwich and a coffee at the counter inside, while she had brought a lunch made at home along with a drink in travel mug. They sat on the retaining wall at the edge of the patio, rather than at one of the tables. It was nearer to the water and the view over the lake was unobstructed. Jonathan was about to mention Stan and Sandra's plans for the weekend, when she threw him a curved ball.

"I don't know anything about your family." Or anything else about you, come to that, she thought. "Are your parents..."

"And I don't really want to talk about my parents," he interrupted coldly. He finished his ham and factory-cheese-slice sandwich slowly then turned to her. "And you don't really need to know. It's such a nice day. Don't spoil it."

But she sat there with her hands in her lap and that appealing look in her eyes. More and more she was making him release his secrets. He was half willing, half stubborn.

"All right," he relented. He knew he'd probably have to tell her eventually, so why not now? "But you won't like it. My father ran away with some woman from work—insurance company from Windsor—and we had no idea where he went; overseas, we thought. I was about eight or nine. Mum worked hard to keep us, any sort of job she could turn her hand to. We were true working poor and I grew up in a shit neighbourhood. Then, my second year at U of T she had this pain..." He blinked his eyes are stared into the distance across the water for a long time. "Ovarian... and that was that. So... so, there you are."

"My God, Jonathan! That was right in the middle of your studies." She took his hand—a bold move this close to the concert hall—and though he didn't relinquish it, it remained passive in hers. She was horrified at the things she was learning.

"Well, you throw yourself into things..." He turned from staring out at nothing, and looked her seriously in the eye. "You know, Kate, it was like you know when Arthur Dent said he couldn't get the hang of Thursdays? Well, add the other six days of the week and that was me."

He smiled a little at a thought. "When I was kid I was sent to Bible school; we used to sing this song—you know it, of course, everybody does—'What a friend we have in Jesus', and I used to wonder, even as a little kid, what kind of friend this was that I couldn't see, couldn't hear, and couldn't touch... let my dad just disappear..."

Some orchestra members came noisily out of the cafeteria doors, saw them sitting on the retaining wall, hushed their talk, and turned the other way. Not brass players, obviously.

"When I was on the bus down to Toronto a while back," he continued when they had gone round a corner, "I sat wondering to myself if I'm one of those people who life just doesn't suit. I don't wear it comfortably, I thought, and I wondered if I shouldn't just take it off and hang it up somewhere."

"No, please don't say that! *Please!*" She couldn't bear to hear him talk like this. She shuddered at the memory of the Toronto hotel room.

"It's okay..." His hand squeezed hers slightly to reassure. "Since... Toronto... and us... you... I'm beginning to get the hang of it... Finally..."

They sat for a short while gazing out at the lake. Cloud shadows were flitting across it making an ever changing patchwork of blue and grey, like an old crocheted quilt shaken in the wind.

"Hey!" he brightened. "Stan and his wife Sandra want to come up and hear us play. And, of course, he wants to keep bending my ear about his crazy hypothesis."

"Oh, that's nice! I'd love to meet them."

"Well, they actually asked after you specifically," he replied. "They're going to book a B-and-B; be here on Thursday."

She thought of his Spartan accommodations and winced at the thought of socializing there. It would be much nicer if...

"Tell you what, why don't I invite you all to my place? I'd love to do it." She bit her lip at the thought of rejection, watching the thoughts cross his face.

I've never been to her place, he thought, and do I want to? She's been to mine, of course, but it'll be that extra bit of sharing, just another strand of her thread winding with mine. The war between the dark shadow and the light; between what was and what may well be. One meeting of eyes; that's all it takes to set a train of choices rolling. Stan and Sandra think we're an item anyway, and so do most of the bloody orchestra. More and more it becomes inevitable.

Then he brightened. Of course, there's the practical side; he hadn't relished the thought of sprucing his place up for just one visit, and ordering stuff from the IKEA in Huntsville that he couldn't send back afterwards because it had already been assembled. And the assembly was a pain in the ass anyway; why could he never get the Billy backing boards to stay on? Then, he'd need some matching crockery and four similar wine glasses. Christ, it just gets too complicated.

The series of thoughts that she watched as they passed openly across his face ended in a broad smile. "That's a great idea. Um... where do you live?"

"48 Simcoe, up at the top end of Main Street and turn right at KFC," she replied, relieved at the crossing of another hurdle.

They stood up and returned to the concert hall, walking side-by-side, not touching.

Symphony No. 9 in E Minor

Stan and Sandra checked themselves into Ivy Lea around three in the afternoon. They were shown up to their room by the proprietor herself, and given an introduction to the curious operation of the bath taps (especially the hot one, which was quite temperamental apparently) plus the protocol for switching on the television and the use of the 9 in dialing out.

They left their bags in the room and went out on the town. Strangely enough, although they enjoyed day tourism in the many small locales an hour or three from Toronto, they had never visited East Gladstone. They were charmed by the main street with its prideful civic buildings and active sidewalk life, delighted at the vistas of lake and windmill, and quite awed by the size and beauty of the East Gladstone Centennial Centre.

They returned slowly to the town centre around supper time and, following Ivy Lea's advice, settled into a booth in *The Glad*, a restaurant right on Main Street, kitty-corner from St Luke's Anglican Church. They had a slow and pleasant meal; slow because the waiting staff gave a whole new meaning to the term casual, and pleasant because the food was surprisingly good. They decided against wine, choosing instead to stop by the LCBO a little way down the street and buy a couple of bottles, a white from Kelowna and a red from Niagara. They were patriotic about their wines and knew that, with care, they could find ones that would compare with any from the world's old wine centres or the upstart California (Stan's appellation).

Just before seven in the evening they were walking up Simcoe Street looking for number 48. It was rather sweet because they walked holding hands. A fast striding figure overtook them.

"Stan, Sandra! Here you are. When did you get here?" asked Jonathan as he slowed down beside them.

"We've been in town for a while, had a look around the place and are most impressed," replied Stan.

"Your concert hall is marvelous," said Sandra. "We can't wait for tomorrow night; didn't look inside yet. Wanted to save that treat."

"Oh, you'll love the interior too. All wood," replied Jonathan, scanning the house numbers. "Ah, here we are. Oops, no, that's 46; other side of the half-double. Here."

There were three bell pushes at the side of the door, each with a tiny brass slot to hold a name label. Jonathan peered closely, found Heinrichs and pressed the button. They had waited a while and he contemplated ringing again, when they heard her feet descending stairs. Kate opened the door. She was wearing black stretch pants and a multicoloured cardigan in which aquamarine dominated. She had left her hair loose about her shoulders.

"Sorry, I took so long. It's the top of the house and I hadn't quite got ready. Come up, come up."

She led the way and they followed in single file up the steep stairs to the second floor. It was an old house, or at least old for that part of the world, and dated from the late 19th century. She opened her door on the landing and invited them in.

"Stan and Sandra, this is Kate; Kate Heinrichs," Jonathan performed the introductions.

"It's lovely to meet you," she replied. "Jonathan's talked about you, and I'm so glad you wanted to come and hear us perform."

Stan and Sandra shook hands in turn, and Stan passed Kate a brown bag that clinked enticingly.

It was no wonder that Kate had found Jonathan's living quarters Spartan; her apartment was furnished with comfortable chairs and a bed/chesterfield, while an intricately designed carpet covered a large part of the floor space. There were pictures on three walls, while on the fourth a window looked out upon gardens and a tiny triangular glimpse of the lake between the trees. A tall bookshelf contained an eclectic mix of titles and subjects in no apparent order. A sideboard with a cupboard below held a small CD player and a pair of little speakers. A foldable music stand with a score resting on it was parked near the window. The room impressed the visitors with its warmth and invitation. On a central low table was a large dish of cheese and crackers, and wine glasses, a bottle and a corkscrew.

"Ooh," cried Kate as she opened the brown LBCO bag, "you've brought one of my favorites from Niagara. How could you have known? Please, please come in and sit down."

Stan and Kate sat on the chesterfield while Jonathan and Sandra took chairs across the table from them.

"We did a short tour of the Niagara Escarpment last year, didn't we dear?" said Stan. "And we found some very good small wineries that don't supply to the big stores. Brought back cases of the stuff! But that one's a good choice."

"Pity we didn't bring one from home," said Sandra. "Should

have thought of that. Maybe a Staff baco noir."

"Let me open one," volunteered Jonathan, who had turned back from admiring a Colville print in a frame on the wall. "What's your fancy? The Niagara?"

Drinks were poured and the two couples took time to appraise each other while they tasted from their glasses.

"That's very nice. Thank you so much," said Kate. "Look, I put out some cheese and crackers. I'm sure you've already eaten, but..."

"Ah ha!" said Stan as he leant forward. "That looks like a piece of Stilton. Never too full to enjoy a little of that."

"Help yourself, please. And the other one's Balderson, place near Perth."

"Oh, we know it well," said Sandra. "One of the best cheddars you can buy."

They busied themselves with crackers and cheese. Jonathan seemed to be doing the food sterling service. He doesn't eat properly, thought Kate.

Stan sat back and sighed with contentment. "Look, Jonathan and you too Kate, I want to bounce all sorts of things off your heads, as you young people say. We've been talking about music—haven't we my dear—but not being musicians ourselves we might not have the full picture."

"Sure. Run it all by us," Jonathan replied for both of them.

"First off, among all the creative arts, music is absolutely prime. Every single culture on the planet has found music indispensable. And in that respect I think it's quite unlike the other arts. I believe a culture could exist perfectly well without painting, without literature, without sculpture, but ultimately if it lacked music it could not be a human culture. Do you see what I'm getting at?"

"It's nice," replied Jonathan, "that you have a feeling that us guys are uniquely different, but..."

"You see," Sandra intervened, "the expressions of culture are additive. We can look at early Palaeolithic sites and find carvings, paintings and so on, that show high cultural sophistication, and we can, of course, see progression. But what of a five-hole flute from the very earliest of sites that show creative artwork? That argues a musical sophistication that predates any other cultural expression."

"I can see the sense of that," observed Jonathan, "because, basically, we have an innate rhythm dictated by our hearts and our lungs and our stride as we walk. And early Man would find a way to exploit that; to express it."

"Exactly," she replied. "And it's deeply embedded. Even the profoundly deaf—those who have never, ever heard sound—have a strong, healthy musical culture, based upon rhythm and vibration."

"I was just thinking of the Mozart Effect," offered Kate, "where it's been shown that even babies in the womb respond to music. If that's so, there must be something genetic rather than cultural."

"Good point," said Stan. "Good point."

"But, hasn't the Mozart Effect been more or less debunked?" asked Jonathan, reaching forward and topping up glasses all around.

"No, that's the thing," replied Sandra. "It hasn't. It's not the effect itself, but the crass way it's been abused by the ignorant. And all sorts of stupid theories arose from the simple fact that people hadn't read the original work. Or, at least, chose to extrapolate in ridiculous ways. Breeding special kids and such nonsense!"

"I haven't read much about this," said Stan, "except the paper in *Nature* back in the '90s, but I certainly see a blip on my bullshit radar."

"Damn right, my dear. You press speakers playing Mozart onto mummy's tummy and breed a perfectly well balanced, cultured child."

"And the corollary, or course," he replied. "Send a few rousing tracks of Guns 'n' Roses down the wires and a perfectly formed little juvenile delinquent pops out of mummy's vagina!"

They all laughed at the ludicrous image this conjured. Kate thought of tiny swaddled newborns with tongue rings, macabre tattoos and Goth hair styles.

"The original study," continued Sandra when the mirth had died down, "showed a temporary enhancement of spatial-temporal reasoning in adult laboratory subjects as tested by IQ. There is clearly an area in the brain which is mapped to respond to specific frequencies. The effect is shown to last about fifteen minutes. Hardly justifies the claims of breeding super-intelligent kids, does it?"

"Damn," shouted Stan, slopping his glass a little. "I wish to God people would read the bloody literature! There is even less excuse for ignorance than ever before in the history of civilization. All you have to do is Google the damned stuff! Or even go to a bloody library! Ah, people! You can tolerate 'em, but you can't like 'em."

"Oops," said Sandra. "Sorry, I accidentally pressed the curmudgeon button." She pointed a forefinger and thumb at Stan's head, pressed the thumb down, mimicking a remote, and shouted "Click! Reset!"

"But you know it's true, damn it." He glowered over his glass for a moment then continued. "The fact remains that music is innate. It is not something acquired by nurture and upbringing, as are all the other arts. I think it's safe to say that societies could do without the written word, without drama, without painting, but they could not survive without music."

"I agree," observed Kate. "You don't ask someone if they like music; you ask them what music they like. Everyone has music wired into them; they simply don't exist without it. And music accompanies every aspect of our lives. We can't get away from it sometimes."

"Damn right," said Stan. "Muzak in elevators, ghastly Christmas music flooding the stores from October onwards, the hideous row they make at hockey games..." He glanced meekly in Sandra's direction while she mimed the mute at him again. "Look, a feller could die of thirst down this end of the sofa; pass the bottle along."

He refreshed his glass, pretending to squeeze the last drops out of the upended bottle, then turned and applied himself to the bottle that Kate had provided.

"Louis XIV had music for every single moment of his day," said Kate, accepting a glass. "But even labourers, farm workers, sailors have their indispensable songs."

"Look at all the sea shanties, for example," said Sandra. "Work just goes better with a song."

"We used to sing all sorts of folk songs—my family—when I was a kid," Kate reminisced. "It's silly really, when you think about it, sitting around the fire with my mum and my uncle deep in the heart of Saskatchewan singing sea shanties, when the nearest ocean is a hundred thousand miles away."

"Remember the *Mingulay Boat Song*," murmured Stan to his wife. "That has special meaning for us, doesn't it my love?"

"Oh, for God's sake, Stan, don't you go on and on to these young people about the ancient history of our *honeymoon*. You senile old bugger."

But before the conversation could resume, and before she could even really stop herself, Kate had started singing in a small but pleasant mezzo-soprano:

"Heel yo ho, boys, let her go, boys
Swing her head roond and all taegither
Heel yo ho, boys, let her go, boys
Sailing homeward to Mingulay."

Then, with surprise to the whole company—himself included —Jonathan took up the second verse. She joined him quickly, a measure or so in, and they sang together in octave unison, their eyes upon each other.

"What care we how white the Minch is
What care we boys for wind or weather
When we ken that every inch is
Closer homeward to Mingulay."

The Wards applauded, the singers bowed, and a spell was broken. But Kate's gaze stayed on his face. Music together. Yes, we move forward...

"That was lovely," beamed a delighted Sandra. "It *does* bring back memories. It's so nice to be entertained by musicians. We love music but neither of us actually *do* it."

"It's not common anymore," observed Jonathan. "Recorded music has so taken over that it's no longer necessary to make your own. The old days of an upright piano or a pump organ in every parlor are long gone."

"Did you not try to learn an instrument, Stan?" asked Kate. "As you are so fond of music?"

"Oh, I tried, but I simply don't have a musical bone in my body; it's just my head that carries all the music."

"Well, that's something, anyway," observed Jonathan.

"Something? I suppose..." Stan sighed. "You cannot know, my friend, how hard it is to be a lover of music—to hear it most gorgeously inside your head—yet not have the musical talent to express it. If a genie came out of a bottle right now and offered me any wish in the world—any wish at all—it would be to sing."

They sat quiet then, each with their own thoughts.

"So!" cried Stan, slapping his hands together and breaking the silence. "Well, I said I wanted to bounce some ideas off your heads, and I have been rewarded in spades. But now, we go to the next level!"

"The next level," asked Jonathan in trepidation, "is your damned 'files', right?"

"You've got it," he replied. "My damned files. You've heard of this New Age idea of channeling energy from some other bullshit dimension? Well, y'know, turns out, just maybe, that it's not such bullshit after all." He steepled his fingers and pressed both index fingers to his nose. "Jonathan, have you filled in your young lady on our... my thought processes so far?"

Kate coloured; she had never been called anyone's young lady before, and the association with Jonathan was especially poignant. She tried 'young lady' on for size, turning this way and that in front of the mirror of her mind, and she liked the fit.

"Yes, Kate's up to speed..." Stan winced "...so let's have it out, shall we?"

"Right. Now, I have told you that I think there is some indefinable place where the lost energy we have measured is being stored. I like to call this the Music Continuum. And it is unique to music; I don't believe the remaining creative endeavours have this characteristic. We have argued, I hope satisfactorily, that music of all the arts is—as you suggested Kate—genetic and not cultural. Hard wired.

"Suffice it to say that every single act of musical creation adds some energy to the Continuum. And it also adds an identity. Each created work—Dvorak's *New World*, Beethoven's Fifth Symphony, Handel's *Messiah*—has a unique 'file', if you like, in which creative energy is stored. And it's not just the initial act of creation that adds energy; the playing of the work is also an act of creation, is it not?"

"Most certainly," agreed Jonathan. "You cannot convert the notes on the page into music without creative retrieval."

"Come to one of our rehearsals," Kate lamented, "and you'll hear that. One sheet of music, eighty different interpretations! But, of course, the boss at the front with the little white stick is the one that calls the shots."

"Ah ha!" with an index finger raised. "This intuitive young lady is leaping ahead of us. Excuse us, Kate, while we try to catch up. Now, I want to ask you musicians something very important. When you play the music what do you *feel*? Do you feel that 'spark' that crosses the gap between yourselves and the music, or is that my flight of fancy?"

"Hoo, that's a tough one, isn't it Kate?"

"Ye-e-s. I suppose you could say that some sort of communication—don't know if that's the right word—occurs between you and the music. But, whatever it is, it's highly addictive. Wouldn't you say so, Jonathan?"

"Absolutely! We train hard, very hard, and every evening, with few exceptions (this one's lovely!), you spend an hour or two practicing. I wouldn't do this if it didn't give me enormous satisfaction. But as to what the satisfaction is, and how I would define it... Tricky."

"Me too," said Kate. "I am driven to play music, always have been, and it's as if there's someone up there working the controls. I would be absolutely devastated if I couldn't play. Does that help at all?"

"Yes, ye-e-s, I think it does. Here's what I think, you two. I think that when you play music there is some part of your brain that is in direct link to the Music Continuum. It mediates the connection. The 'spark', the drive, the satisfaction—whatever you wish to call it—is a small packet of energy leaking back out. In small doses it is a stimulant to the creative process."

"Stan, Stan," pleaded Jonathan, "you're pushing this too far. Sure, it's a hypothesis, but if you want to bring it up to the level of a theory, you're going to have to present some data. So far, I haven't heard anything that couldn't have come out of a sci-fi author's head."

"Bear with me here," replied Stan, somewhat chastened. "Kate, has Jonathan brought you... ah, up to speed on the musical phenomena? Mozart and Vaughn Williams?"

"Yes," she replied. "Different results because of the... size of the file?" Oh dear, she thought, am I becoming beguiled; what weird world am I being wooed into?

"Not file size, so much as fullness. I believe as the flow into them continues it becomes slower and slower, stops then reverses. And this is all to do with how many times the piece of music has been played. And that, of course, ties in with the date of composition and the piece's popularity. Leakage in the form of reflux can occur benignly. Without a maestro, I believe the reflux is distributed through all members of the orchestra, and of course it's diluted."

"Bit like breathing deeply at a folk concert," Jonathan observed laconically. "Everybody gets some."

"Maybe I'm just being stupid," said Kate ignoring the wit, "but I don't understand why the maestro gets hit when the whole orchestra is playing the music. It seems unfair."

"The key issue, I believe, is that the energy transfer is mediated in the brain by the *playing* of music. When you play, the energy reflux passes through you benignly, but the maestro isn't playing anything."

"But, he's reading the music, and that counts surely? He's playing it in his mind."

Stan sighed. "I know. It's a conundrum and I'm damned if I can see a way past it, unless the actual mechanical act of making music is the key. A physiological basis..."

"Sounds like conducting *Messiah* from the keyboard would be a great idea," Kate observed. "Lets you be the maestro, yet still feel safe."

"Exactly! Or lead a baroque orchestra from first violin."

Jonathan sighed and raised his hands in mock supplication. This was getting ridiculous, and he was irritated with Kate for being so gullible.

"But why just classical music?" asked Kate. "What's so special about classical music that our people are being targeted?"

"Yeah, why hasn't Mick Jagger been blown to smithereens?" asked Jonathan. "He's been at it for ever."

"Simply this: The symphony orchestra has got stuck. In all other genres of music, the acts of creation far outweigh later acts of creative interpretation, because the art is always moving along. And it would still be so in the sphere of classical music if we didn't keep playing the old chestnuts over and over again. We love them. Look at the flyers and brochures of any symphony orchestra on the planet and what do you see? The 19th century! We can't stop playing the stuff! The files are bursting!"

"So, by extrapolation," replied Jonathan, "if *The Stones* keep going for another century—which, judging by their track record, is highly likely—then Mick and Keef are gonna blow up?"

"Well, I was thinking primarily of classical music..."

"Ha! Classical!" interrupted Jonathan, spreading his arms and addressing the room at large. "You see, folks, this is where I sort of lose it, mostly because it's so... what's the word? Condign! Yes, that's it, condign. The maestro hogs it all to himself—as these self-aggrandizing ponces are prone to do—and he gets it full force. Wham! Serve the bugger right! We literally love them to bits. Sorry Stan, but it's just *too damned good* to be true!"

"Jonathan," said Stan with the sort of laboured patience he would show to a first-year undergrad with failing grades, "if you can provide me with a better hypothesis, then go ahead."

"Look Stan. It's a question of belief. How can I believe your hypothesis of this Music Continuum, something that is impossible to perceive or to measure and which, you say, we humans may *never* perceive or understand anyway? Man, that's a tough sell."

Stan looked him in the eye for a long minute, smiled slightly and raised his almost forgotten glass in a toast. "I'll have you on side, by God. This old bastard isn't done yet." He drained the glass, looked quickly at his wristwatch and made to get up. "It's late now; come my dear, we mustn't presume on the hospitality of these young people any further."

Kate and Jonathan got to their feet and saw the older couple to the door.

"How about we resume this discussion while we're still in town," asked Stan. "Are you available at all...?"

"We've got a bit of work to do tomorrow afternoon at the hall. Kate, how are you fixed for tomorrow morning? Good, then where should we meet?"

"Oh, come back here, please," pleaded Kate. "This has been absolutely marvelous. Please?"

"We would be delighted to," answered Sandra. "How about around ten? Would that suit us all?"

They all agreed, and Stan and Sandra started towards the stairs. Stan hung back a little and turned. Jonathan saw he was laughing silently. "Anchovies; green peppers!" he chuckled just within Jonathan's hearing, and followed his wife down to the street.

"Do mind the stairs; they're awfully steep," called Kate.

She closed the door and returned to the living room.

"Lovely people," said Sandra as they walked gently back to Ivy Lea along streets that were cooling from the daytime heat. "He reminds me a bit of Peter. D'you think so?"

"Yes, a little. Peter's in such a different situation, of course—mining up North, engineering, flying planes—but there's something about him... Maybe... Perhaps we miss Peter just a little, and that's what rings a little bell with us."

"Well, he and Zenia will be back at Christmas with Colby. I'm so looking forward to seeing how he's grown." She recalled Stan's reaction when the kids had announced their choice of name: Colby!? Colby's a bloody *cheese*!

She paused for a moment with the little one's face in her

mind's eye. "Isn't Kate sweet? What a lovely girl. And the singing!"

"Sweet..." he chewed the word around for a few paces. "Yes, she is sweet, but there's a hard nut in there, unless I'm very much mistaken."

"Well, I think, if you get to their professional level, you have to be a strong personality," she observed. "Some of the high-flying ones can be right bastards, more's the pity."

They turned a corner onto Main Street, a much more populated thoroughfare with its cafés, bars and stores that catered to the tourist trade. Many of the places were still open, and the street was happily and noisily populated.

"But did you notice, Stan, that they hardly ever touch each other? Those two? And, you know, the way he had to find the street number, the way he looked around the apartment, the way he examined that Colville print, I don't think he had ever been there before. Sort of funny for a boyfriend, eh?"

Stan felt a little uncomfortable; although he had told her a great deal about Jonathan's unloading of his history, he sensed there was much more that had not been said. "Oh, I know, I saw it too, but not much point in speculating, eh?"

"I agree," she replied. "None of our business. But one does wonder..."

Kate came back into her living room and closed the door.

"Well, what do you think of Schloss Heinrichs?" she asked, spreading her arms in an expansive gesture.

"You have a very nice place here." He hefted the second bottle. "There's just a smidgen left in this one. May I?"

"Thank you, kind sir," and she held out a glass.

"What did you think of them?" he asked with an expectant expression.

"They're wonderful. They're knowledgeable, they're witty, and just... well, plain alive I guess." She looked a little shyly at him. "I never heard you sing before. Whatever possessed us?"

"Stupid impulse." His eyes slid away from hers. "But they do that to you, those people. Couldn't stop myself. Sure, they're a generation older than us, and they lay it on a bit too, but they're still young at heart."

"Yeah, like that Tom Petty one, eh? 'My old man was born to

rock, he's still trying to beat the clock'." They both laughed and drained their glasses.

"And that thing with the remote clickie and the curmudgeon button!" he smiled. "I just about cracked up."

"Well, let's see what working with him brings. I know you're totally skeptical..."

"Yes, I am," he interrupted. "Utter bullshit!"

"...and it really is completely crazy, but I think it might be good for you. Throw yourself in, like you do with your music."

"You know," he observed holding her eyes. "I am very lucky. Between you and the Wards I'm finding a place to stand."

She said nothing, but reached up and gave him one of those delicate little pecks on the cheek.

He turned to the door, said "Goodnight" softly and was gone down the stairs.

The Wards arrived at 48 Simcoe Street promptly at ten o'clock next morning thanks to Stan's obsessive and irritating punctuality. Kate came down to meet them and led them up the steep and narrow stairs. She had chosen a knee-length dress of pale blue, cinched with a light leather belt at the waist. She wore very little make-up.

"I know, so soon after breakfast you won't want anything to eat. But Jonathan and I don't have to be at the concert hall until at least two, so if you want me to fix you some lunch, that's no problem."

Just as they were entering the room the doorbell rang again. Kate went quickly down the stairs to let Jonathan in, while Stan settled onto the chesterfield as he had the night before, while Sandra examined the framed prints more closely. As soon as Jonathan entered the room, with Kate just behind, Stan was upon him.

"Jonathan, Kate," he began, rising from his seat and rubbing his hands together, clearly eager to resume where he had left off the night before. "Let's talk about belief..."

"Before you even start," Jonathan held up his hand, "I was listening to a podcast just before I left home this morning. Another maestro; Handel's *Messiah* this time. Just last evening in Rio de Janeiro. During a performance. Quite the pandemonium, as you can imagine. 'The trumpet shall sound, and the dead shall be raised' and up he went right on cue. Bits made it into the first balcony..."

"Jonathan, no!" cried Kate. "You *mustn't* say such horrible things! It's not even slightly funny!" She looked as if she were about to cry.

"Oh Kate, I'm sorry, I really am. It's just... if we can't lighten this thing up somehow..." His face showed remorse and Stan, at least, knew the jocularity was a costly mental sleight of hand.

"I know, I know," she replied, "it's just that... But my God, everybody, what is *happening*? It can't go on like this!"

"Well, the journalists may think it's some sort of international terrorist," replied Stan. "But, of course, I know that's not the case. *Messiah* was..."

"The guy on the podcast," interrupted Jonathan, "christened him the Symphabomber."

"Oh, no!" wailed Stan. "Not again! *Please*!"

Jonathan noted the puzzled wrinkles on Kate's brow. "He has a thing about un-a-versities," he explained, "and now it's been transferred to symph-a-nies."

The puzzled expression on her face remained; she clearly didn't get it.

"Tell you later," he smiled without humour.

"So," resumed Stan thoughtfully, "as I was saying, *Messiah* is now no longer a threat to the maestros of the world."

Jonathan rubbed his face hard from forehead to chin with the palms of his hands. "As I told you last night, you have yet to give us even one observation that would support such a conclusion. In fact, quite the reverse; you have shrouded it in mystery. I'm not one of those who will accept something at face value; I need supporting evidence, and you're not providing it. It's not an act of faith."

Sandra and Kate sat by while this dialogue continued. This was an impasse. Sandra had come around to Stan's view because she knew that in their long life together this intuition of his had never failed him, while Kate had decided to sit on the fence and watch developments.

"I think it *is* an act of faith, Jonathan. Let me see if I can convince you that in your scientific career you have taken other such acts of faith, and have come through to the other side with your rationality intact."

"Try me."

"What about imaginary numbers, then? Tell me what you

know about imaginary numbers. Let's hear your views in simple terms."

"Imaginary numbers?" interrupted Kate.

"They're not really imaginary, Kate. That was just a derogatory term for them way back in the 17th century. They exist in a manner of speaking; it's just that they are represented at right angles to the familiar real numbers." She frowned.

"Derogatory?" mused Stan with raised eyebrows. "Continue. Elucidate!"

"Okay, your real numbers exist on a line centered around zero; negative numbers on one side, positive numbers on the other."

"But the key thing is the asymmetry, is it not?"

"Yes, when you multiply two positive numbers, the result is positive. But when you multiply two negative numbers, the result is also positive. It's fundamentally asymmetrical. However, with imaginary numbers you can multiply them and arrive at negative values."

"Aye," observed Stan to the ladies, "he knows whereof he speaks."

"Oh, come on Stan! We did this stuff in high school. Well, at least I did. Anyway, the defining equation is the square root of imaginary number 1, which is minus 1. It's a quadratic polynomial with no multiple root..."

"Yes, yes, and they turn out to be additive and multiplicative inverses of each other, do they not? Good! But of what use are imaginary numbers, pray?"

"All sorts of theories on electronics, aerodynamics, many other fields would be impossible without imaginary numbers. Even acoustic descriptions of how my damned oboe works!"

"Excellent! So let me summarize." Stan was clearly in the lecture hall in front of his beloved and hopelessly antiquated chalkboard. "You are speaking of numbers that don't exist, yet we decided they ought to, and numbers that are essential to a mathematical description of the universe."

"I suppose you could say that."

"Oh, I do say that! Now, let me ask you about the wave/particle duality..."

"Ah ha, I see where you're going; another philosophical test. Okay, all subatomic particle exhibit properties of both waves and particles. It's a fundamental concept of quantum mechanics. And, yes, it's a paradox."

"You talked about this to me the other day, didn't you?" Kate sang out from the adjacent kitchen where she had just gone to assemble some coffee. "And, don't you have to decide which property you will choose before you even begin to study them?"

Stan's eyebrows rose again and he nodded with approval in the direction of the kitchen.

"Yes, of course," Jonathan replied. "It's complementarity. You can view a phenomenon as either a wave or a particle, but not both simultaneously."

"And you have no trouble stretching your belief to encompass that?" asked Stan.

"No. The explanation is that the duality can either be a basic property of the Universe, or it could be an emergent, second-order consequence of the observer's various limitations. The jury's out."

"But, you can stretch your mind to encompass this... this... nonsense?"

"As a physicist, you have to."

"So, what is it about imaginary numbers and the wave/particle duality that your excellent brain can encompass, accept and work with, while my hypothesis on lost energy and the Music Continuum continues to be anathema to you?"

"Show me an application for imaginary numbers and I will believe in them. Show me a single photon passing simultaneously through two slits and I will believe in the wave/particle duality. So, show me some numbers Stan! Show me some numbers!"

"We're going to do that, you and I," replied Stan, "but it will take some time and energy. And let me say that I am very glad that you are not one of those who take everything at face value. Your skepticism is exactly what's needed to keep me... us... on the straight and narrow."

Kate brought a tray of coffee into the room. Some time was spent in pouring, and milking and sugaring to taste.

"So far," resumed Stan, "the only numbers I can show you are those you already know. You know that Mozart allows very little energy to pass and that with Vaughn Williams it is measurable. But these data allowed me to make the inference that, because the Mozart was older and more played, the lack of passing energy meant that its file was likely to be fuller. On the other hand, the energy transfer from the Vaughn Williams might, with the same inference, imply that the file was not yet filled. Am I on the right track?"

"Well, in my branch of science proofs are a lot more rigorous," he replied with a gloss of sarcasm. "Yes, you're on the right track if just two observations suffice to allow you to make such an outlandish inference."

"And by the same outlandish inference, *Messiah* is no longer a problem because, as I see it, the file is now empty. Or, at least, the pressure has been relieved. It could, of course, refill and overflow again. How can anyone know?"

"All right!" cried Jonathan. "I fold!" And he made a gesture of throwing down imaginary playing cards onto the table. "But, by God, we'll need to get lots more numbers, if only to give your hypothesis some sort of real scientific challenge! And, most probably, to see its wreckage come crashing down in flames and smoke like the bloody *Hindenburg*."

"He wishes me well, does he not," twinkled Stan to his audience. "Of course, we need more data. I have a three-pronged approach in mind: firstly, would you agree to come back to the lab and perform some more experiments, so that we can assemble a larger and more representative data set?"

"Absolutely. But even with all the data in the world, showing beyond all doubt that this bullshit Music Continuum exists, and that bullshit energy flows in and out of it, you still will not have established a link between it and the series of catastrophic disembodiments on the podium!" Kate shuddered and shut her eyes. "That link, Stan, with all due respect, is in your mind and nowhere else!"

"And that, my friend, is the second prong. We need to amass data and perform a statistical analysis of the occurrences in order to establish the presence of a pattern. Firstly, we need to know specifically what music was being played when the deaths occurred, and then secondly—perhaps anecdotally—how popular the pieces were. Now, how many deaths have there been?"

"I think it's around nine or ten," said Kate in a small voice. "But you'd still need to filter out deaths from natural causes, of course."

"And that, I suppose," observed Sandra, who had remained a silent observer thus far, "could only come from the results of postmortems."

"News reports might suffice," Stan offered. "But that's a fence we'll cross when we come to it. If it's possible to establish even the shadow of a pattern, we may be able to get somewhere. Perhaps you young people could do two things: compile this list of the deaths and what was being played, and then try to arrive at an ordered list of, say, the first ten or fifteen of the most popular pieces from your repertoire. Could you do that?"

"On our own, I don't think it would mean much because of our own preferences," observed Kate, "but if we got the opinions of everybody in the orchestra it would be a better statistical sampling, wouldn't it?"

"What, circulate a questionnaire, you mean?" asked Jonathan.

"Sure. We don't need to tell anyone what it's for. Some research we're doing on audience preferences; something of that kind."

"Sound harmless enough. Would that do Stan?"

"I'm sure it would," Stan replied. "How many are there in the orchestra? Fifty?"

"No, eighty," replied Kate. "Great sampling. And I'll bet," she added, "that we'll find a ton of stuff on the web. We could Google the Top 20 or even the Top 100 and see what comes up."

"Good! Yes, do it please."

"And the third prong?" asked Jonathan.

"The third prong...?" Stan mused. "The third prong would be a predictive model... Some way to predict which pieces of music were ripe for reflux... But that," he brightened up, slapping his hands together and steepling his fingers on his chin, "is yet nascent. First things first."

"It seems to me," said Jonathan, like a dog to a bone, "that your third prong is in essence a risk assessment protocol, and I would think—assuming of course that *any* of this isn't pure science fiction—that exactly when a reflux will take place would be almost impossible to predict."

"Elaborate."

"Okay. You have three unknowns: the initial size of the file on first creation, the number of times the piece has been played, and the capacity of the file. In order to create any kind of risk assessment model you would need to know two of these. And that just ain't possible. You might find out how many times a piece has been played, but I strongly doubt it, and the other two are 'way out of sight. You don't even know where the files *are*, let alone what's in 'em!"

"Well, let's shelve that and concentrate on the first two prongs." He dusted his hands together. "We have work to do."

Stan and Sandra left later in the morning for a little tourism, kindly refusing Kate's offer of lunch, and she and Jonathan remained chatting about the strange turn their lives were taking. It was a peaceful, gentle and slow time with lots of long but comfortable pauses in the conversation. It was fine, Kate thought, as long as they stayed with generalities.

Towards twelve-thirty Kate put the kettle on and laid out a plate of cheese, crackers and vegetables. They had a quiet, contented lunch then headed somewhat reluctantly to the concert hall, detouring by Jonathan's place to collect his instrument.

Visitors to the East Gladstone Centennial Centre are always impressed when they step through the double doors from the foyer into the auditorium. The wooden beams springing away from the floor carry the eye effortlessly upward to the nexus above the stage, giving an organic and naturalistic expression to the building. It must be said that the acoustics of this form of interior support were not as well thought out, and on completion of the structure in 1968 it was found to be too resonant for musical use. This failing was cleverly alleviated by hanging sound absorbers from the beams in such a way that sound traveling upwards would no longer be reflected from the roof. This stop-gap measure was made to actually enhance the natural ambience because the sound absorbing surfaces were fashioned in the shape of the trillium flower of Ontario, painted white and complete with tiny fiberglass pistils and stamens of bright yellow. The effect of these giant flowers hanging above the stage was magical, and the viewer felt reduced to insect size beneath the giant blossoms.

Sandra and Stan Ward looked upwards in delight at this unique interior as they made their way to front of the stalls. They had arrived in plenty of time for the seven-thirty face-off (Stan again) and so they had time to watch the musicians filter in and take their places. Scores were sorted out and placed on music stands, and warm-ups and tunings were attended to. Sandra did have to admit to herself that these preparatory stages in the concert were all part of the entire package, and contributed to the overall experience, although she drew the line at Stan's coarse remark that if you arrived as the concert was beginning it would be all orgasm and no foreplay.

"Did you bring some crunchy candies in nice crispy, rustling wrappers?" asked Stan in a mock stage whisper.

"Yes," she hissed. "And I hope you're working on your cough;

I want it nice and moist and fruity right after the opening bars."

"Roger that!"

A gentleman two rows in front swiveled his head to face them, exposing a long intolerant nose, close-set eyes and yellow incisors. Clearly, he was of a sober disposition and resented their lowering of the tone. Stan grinned back, putting on an empty bumpkin face. They spotted Jonathan very easily as one of the orchestra's two oboes, but it took a few moments to locate Kate among the second row of violins; the strings were all rather anonymous in their severe black and white clothing. Neither of their musicians looked out into the auditorium; it was if their audience didn't exist.

The seats around them began to fill; even for a Friday evening the turn-out was quite impressive. Presently the lights lowered and the new concertmaster appeared from the wings to a light applause, stepped to the front of the orchestra and indicated to first oboe that he may now give the musicians their pitch. The audience settled comfortably into their seats while this fustian ritual was being played out. A pause, then the maestro *pro tem* stepped forth to more applause, bowed to the audience and turned to his musicians. (Kate and Jonathan had filled the Wards in on the latest EGSO dynamics.)

Sandra leant over and brought her mouth close to Stan's ear, and in a real whisper, said, "If he explodes on the podium right in the middle of the *New World* symphony I shall be very cross with you."

"That, my dear," Stan whispered back, "was in extremely poor taste."

Even with the quietness of their whispers, long intolerant nose turned again and fixed them with his eye. He was not having a good day. The baton swished down, the music began, and he perforce took his acid attention elsewhere.

The *Enigma Variations* was an old friend, and they always found joy in every iteration they attended. This was the crux of the problem, thought Stan as 'Nimrod' washed around him; we love this and we would never want it to stop being produced. Sure, we're stuck in some ways in a comfortable place, but as long as there are still enough of us to enjoy this, let the music play. The final bars of Variation XIV, the Finale, closed and the applause welled up. The maestro bowed mightily and then turned to acknowledge his musicians. Better round the other way, thought Stan as he applauded; a bow from the musicians first, then the conductor. After all who's output are we applauding here? Typical inversion of worker and boss.

They played the usual suite of Brahms *Hungarian Dances*, numbers 4,5,6,7 and 10 from the two books published in 1869. The number 5 in f# minor—the one that everyone knows—had a charming section where the oboes and the strings engaged in some fine work. This was their chance to watch Jonathan perform. There was a lot of show-offy solo fiddle work in number 7, and the stand-in concertmaster did very well. Unfortunately, Kate's role as literally second fiddle, made her less easy to distinguish.

"Well, I think they acquitted themselves mightily," announced Stan as they headed for the foyer at the intermission. "It's nice to know someone in the orchestra, isn't it? It gives a little tension to the performance."

"Yes," agreed Sandra, "but I think it would be less enjoyable if they had to do a tough solo; you'd be tense all the time, willing them to do well."

"Well, Jonathan's got some tricky stuff in the *New World*. That'll rack up the tension a bit. Ah here's the line for the gents. See you shortly."

"Right. I'm going round to the other side. Meet me over there by that railing. I doubt if there will be time for a drink; the line-up's probably huge by now."

"You people really ought to learn how to do it standing up!" he replied much too loudly.

"Don't be so gross, especially in public!" she hissed. "You'd do well as a city planner, you would; equal number of washrooms for both sexes, and be damned to time and motion studies."

They parted ways, each unto their own, and when they finally met by the railing there was a long line at the bar.

"Well, it could be worse," observed Stan. "Last thing I want is to empty the tanks, then go and fill 'em up again. Let's head for our seats before the bell."

In the second movement of the *New World*, the largo, it was the turn of Jonathan's colleague Graham Swann to shine. He took the solo for cor anglais and shook them by their ears with it. The haunting richness of the instrument, pitched a perfect fifth lower than the oboe, was absolutely transporting; this gorgeous moment would stay with them for ever. Around the middle of the fourth movement there was some fine work for the woodwinds, in which the oboes again came to the fore, and the concluding bars where the horns introduce the theme so softly and the ensemble swells to the finale were quite stunning.

In the roar of applause Sandra turned to Stan and yelled in his ear, "I don't remember when I've enjoyed a concert so much!"

"There is absolutely nothing like a live performance," he shouted back. "Don't care what anybody says, home entertainment will never hold a candle to this."

"As long as there are enough old fogeys like us to sustain it, of course."

"Oh, no my love, don't burst our little bubble..."

Stan phoned Kate and Jonathan after the concert and invited them to breakfast at Ivy Lea. The Wards' landlady was pleased enough to have them as guests, so at eight-thirty all four sat in the sun-filled breakfast room and enjoyed eggs, bacon, toast and orange juice.

"Marvelous concert you two," enthused Stan crunching his last piece of toast. "We were saying that there is absolutely nothing to rival a live performance. We'll have to come again."

"Most definitely," replied Sandra. "This is going to become a fixture on our entertainment circuit. It really isn't far to drive and, apart from the concerts, there's lots to see and do."

"So now," said Stan. "It was extremely useful to discuss all my theorizing with you both, and although I know you remain skeptical Jonathan, I hope you'll agree to compile some numbers. If you two can produce some statistics—what is being played, what is popular and, in particular, what music was on the program on those fateful occasions—then we might possibly see some trends. Would you be able to do that?"

"Yes," Kate replied first. "I'll get on with that questionnaire on what our people think are the most popular, most played pieces. And I'll check a few sites on the web too, see what I can come up with. Sort of Top 20 symphonic hits."

"And meanwhile," put in Jonathan, "as I said, I can do some searching on the web too, and try to pin down the concert programs."

"Good!" Stan thought for a moment. "I'm going to have to raise this whole thing with the team. I can't keep fiddling around in the lab's downtime, but I am in a quandary as to how to broach the subject. You ladies think Jonathan's skeptical; you should meet Ken Livermore! But, Jonathan, we really do need to play some more music, get more data. When can you come back again?"

"I'll check our schedule for the next week or two," replied Jonathan, "and I'll see if I can shake a few more coins out of my piggy bank."

"I'm sorry. I wish I could help. There is a small fund for our student volunteers..."

"No, no, I was joking; I wouldn't think of it. The money's not an issue at all, although the time is another story. I can miss the odd rehearsal at a pinch, but I've been really pushing it."

"Well, see what you can do, and then get in touch will you? You can always stay at our place; we have a spare bedroom, save you the cost of a hotel. Meanwhile, I'll have to do some mighty hard diplomacy on the lab front. Can't fathom how I'm going to handle that..."

"Thanks for breakfast," said Kate as she and Jonathan stood up to leave. "It's been really great meeting you both, and I hope to see you again next time you're in East Gladstone."

"You should come down with Jonathan," said Stan. "Stay at our place, make a little vacation of it." He winced as the toe of Sandra's shoe caught him on the shin.

Colour rose in Kate's cheeks. "That... that would be... it's difficult to get the time... But... You're very kind. Thank you."

It was surprisingly hard to do the survey of the orchestra members' Top 20, and it took Kate much more time than she could really afford. Firstly, she had to speak to most of them personally, explaining that this was a matter of interest to her alone, and that the information would be used for no other purpose. She felt a little uneasy at this, and hoped this would actually be the case. Secondly, she had to emphasize that their lists should not be compiled from personal favorites, but should represent a typical sample of the music they had played over their years of performing. She wished they all been as nice as Bill Baines, the bassoonist; he had been around for a very long time and had seen much, but it was the gentlemanly way he dealt with her request that warmed her to him. You play with these people for years, yet sometimes you don't really know them...

Finally, once all the returns were in—and not by any means

every member of the ensemble responded—she had the onerous task of number-crunching, producing a definitive list by rating the answers on each sheet and transferring the data to a master spreadsheet. When she was done she looked at what she had, ran her eyes down the list once again, and thought, well here's the ultimate and definitive list of the good old orchestral top of the pops. There were no surprises.

Harold Gropius, the orchestra manager, accosted Kate in the hallway one morning while she was halfway through her project.

"I hear you have been going around doing a survey among the musicians. What's this all about?" He was holding a blank copy of Kate's questionnaire in his smooth, short-fingered hand. His nails were curved and tapered, and looked highly polished.

"It's just a little idea I had regarding our favorite music. I wanted to know if we all shared the same musical passions." This smelt highly of bullshit, but Kate knew that the little man was not a musical sophisticate; smooth running of the machine was his responsibility and focus.

"Well, I think you should have cleared this with authority first. We can't have the Board thinking that someone is critical of our offerings. As you know, the Board works very hard to satisfy the wide-ranging tastes of our audiences."

"Oh, Mr Gropius!" cried Kate. "The thought never entered my head! The information is for nobody's use but mine. Mere curiosity. You know full-well how we love our repertoire."

"Well, you must promise me that this information will go no further."

"Absolutely, Mr Gropius, you have my word on it."

"Well, then, I wish you a good day," and he bustled off to see to some aspect of orchestral management that it would have been impossible to leave to underlings.

Meanwhile, Jonathan had the task of compiling a list of all the deaths at the podium, and finding out what pieces of music were being played when the awful event overtook them. He decided, wisely as it transpired, to also include the entire program for the concerts in question. Like Kate's experience, he found the work time-consuming; in his case he was working with old news reports of orchestras throughout the whole world, and some surprisingly sparse information. When his list was finally compiled he looked it up and down and smiled; well, he thought, not one single piece of what I would call unusual or rare music; all of these are right up on everyone's Top 20 classical hits. Be interesting to see what Kate's research yields, although I am suspecting a scary pattern here.

Jonathan and Kate met in the foyer after rehearsal and walked into town, each with a laptop tucked under an arm. They had decided to share the results of their research in a neutral location, far away from the eyes and tongues of their colleagues. They chose a café on the main drag, chiefly because it had good Wi-Fi, but the coffee wasn't bad either. While Jonathan joined the line at the counter Kate grabbed a table, pulled two chairs around side by side, and opened their laptops.

He returned in a minute or so with two cappuccinos and a couple of nutty-fruity bars, one of which she declined. She had a horrible suspicion that she was looking at his supper.

"Okay," he began, "it took a lot of messing around to get all the info. I had to find the dates of death of all these guys, then locate the concert programs from those dates. One of them, of course, was dead easy; our guy. Look, I did leave out our first maestro; I swear that was coincidental, and there is nothing to say it wasn't a genuine heart attack, but I've kept the data anyway. Some of the orchestra websites were great—had their whole season listed—but I had to e-mail two of them because they'd updated and wiped the out-of-date stuff. Anyway, I have a pretty definitive list, and I also have an eerie premonition. But, first off, what did you get?"

"It was hard work, too. God knows what anybody did for research before the web." She opened the laptop and booted up Firefox, her preferred browser.

"Okay, first the web search. I went on Google and tried to locate sites that listed the top twenty, top fifty, top hundred, whatever. Problem is, classical is defined too broadly. The label 'classical' covers a much wider range that our repertoire."

"That's the trouble; the word classical has become quite meaningless, or at least so broad as to be non-specific. Used to be just Haydn, Mozart, that bunch."

"Right. So then I tried 'symphonic' but I drew a blank. Too specific, I guess. So here's all I found, bookmarked; check these sites out," she opened them in turn. "See, this one rates classical music according to popularity, but apart from the fact that half this stuff is not symphonic, there are several other issues. Firstly, their ratings are more likely done from sales of recordings rather than attendance at live performances, and secondly they're listing snippets and excerpts rather than whole works."

"It's the universal problem of attention span. All this stuff looks like samples on an easy-listening CD for the car stereo."

"Absolutely. Great moments at the symphony. High up this list," she opened another tab, "they've got good old Pachelbel's *Canon* in D. I mean, really, what's that all about?"

"Oh, Pachelbel's *Canon* always makes the cut," he observed. "It's one of those bits you can get lots out of if you're really stoned." He breathed in deeply, held it, and than said in a strangled voice, "Like Pachelbel, TacoBell, Tinkerbell, Mirabel, Ma Bell; it's so like y'know, these cool words, they're all like connected... Know-wom-sayin'?"

He let go the breath explosively and they both laughed.

"Anyway," she continued. "Fact is, if we look at these lists we can delete a whole load of pieces that fall outside the symphony orchestra repertoire. They all love Bach's *Toccata and Fugue* in D minor—can't get enough of that—so we can whip that out for a start. Pachelbel can go as well; it's baroque and you don't need a damned conductor."

"Oh look," he exclaimed, "here's *Also Sprach Zarathustra* on this one—boom-boom-boom-bom bang—scarcely a minute and, who the hell listens to any more of it anyway?"

"Yeah, it's all fragments isn't it?" she said, scanning down one of the sites. "Look, here's the Hallelujah Chorus from *Messiah*. And *Eine Kleine Nachtmusik*, but only the Allegro."

"Exactly; dum, dum-dum, dum-dum-dum diddley-dum, and then they get bored." He scrolled down a list and his eyes suddenly lit up. "Hah, I knew I'd find it! Here's the Lone fucking Ranger, rated fifteenth. I'd swear Rossini would be totally forgotten if it wasn't for Clayton Moore and Jay Silverheels."

"And what list would be complete without the *Flight of the Bumblebee* and the *Hall of the Mountain King*?" she asked. "And, yes in case you were wondering, they're both here. And then... Where the hell is it?" She opened another site and moused up and down. "Ah, here we are: Bach's *Air on a G String*. Why *do* people love it so?"

"I have a theory on that," he replied, "and it's very simple. It was transposed into C major so as to be played on the G string of the violin, right? I'd swear if it was transposed for the D, A, or E strings nobody would have heard anything about it. It's because of the G-string association, mark my words."

"You're just a dirty old man," she smiled. "So, in the end, if we boil a lot of the fat out of these lists, selecting specifically for full-length pieces likely to be played by a symphony orchestra, we come up with a very short list of the usual suspects. Here's my boiled-down spreadsheet."

She booted up Excel and opened the file.

"Yup, they're all here: Beethoven's Fifth, the 1812, Schubert's *Unfinished*, Bruckner's Fourth, *New World*, *Plump and Corpulence*, Beethoven's Ninth..." He was beginning to look both intrigued and perturbed.

"Now here's the results of the EGO survey. What I refer to as our expert sample. And, God, that was tougher than I thought. Got a talking-to from old Gropius into the bargain. I only got about sixty-five responses."

"Sixty-five out of eighty is pretty damned good for any survey; around seventy-five percent is not bad at all. Must be your charm. I can guess who *didn't* help you out."

"Yeah, the usual suspects." She took along drink of coffee, leaving a white moustache on her upper lip. She licked her lips and opened another spreadsheet. "Here we are. Notice some similarities? Same old pieces; roughly the same order."

"Holy shit! Ho-lee shit! It's exactly what I thought!"

"What? What is it?"

"Kate, look." He opened up an Excel spreadsheet on his laptop, and placed the two computers side by side. "Here's my list of all the deaths at the podium; what they were playing."

There were ten.

"They... they're all on my spreadsheets!" she cried. "All of them!" They looked into each other's eyes. "Oh, my God!"

He thought for a moment, and as Kate looked into his face she could almost see the gears turning. "Look, this could be a self-fulfilling exercise. Yes, they're the most popular pieces; yes, the maestros died while conducting them. But that doesn't signify much..."

"Yes it does," she replied, "you're grasping at straws. Look at what else was on the program that day. Here's Beethoven's Fifth in Canberra, and look at this; Shostakovich Fourth, and some stuff I've never heard of by Percy Grainger. Neither of those make it on the popularity list."

"You're right, check this out; death during *Pomp and Circumstance*, and they were also doing a Haydn symphony and a Piano

Concerto in C Major by John Field; nice pieces, but hardly up there in popularity."

The remaining incidents showed similar results; the maestro had passed over while conducting the most popular piece on the program, and in each case the piece of music was represented on Kate's Top 20. There was no question that this small sample of results was showing exactly the trend Stan Ward had predicted.

Jonathan sat in thought for a long while, sipping his cooling cappuccino. "I begged Stan for numbers, and now I've got numbers..."

They finished their coffee while they sat immersed in their own thoughts in the clattering aromatic café, then Kate rose with their empty cups and returned them to the counter. She came back in a few minutes with two large medium roasts with half-and-half already added.

Jonathan sighed and broke the silence. "I've resisted coming round to his view because it's so crazy. I've tried and tried to see some other more rational explanation. I'd even prefer the bloody Symphabomber because then the whole foundation of my thinking... my scientific background... wouldn't have to be... well, retooled."

"What we're seeing," observed Kate slowly, "is evidence of an entire hidden universe, complete with its own set of rules. I'm feeling tiny and helpless..."

"Not so fast," he cautioned her. "Yes, Stan has connected the dots; he has produced a hypothesis which can explain the results we have produced, but like any hypothesis it is only one of an open-ended set of possible solutions."

"How do you mean?"

"I'll give you a great example; when Stan first introduced this idea of the 'files' I was as skeptical as I am now. You remember I told you I cracked up laughing, which pissed him off a bit. I told him I could imagine Zeus up on Mont Olympus hurling thunderbolts down at people because he was sick of Mozart. Well, that is one alternative hypothesis that can explain all the facts we have. The energy lost during playing music goes up to Mount Olympus and Zeus forges it into thunderbolts and fires it back down. Now, I'm not saying it's any closer than Stan's—it's easily as fantastic, mind you—but as a hypothesis it is equally valid."

"So Stan's theory..."

"It's not yet a theory," he interrupted. "People confuse theory and hypothesis all the time. Sorry, I wasn't trying to criticize you,

Kate, but it's a very common confusion. You've heard the Bible-bashers talk about evolution as 'only a theory'? Well, by the time you get to call something a theory it has to be pretty damned solid. Gravitation is a theory; acoustics, electronics, thermodynamics, they're all rooted in theories, and they only get to be theories by a great deal of systematic examination. 'Only a theory' betrays a misunderstanding of what a theory actually is. Had they said 'only a hypothesis' that would be a different story."

"So, Stan's... hypothesis might not be valid?"

"It joins the dots between 'here's an observation' and 'here's another', but it lacks any solid proof."

"So, what's the next step?" She sipped some more of her coffee, looking down into the cup as if seeking inspiration there.

"Well, I'll go down to T-O again and play some more music. Fill in data from that end, at least."

"Jonathan, look at me." She swiveled round in her chair to face him and held his eyes; hers were bright with moisture. "Tell me what we're doing. Please. It's all very well to talk about files and refluxes and the Music Continuum; all these lists of music and... Jonathan, people are dying horribly. *Please*, what are we going to *do*?"

He took both her hands in his. "I don't know, Kate, I just don't know. Even if we have shown cause and effect, what possible hope is there of convincing the symphonic world of these findings? Whichever way you look at it, it's laughable. Hey guys, here's a list of all the stuff you can conduct if you wanna get blown to bits."

"Oh, stop it Jonathan! It's breaking my heart that we know this much, yet we're so powerless to do anything!"

"I do feel the same. I really do. There's got to be something..."

"Do you think, perhaps, that if it continues they'll stop conducting any music at all for fear of coming to harm? Do you think it'll all come to a stop?"

"I just don't know." They sat for some while, still holding hands, then as a memory passed over his face he squeezed gently then withdrew.

"We're a funny pair, aren't we? You and me," she murmured.

He nodded, lips gripped between his teeth and eyes closed. "But, we go forward..."

This was one of his 'moments'. Things had changed a lot since Toronto... since Kate. Before she had broken into him, the nights when the defensive walls are down were peopled with horrors and demons, and it was his task on first waking each day to erect the barriers anew, batten down the hatches and keep it all tight and controlled during the waking day. In some ways she had made it worse, because since Toronto the enemy had now advanced into the light. The nights were no longer haunted—peace reigned there, and that was where healing took place—but now the barriers were more permeable because the demons crept up by day and showed their sudden faces. But daytime demons could be faced and defeated one by one. At night you have no help at all; you are tiny and defenceless in a blackness where common sense and logic have no sway, but by day there was his ally Kate.

He wanted so hard to tell her all this; to lean fully on her, but he knew he must not. This was his battle, and he could fight it, *must* fight it, alone. If he occasionally took a brief furlough from the battlefield with her arms wrapped around him, well, that was a fair rest for a soldier. The war would not last forever.

But this was not one of those times. He stood and smiled down at her, thanking her from all his heart with his eyes, and bade farewell until tomorrow.

As soon as he returned home Jonathan placed the laptop on the table, flipped it open and called Stan on Skype. As soon as Stan's face appeared on the screen Jonathan began with no preamble.

"You'll be delighted to know that our numbers validate your hypothesis."

"They do? Tell me more!" His face lit up and suddenly he looked very pleased with himself.

"Kate's listings of popularity correspond very well with my breakdown of the deaths and the music that was being played at the time. Let me e-mail the data as Excel attachments right now." He had got Kate to e-mail her results to him before they left the café. He kept Stan waiting while he opened his e-mail account, selected Stan's address and fired off the attachments. "That's a U of T server, isn't it? Good, should be pretty quick then."

"Oh, this is excellent, absolutely excellent!' he clapped his hands together, shaking the table and turning his image into a dancing blur. "You two have done some good work. So, all popular pieces, and thus fully loaded and ready to belch when the baton swung down."

"If you say so. All nine deaths are tied to nine pieces of music in Kate's Top 20. The correspondence is uncanny, but this doesn't mean I buy your Music Continuum hypothesis."

"Well, I hardly thought it would be *that* easy. But at least you're coming around to the idea that the incidence of the deaths can now be related to the music, and that's a huge step." He looked down briefly. "Ah, here's your message. Let's have a look here..."

"Tell you what Stan, check over those figures..." Jonathan was going to leave him time to study the data and have him call back, but Stan was hopping with excitement.

"Oh, I see 'em. It's as clear as a bell. This is just marvelous!"

The old boy's enthusiasm had a paradoxical effect; instead of being happy for him, and happy with him, Jonathan became irritated. He had the strange vision of a physiologist being delighted with results gained from vivisection; death embraced in order to consolidate and verify a hypothesis.

"Damn it, Stan," cried Jonathan. "We can't go on like this! Now Kate and I have seen this pattern we're feeling guilty and as frustrated as hell that we can't do anything about it!"

Stan's image on the screen took on a serious tone, and he looked directly into the camera. "Do you think I don't worry about it too? But, just like you, Jonathan, I try to mask my true feelings with levity. Can we really deal with the world if we don't do that?"

Jonathan sighed. Some things can never have a light side.

"True, but something has to be done. As I see it, we have exposed just a trend; there is far too little data in what Kate and I have been able to do. We need more information, we need to make predictions, and we need to be able to sell the idea to anyone who might listen."

"Tall orders, all. Look, I'll tell you what I'll do. As you know, we have a little fund here for paying our experimental subjects. Why don't I commission some students to do what you and Kate did, but on a much larger scale? If we can do a worldwide survey on the web—what orchestras are playing, when they're playing it —we might be able to develop prediction protocols."

"That would be great. Maybe a calendar year of concerts, catch as many orchestras that have web presence as you can. A much larger data set will help a hell of a lot."

"Excellent! I'll get on to it. But, my goodness I am so pleased that we have at least some data to back up my senile ravings. I have no idea what I would have done had your results proved inconclusive."

"But you were sure, weren't you?"

"Yes, but you know what a nagging doubt can do to one's psyche. Now, when can we get together again? Have you checked your schedule?"

"I'm free as of next Monday for a few days. Have to be back by Wednesday morning as we're getting ready for the following weekend. Would that be okay?"

"Perfect. That'll give time to get some more results. Could we meet at the lab as soon as you arrive? I would like you to be present when I open the topic of our results with the team, although I still don't have a clue as to an approach."

"I'll call as soon as I get off the bus."

"Good. Let's plan to meet the team right after lunch. Say, one o'clock?"

"That's fine; I can get the later bus, have a leisurely start to the day. See you then. Bye."

He left the laptop turned on, opened one of his music folders, and selected the evening's practice pieces. Before beginning in earnest he went to the fridge and grabbed a bottle of Smithwick's which, with the two nutty-fruity bars he had eaten in the coffee shop, accounted for tonight's supper.

The weight of depression lifted as he went through his exercises, not because anything was resolved but because he had filed it elsewhere while his mind concentrated on the job at hand.

Symphony No. 4 in E-Flat Major

It was as frustrating as hell for them to know that the deaths at the podium might be prevented, but Kate and Jonathan both recognized the impossibility of acting on the information. Who would listen to a couple of bit players from a musical backwater, who claimed that you could cheat death by avoiding conducting music on a prescribed list? It was laughable at best, and more likely professional suicide. However, only a day after their café meeting when their data had come ominously together, an announcement was made that would at least protect their own conductor from harm at the hands of invisible forces.

Stefan Kulikofski was having second thoughts. Yes, he wanted with a passion to be the maestro of the East Gladstone Symphony Orchestra, and his bid to win the place was looking more and more favourable, but the news reports were ominous. Eleven maestros around the world had now died while conducting, and the media were making much of it. He told himself repeatedly that the statistical probability of being struck down himself was minimal, and that surely lightning would never strike twice, let alone three times, in the same place. Still, he was deeply uneasy. And fear eroded performance; rehearsals were more fraught than usual, and the effort necessary to wind up the tension before a concert was greater. It was enervating and discomforting.

Of course, what Kulikofski was experiencing could be seen worldwide; wherever a symphony orchestra was preparing for a concert there was a maestro in potential danger. While the 'it couldn't happen here' anodyne helped ease the strain, it was obvious to them all that there were eleven poor souls around the world to whom 'it' *had* happened. At first, among the international brotherhood there was a counter argument that what they were seeing was only the work of probability, and that media attention was driving the agenda. While the symptoms mimicked heart attacks this was all very well, but once the violence was ratcheted up the argument became untenable.

There was another cadre of maestros to whom the idea of danger at the podium was actually alluring. The image of strutting into the breach in a damn-the-torpedoes stance, braving the worst the world could hurl at you, was more than beguiling; it was heroic, it was magnificent, and it was highly sexy. Leading great orchestras in bringing to the world the finest music that human civilization had devised was a calling of epic proportions, and even more so when under enemy fire. There were shades of Piper Findlater skirling away with his feet blown off at the battle of Dargai Heights.

There was also a new and rather bizarre twist to this stance of selfless heroism; the usual symphony-going clientele was augmented by sensation-seekers who, like some spectators at air shows, were only there in hopes of witnessing the unspeakable.

But worry is a worm, and perhaps because Kulikofski wasn't truly of that front-line maestro material—he had very little of the swagger, arrogance and disco-ball scintillation of the true blue podium hog—he had caved before many others would. He approached the orchestra's manager and announced that he refused to conduct another concert until the Symphabomber had been brought to justice. No arguments about commitments, no threats and no inducements could change his mind.

Like most smaller orchestras in North America, the difference between success and failure is one series of concerts away; turn away audiences for a long weekend of concert activity and you might as well pack up the music stands and shut the doors.

For Kulikofski, the worldwide death count creeping nearer to the round dozen was his focus. Everything in music that is fine, beautiful and spiritually uplifting took second place to an assured old age, lolling in an easy chair and browsing through a hard copy of the *Grove Dictionary of Music* while jotting marginalia.

News of Stefan Kulikofski's withdrawal from the spotlight hit the orchestra members as they arrived for a Monday morning rehearsal. Harold Gropius fussed onto the stage long after their new maestro should have made his appearance, and announced that the gentleman was indisposed until further notice, and that they should await further instructions. The fact is, the little manager was utterly out of his element and was playing for time until he could locate and convene a quorum of Board members. However, Blair Watts, one of the first violins who was a personal friend of Kulikofski's and knew of the decision from the man himself, spoke up.

"Why don't we lay the cards on the table, Mr Gropius?" he called from the side of the stage. "Stefan has decided to step down temporarily, has he not?"

"Well, yes, yes... It's... it's all very sudden. As soon as we... the Board, has... have found a replacement we will let you know."

"But, what do we do now?" asked someone. "We've got work to do, and a big show this weekend."

"Stand by, stand by," was all he could offer, and he quickly disappeared like a cockroach under a kitchen cabinet. He left an uproar behind him; they were clearly being treated as mere cogs in a machine, and they were deeply offended. A small faction was all for marching off to the little toad's office and demanding solutions, while another was keen on setting up the coffee cups and talking it through. Another faction took this news as the harbinger of a day off and headed out of the doors to await instructions from home.

Little could be accomplished for the rest of the day. Musicians sat around talking about it and about, either at their chairs in the hall, or around cups of coffee and tea in the cafeteria. They all knew this situation could not continue; unless something happened in the next few days they were out of a job. It was that simple. And one unemployed musician in these hard times was problematic; eighty of them all at once was a disaster.

Jonathan and Kate's table in the cafeteria was dominated by a faction that felt they could probably play the pieces on the upcoming program without a conductor.

"Look," said Steve Mah the wisecracking trombonist, "tell me in all honesty, once you're there on stage and you're sitting in front of the music, and you begin playing, just how often do you even look at the guy?"

"In fact," remarked Rick, one of the horn players, "he can actually be one hell of a distraction. I was in Montreal a while back doing the Beethoven Four. There's this bit in the second movement where first horn comes in on a pianissimo high C, okay, and this idiot stares directly at me—right there in the middle of the damn concert—and puts a finger up to his lips like he's shushing a baby. I just about blew the whole damn' passage! What a stupid cretin!"

Pete Lalonde, the analytical clarinetist, observed, "That's all fine and dandy if it's the early classical stuff; Haydn, Mozart, even early Beethoven. But imagine doing Brahms! Or anything later!"

"Yeah," put in Liz Straker. "That'd be impossible. But I've played with enough baroque orchestras to know that it's perfectly feasible for the earlier stuff."

"But they're smaller ensembles, don't forget," said someone else, "so control is a lot easier."

"But look at this weekend's program," continued Lalonde thoughtfully. "Beethoven three, Mozart piano concerto, Haydn; all possible."

"Well," replied Mah, "you don't know how successful it'll be until you try it. Wonder what the public will think when they see us flying the missing maestro formation?"

"Trouble is," said one of the double basses, usually a silent observer in their little group, "the public expect to see a conductor up front. It completes the picture."

"P'raps we could borrow one of the Sony Corp's robots," wondered Steve. "We could dress it up in a tux; nobody'd notice."

"Yeah, but you couldn't have it strut on from the wings at the beginning, could you," observed one of the other trombones from the end of the table. "Caterpillar tracks and all."

"How about popping out of a trapdoor in a cloud of smoke, like the genie in what's-it-called?"

"What is it about friggin' brass instruments," cried the double bass, "that makes the people who play them turn stupid? Here we are just about to lose our jobs for Christ's sake and this yo-yo's cracking jokes!"

Steve Mah subsided into the silence that followed.

"What I'm trying to say," resumed double bass in an aggrieved tone, "is that it's not the public we have to worry about. What about the music establishment? A couple of hundred years of tradition? That's the issue."

"We have to try it," stated Jonathan. "We're small potatoes; we might just fly under their radar."

"What is there to lose?" asked Kate. "Only our jobs. So let's do it."

"We should get Stefan back here as concertmaster. He can run us perfectly in that role," said Lalonde. "Where's Watts? Let's get him to contact Stefan."

"Wait a minute," said Jonathan. "We've hardly got a quorum at this little table, have we? And half of us buzzed on caffeine. Let's contact as many of the players as we can, *then* talk to old Stefan. And only after that should somebody talk to Gropius and the Board; that's if Stefan doesn't want to do it himself. I can be the spokesman if everybody agrees."

This offer pleased Kate in particular. She was delighted that he had offered to do this because it indicated a thawing of his aloofness, but she also saw new respect in the eyes of the others. First oboe should take the lead.

It was late afternoon by the time all the discussions had taken place, and Kulikofski had been sounded out. He had agreed to let Jonathan address the Board in his stead, figuring perhaps that his absence would be construed as diplomacy. The Board members had been dragged away from their various duties around the town and had been assembled in the main boardroom of the concert hall. Following instructions from Mr Gropius, Jonathan ascended to the upper floor, knocked on the impressive wood paneled door, and entered the holy-of-holies.

The Chair of the Board, a florid gentleman whose face bore the unmistakable signs of a lifelong love affair with bottles and cutlery, motioned him to a chair placed some few paces away from the table where all seven of the Board sat in an auspicious row. Seated thus before the inquisition, it took him a few moments to gather his thoughts. They gave him no assistance with either word or gesture.

"I know the absence of our maestro might entail suspending our productions," he began, "but on behalf of Mr Kulikofski I would like to suggest an alternative strategy. Do without a conductor and let Stefan lead from first violin. The smaller baroque orchestras do it all the time. Their leaders also conduct from the keyboard, but of course you couldn't lug in a harpsichord when you want to play Mahler." Oops, what the hell made me say that?

"Mahler...? Harpsichord...?"questioned a small lady with a blue rinse and half-moon glasses.

"Do without a maestro?" asked the Chair. "That's inconceivable!"

"What sort of rubbish is this?" demanded a Justice of the Peace. "I didn't come here to..."

"Madness! Madness..."

Jonathan held up his hands and waited for silence. "Let me be quite frank with you. For the earlier classical repertoire the great majority of symphonic players are quite capable of playing the music from the score, in harmony with all the other players, without reference to the baton and the gestures. That's what we do, and we're trained to do it. And look at the program for this weekend: Beethoven's third, the Mozart piano concerto and the Haydn; all quite possible."

He forbore to mention that most of the time he played better without the distraction. In present company that would be a curry fart at a wine tasting. And one glance at blue rinse and half-moon made him bite his tongue before accidentally letting slip the old orchestra staple: the maestro is like a condom; safer with, but more fun without.

"But, what about the pianist? Brault from Montreal," asked the Chair. "Whatever would he say?"

"I wouldn't be surprised if he'd be delighted to lead from the keyboard," replied Jonathan, knowing full well that this particular gentleman would revel in the attention. He'd played with him before; his sense of his own importance was immense. "It'd be a great expression of his..." ('ego' was on the tip of his tongue) "...musicianship," he concluded.

"Even so, the maestro applies his stamp, his character, his signature to the music! Without him it's... it's..." spluttered the franchisee of the local Canadian Tire store.

"Business as usual," finished Jonathan. "Yes. Listen, when Sir Arthur Compton came in to conduct us in one single concert last spring, how much time do think he had to impose anything upon us? Not a great deal, although he is far better at it than most. We had one rehearsal where we went through the pieces just once—Brahms, Beethoven and Mendelssohn if I remember rightly—and that was that. As we had all played those pieces many times before, all he did was point out a few nuances that he favoured, and we went with it. Now, of course, you couldn't do the Brahms or the Mendelssohn without a leader—they're rhythmically far too complex—but for this weekend there's nothing that couldn't be done perfectly well by a music director during rehearsals."

"Are you trying to tell me that flying guest conductors in—at great expense, I might point out—is a complete waste of time and money?" rumbled the Chair of the Board. The broken veins in his cheeks were becoming more pronounced, and there were little white flecks at the corners of his mouth.

"No, of course not. We're very fortunate with this week's program, that's all. For the classical stuff and the earlier Romantic we can pull it off, but beyond that... no, a conductor is essential."

"So, whatever are we going to do in the future?" wailed blue rinse and half-moon. "If this dreadful business isn't stopped it'll be the end of the symphony orchestra."

"It's getting worse and worse," observed a thin gent with a van Dyke beard, who has so far not uttered a word. "Orchestras are packing up rather than... hmm... facing the music. Police seem to be powerless."

"This is the end of it all," put in Canadian Tire. "Beyond this weekend it's curtains for us. Look at the program for the rest of the season! How can we manage?"

Good God, thought Jonathan, what we're seeing here is being played out in boardrooms around the world. And, yes, we're up shit creek after this weekend. Johannes Brahms was looming on the horizon, and beyond that was the impossible Carl Orff; try *Carmina Burana* without a stick-wagger!

"Back to our immediate problem," the Chair slapped his palm on the table. "We have to deal with this weekend. It's quite a departure from practice, but I see no alternative..."

"But we do have to honour the program for the rest of the season," observed van Dyke. "And we can't afford to lose revenue."

"This weekend," reminded the Chair, "is what we're dealing with. Let's focus people. Do we try it?"

"You've got us by the short and curlies," observed Canadian Tire in Jonathan's direction. "Just one weekend without revenue and we'll be in a hell of a hole. We have to try it, don't we?"

"We just have to go with it as a stop-gap, just for this weekend," admitted the Chair, "but I can't imagine what we'll do beyond that."

"As I said," Jonathan rose to leave, "there you have it; if you believe we can do it, we'll give it a try. Stefan is all for it. We all know we can do it."

"Good. It's settled. Thank you."

The process of working without a maestro proved to be an interesting and eye-opening experiment. The rehearsals were surprisingly routine, because Stefan Kulikofski led the musicians from his chair quite fearlessly, confirmed in the knowledge that the Symphabomber would only strike at a maestro.

One absolute necessity during rehearsal was constant and detailed marking of parts. Only the briefest of penciled notes were written on the scores because they would have to be read on the fly. A wide range of shorthand notations had come to be used. One of Kate's quick notes, a sketched pair of eyeglasses followed by '1 ob.', meant 'watch first oboe', a direction she always had pleasure in following. There were many places where Kulikofski had them stop and explained what he wanted, but it would not be possible to rely upon a cue from his chair at first violin. Those cryptic symbols became extremely important, and the musicians learned to be even more studious than usual.

One feature of Kulikofski's tenure stood out from that of his predecessor: he always gave the musicians time to make their notes upon the scores, instead of launching immediately back into the music and then berating them for wasting rehearsal time by not being ready.

The three concerts that weekend were a revelation. Yes, they could manage extremely well without a maestro to lead them. With the string section carrying the tempo, and the added labours of their more intense and studious rehearsals, the musical effect was indistinguishable. Their pianist rose to the occasion magnificently, as Jonathan knew he would (the arrogant pissant) and, had the audience members closed their eyes, they would have noticed absolutely no difference in their concert-going pleasure. Nevertheless, the carefully worded insert in the concert program, referring to the EGSO's search for a new maestro and the onerous duties of concertmaster, reminded audiences that this was indeed a stop-gap measure, and that no great symphony orchestra could carry on long without solid leadership from the podium.

And what the East Gladstone Symphony Orchestra would be able to offer from here on was a moot point. The program for two weeks hence included the Brahms Symphony No. 1 in C minor, and with the increasingly slender possibility of getting a stand-in maestro (there were few out there anyway, let alone in the present climate) and in the absence of any other strategy, the Board had decided to continue the maestro-less approach. The concert schedule had been planned, the brochures and programs printed, and advance tickets sold. You couldn't just scrap the program and offer only music that could be handled with a vacant podium. The show must go on. So now Stefan Kulikofski was faced with a Brahms symphony that he, and the rest of the musicians, had huge misgivings about.

Only once in a few years did the CBC do a live transmission of an East Gladstone concert, so why, oh why, did it have to be now? While it was true that the loss of one weekend's revenue by cancellation and ticket refund would probably be the death knell of the orchestra, it was also true that going ahead and mangling Brahms One for the whole world to hear would be equally terminal. Nevertheless, Kulikofski went stoically ahead, if only because there was little else he could do. He had eleven days to test the concept of doing something really complex from his place at the concertmaster's chair, and he didn't relish it one little bit.

Jonathan felt bad about abandoning Stefan Kulikofski when the poor guy was really up against the wall, but he was torn between staying in East Gladstone and abetting the impending orchestral gong show or going down to Toronto again and working with Stan Ward in the hopes of finding some sort of solution. The research won the battle but he was filled with guilt and unease.

At Stan Ward's request, the physiology team was to assemble in Livermore's small office on Monday afternoon at one o'clock. As promised, as soon as Jonathan got off the bus in Toronto just before twelve thirty he gave Stan a call. Stan was excited; he had sheets of preliminary statistics that his students had compiled, so he asked Jonathan to hurry to the Medical Sciences Building for a brief meeting in the cafeteria before getting together with the team. Instead of a leisurely walk up University Avenue, he took the subway one stop from St Patrick to Queen's Park, wondering if it had really been that much quicker.

They sat at a cafeteria table and Stan spread the print-outs in front of them. Jonathan wished he had more time to check them out, but there were hundreds of entries and, as yet, no collation or tabulation of results.

"The kids'll get the stats done as soon as possible, but I thought you'd like to see these anyway. They've done a very thorough job; most large city orchestras around the world, and both past programs and future offerings. So you get to see what was done and what's to come. This way we'll have more solid stats on popularity, and a way of seeing when and where the more popular ones are being played. Of course, they had to draw the line somewhere, so the smaller outfits like yours didn't make the cut. What do you think?"

"This is just what we need, Stan. Guess we don't have time to go over 'em now?"

"No, we ought to have been upstairs," he checked his watch, "two minutes ago. Come along."

Chairs had been wheeled in from the lab and distributed in a half circle around the desk. The coffee ritual with mismatched mugs was well underway when Stan ushered Jonathan into the room.

"John, this is Dr Jonathan Rycroft," said Stan, introducing him to John Rolfe, the one team member who was absent at his last visit. "My musician, but also a physicist in his own right."

Jonathan put his overnight bag and oboe case on the floor beside a chair, shook hands with Rolfe, and sat down.

"So, Stan," began Livermore, "this does not bode well. What's the story?"

"Quite simply, Ken, the anomaly that I noticed away back is quite real. Jonathan and I have done a number of runs, and there is no question that when he's playing music the figures don't add up. There is a microscopic energy loss, and much as we might like to, I can't really see us brushing it off. So, I'm throwing it out to all of you. What do all of you want to do about it?"

"Well," replied Livermore, "as you know, the publication of the results is well underway and the editorial office has responded really favourably. Frankly, Stan, just about the last thing we need are questions on the accuracy and reproducibility of the methodology. What I'd suggest we do right now is to get you to give us a demonstration. Let's go to the lab right now and hook Mr Rycroft up."

"It's okay," replied Jonathan, "you can call me Jonathan, if you like." Or *Doctor* Rycroft, he almost added, if you would prefer formality.

They moved *en masse* into the lab and entered the electrostatic cage, and while Stan got Jonathan seated on a chair beside the exercise bike and began hooking up the many monitors, probes, sensors and electrodes, Khan started switching on the computers and booting up the programs. While this was going on Jonathan was assembling his oboe, and exercising his fingers while sucking on a reed between his lips. Once all was ready the research team either sat at chairs behind the rack of monitors, or stood in the small space between the table and the exercise bike.

"Start with whatever you like," instructed Stan, "and when I sa-a-y... Now!"

He played a few random selections of material he had been working on, none of it too difficult.

"There, you see!' he heard Stan exclaim as he played.

Out of the corner of his eye Jonathan saw Livermore peer closer to the monitor and acknowledge the result. Stan and he should have discussed the 'play list' before starting on this demo, he thought, but maybe he'll give me some advice. However, without any guidance and not realizing consciously the implications, he switched to the Mozart piece that had got Stan so excited.

"Nothing!" he heard Livermore say before Stan stepped in. "Okay, Jonathan, let's switch to something else, shall we?"

Now he felt foolish because he'd unwittingly thrown some confusion into the mix. Damn it, he knew that piece was showing nothing! A little flustered, he made a second mistake although he could hardly know it was one at the time. He switched to the first oboe part in the opening movement of Bruckner's Fourth Symphony, a little before the 40th measure.

"No!" he heard Stan shout. "It can't! It just can't!"

"Well, it is, isn't it?" replied Livermore in a tone that dripped acid.

"What is?" asked Rolfe and Wong almost simultaneously.

"It's reversed," Stan answered in perplexity. "We're not losing energy; we're gaining it!"

They all gathered around the monitors, pointing and talking, while Jonathan played on and on. He had never felt so exhilarated; had never felt so close to the music, so deeply entwined in it, so filled with the glory, the intricacy, the ecstasy...

"I think he's alright now," he heard someone say, as if from a long distance. "How are you doing? You gave us a bit of a worry there."

He found that he was still sitting in the chair, instrument still in his hands and his limbs still hooked up to all the gizmos, but it felt as if a great gulf of time had passed. Celia Wong was checking the pulse in his wrist with a cool forefinger, and Stan Ward was eyeing him with a quite inscrutable expression. Makharam Khan sat behind the monitor with a faraway expression in his eyes. The disorientation lasted a few minutes then, with a nod and a half smile, Jonathan sat up straighter in the chair. He realized that something quite unplanned had just taken place, but until he understood what it was he was content to play it very cagey.

"Sorry about that," he said. "I must have got light-headed. I didn't have any lunch, and breakfast was a long time ago."

Ken Livermore was standing against the side of the cage with his arms folded across his chest and Stan was sitting slumped in one of the chairs. The others sat or stood, waiting for one of the chief protagonists to make a move.

"Shall we continue?" asked Stan into the silence, observing Jonathan's far-away expression.

"No, no, it's fine," replied Livermore in a distracted voice. "Just fine. Let's go back to the office."

"Here," said Robin Tokarek to Jonathan, handing him a granola bar. "This should tide you over. I get hypoglycemia sometimes, so I always carry some defensive armour."

Jonathan thanked him, tore the wrapping off one end and bit down on the bar. The flavour and texture brought him somewhat back to earth.

They assembled in the office, sitting in a half circle in silence about Livermore's desk. Perplexity was written on the faces of Rolfe, Tokarek and Wong, while Livermore's face reflected plain annoyance and impatience. Kahn's expression, on the other hand, showed animation and, almost, excitement. On first glance Stan Ward appeared downcast, but a slight exchange of looks between him and Khan revealed something more intriguing.

"So," began Livermore, "we get energy loss, we get energy gain, and then we get absolutely screw all. In other words, all over the map. Got any ideas?" This question directly to Stan, who just shook his head slowly and remained silent. "Anyone else?"

Makharam Khan spoke into the stretched silence. "I thought I'd got all the bugs out when we had this anomaly before, but I obviously didn't. Lemme look over the whole lot again and see what I can do. Would that be okay with you, Ken?"

"Sure, works for me," replied Livermore grumpily. "And the sooner the better. I haven't enjoyed having this doubt hanging over us and now it's just got worse. It's a critical time in our research and we just can't afford any more glitches, damn it!"

"Stan," said Khan, "why don't you and Jon and me..."

"Jonathan," he replied automatically, returning from somewhere else. He loathed being called Jon. "I don't call you Mak."

"Oh, right, sorry Jonathan. Why don't we get together over a coffee or two and talk this through?" Jonathan noticed that he fixed Stan with a quizzical expression quite out of keeping with the dour tone of the discourse. There's something here, he thought, that I'm just not seeing.

Jonathan picked up his bag and oboe case in silence, and the three of them reconvened in the cafeteria on the first floor. While Khan was joining the line and buying three large coffees Stan leant forward over the table and whispered.

"We have to play this carefully. I don't want to give anything away, so let me do the talking and let's keep it neutral. What we saw today is potentially..."

"Okay, guys," said Khan as he placed the tray with three tall paper cups on the table, "spill it. There's something going on here, and it ain't just a little glitch in my wiring. Uncle Ken hopes it is, but it ain't."

Stan took his time, adding cream into his coffee from little plastic pots, and stirring far more thoroughly than was necessary to achieve complete mixing.

"Makharam, I am as confused as everybody else. I thought I knew what was going on, but clearly I don't. If the anomaly was predictable..."

"But, I think it is! I'll bet that if we went up there right now, and played the same pieces in the same order we'd see the same results."

"I don't know what you're talking about. The selection was random, wasn't it Jonathan?"

Jonathan nodded, not wishing to elaborate on quite why he had chosen either Mozart or Bruckner, both of which had caused problems. He ran through the alternative scenario in his mind; had he played all the pieces from previous tests that had yielded net energy loss, they would be up there in the lab right now discussing the anomaly with the whole team. As it was, Stan had been made to look like a fool and Khan, for some unfathomed reason, was sniffing around like truffle-hound. But what had *happened* up there?

"When I was at U Cal," Khan continued, taking a good long drink of coffee, "I heard of some weird research with musicians focusing on the medial parietal lobe and the caudate nucleus. They were doing imaging of the brain while music was being played and listened to. Thing is, they could never get consistent results, and it seemed that different music gave different levels of effect."

"Same issue with us perhaps?" observed Stan innocently. "An instrumental error of some kind?"

"Come on, Stan!" urged Khan. "We've worked together on this stuff for a good few years. We're coming to know how each other thinks, and I'd swear you're not leveling with me."

Stan looked at him for a long time, taking slow sips of his coffee, assessing the situation. Finally, he appeared to come to a decision.

"Look, Makharam, you may be right. There might be more to this than meets the eye. If you will indulge me, give me some time to think things through. Today's results have hardly clarified anything in my mind, and have in fact made things a damned sight more confusing. So, cut the old man a bit of slack, would you?"

"Fair enough. We'll talk later." And with a quick handshake to Jonathan, a pat on Stan's back, and a last slug of coffee he was out of the door.

Stan let out a huge breath. "Now, down to business. First of all, what the hell happened to you when you played that last piece?"

"You tell me! Stan, I have never been so deep into the music before! Sure, you get inside it and it runs away with you, but never like that. Never! Holy shit, it was magnetic!"

"What piece was it?"

"Bruckner's Fourth; first oboe from the first movement."

"It's on your initial list, isn't it? The symphony? High up in the popularity poll?"

"Oh, Christ, yes! Of course it is."

He was getting an eerie feeling, as if there was something he ought to know just around the corner of his mind.

"Energy goes in," mused Stan with his fingers steepled in front of his chin, "then it stops going in, then... it starts to spill out again."

"So, what I was feeling was the energy coming out of... Stan, this is getting just too weird."

Then, in an instant, he had turned the corner in his mind and met the full-frontal truth of what Stan had been preaching. The Music Continuum, the files, the reflux gelled in his mind into a reality that could lie parallel to the comfortable one that his body occupied during its waking hours. This was not an apotheosis based upon information, but one based in belief and feelings and emotions. He could not accord it the full status of demonstrable truth, but he could make room for it beside the structure of what he believed to be true. I wonder, he thought, if this is what religious experiences are all about. A truth based in faith, not a faith based in truth.

"Yes, it's coming out," murmured Stan. "What you experienced, my friend, was the energy from an overloaded file finding its way out... but benignly. You get caught up with the music, do you not? You and Kate told me that it's what drives you; it's almost an addiction. Today you really felt it."

"It was terrific and also terrifying. I'm attracted and repelled; it's as if there was something terribly wicked but also incredibly enticing. It's the bloody apple in the Garden of Eden."

"The Bruckner's on the list," mused the professor emeritus, "but no one has died from it yet..." He sat deep in thought with his palms together at his chin, then came to a sudden decision. "I'll get the students cracking with those stats. Jonathan, listen to me carefully. I think we need to do more of this. I think we need to identify some more of those overloaded pieces. And the only way is by playing them."

Jonathan was suddenly wary; he sensed a loss of control, he sensed that he was no more than an experimental white rat, but more than anything he sensed terrible danger. But it was a beguiling prospect, to feel that close to the music, to be right inside it and be part of it. But the danger! Conductors were dying from this very ecstasy!

"Why? Why do we need to do this Stan?" He already knew the answer. "Why do *I* need to do this?"

"Because we have to find out all we can. It's essential."

"So, you expect me to be some sort of lightning rod? Let me get this straight; I lay my life down in the service of research, put myself right in the way of danger—these people *explode* for Christ's sake—and for what? To protect a few maestros?"

Faces at adjoining cafeteria tables turned their way, shocked and curious.

"Not just the ones you're critical of, Jonathan. These were decent people, great conductors, highly talented musicians, fine human beings..."

"But I would still be like the canary in the mine! Stan, Stan, the canary drops off the fucking perch! *That's the whole point*!"

He looked around and glared at one particularly curious onlooker.

"Honestly, Jonathan," replied Stan in a hushed voice, hands patting the air down in front of him, "I don't think there's a chance of this causing you harm. I am certain that the conductor, by his very position, concentrates the force."

"Sorry, but you haven't been there. It's a spiral. How do I know what'll happen; how deep it'll go?"

Jonathan sighed. He knew that he had now come to the crux of the issue; this was no longer an academic exercise, if it had ever been in Stan's mind. Merely studying the problem in the abstract was no longer good enough.

"Not just a thought game, is it? Not just a fancy academic exercise?" He held Stan's eyes.

"It hasn't been for while. Ever since... do you remember I phoned you up, all excited about Mozart? It was from that very evening, a spark of intuition, and I realized that something would have to be done..."

"Preventative measures?"

"No, *preventive* measures. Preventative is a noun, so the only way you can take a preventative measure is to lay a ruler alongside a condom."

The heavy atmosphere was suddenly shattered. Stan smiled broadly and Jonathan laughed out loud. The guy had such a way of bringing things down, letting the steam out of the boiler.

"Condom! You don't let up, do you?" he shouted.

Faces turned their way again.

"No, not as long as you wish to measure preventatives, I don't." He paused. "But no, it's not an academic exercise," he sighed and stared for a while into the distance. "And there's the issue, my boy. Just how in hell *can* we publicize what we know? Just where in God's name do we go from here? And while we dither, they die."

"I'm so pleased you're staying with us Jonathan," greeted Sandra as soon as they were in the front door. "I've only just got in from work I'm sorry to say, so supper'll be a little late. Lucky I got home first, or Stan would have been responsible for whipping something up. Stan, open something while you're waiting, will you. It's probably going to be fish (fish alright with you, is it Jonathan? Good) so make it a medium dry white."

He and Stan had come back on the subway from Queen's Park, speaking only in generalities, tiptoeing around the key issues as they both knew that gentle ambience and relaxation were the first essentials.

"Do you need any help in there?" called Stan.

"No, just get glasses and open the bottle. Oh, wait, put some knives and forks on the table, oh and dessert spoons and forks too. There's an apple pie here that wants looking at."

Jonathan dropped his bag and oboe case at the door, and they went through to the dining room. Stan quickly took cutlery from a drawer and distributed it, then led Jonathan through into the living room.

"Sit here a second while I go down to the cellar for a bottle."

Jonathan's mind was in turmoil. The experience he had had in the lab combined with the revelation, or whatever it was, in the cafeteria had left him confused. The journey to the house had merely placed everything on hold, and now he was bursting to talk it all out. Stan came back with the bottle and glasses, poured for three, and took one into the kitchen. For God's sake, thought Jonathan, get your ass back in here. He began as soon as Stan had handed him a glass, and before the man's rear end had settled into its favourite chair.

"So why me? Why now? Why aren't musicians around the world having exactly the same sensations? It doesn't make any sense."

"You're right, and I just don't know..."

"It's crazy. You have no idea what it was like. It's never been like this before; it couldn't be. We wouldn't survive. So why? I just don't get it!"

"I've got to think this through. This has been the most confusing day. But things are clarified in some ways... There is a pattern here."

"Only the Bruckner! The Mozart, the other stuff, just fine, no problem. But the Bruckner..."

"Why not play the same piece again right now? Just a few measures."

Without a word he fetched his oboe case from the hall, assembled the instrument and sucked on a reed. After a few simple warm-up scales, he began playing the first movement from Bruckner's Fourth from measure 30 right through to 96. It was lovely music, and Sandra paused from her work in the kitchen and stood by the door enjoying it.

"Well, how was it this time, then?" asked Stan breaking into Jonathan's silence as he sat nursing his oboe, eyes unfocused.

"Just fine. Just like any other time," he said quietly.

He was very troubled in his mind. He had played some of the loveliest music he knew, and as well as he was able, but this time he had been quite disengaged. He had tasted the real thing back there in the lab, and he wanted more. Would music always be like this now? Once you've been... *there*... will everything else appear in monochrome?

"So, not like back there in the lab?"

"No," he replied sadly, "not at all. Just the usual."

"So, what in hell went on back there that isn't happening here? This is utterly paradoxical. Maybe it's the cage..."

"I suppose a good test would be to go back to the lab and try it again there," replied Jonathan quietly, more than half hoping Stan would agree. "That would sort it out."

"Supper's going to be on the table soon, this is a nice glass, and these old bones don't want to shift anywhere tonight." He tried not to show it, but Jonathan was disappointed. "Except, of course, to climb them stairs to bed."

"Okay, but I wish I had some clue as to what's going on." His confusion and disappointment showed in the angle of his shoulders.

"Oh dear, oh dear," sighed Stan. "I had no idea we'd get so enmeshed, you and me. When I first asked you to help me with this little project, I had no idea it would become so complicated. I am so sorry it's drawn you in like this."

"No, no, it's not a problem. It's been fascinating getting drawn into this other world of yours—I mean, being brought back into science—and I've learnt so much. See, I always throw myself into things; it's a way of... It's... it's good to be deeply involved. Right now I'm just horribly confused."

Dinner began rather quietly and Sandra took up the conversational slack with observations about her day at the Department of Anthropology, complete with pointed comments about some of her colleagues. By the time the apple pie appeared things had perked up considerably, and Stan felt able to fill her in on the ups and downs of their day. He described the results and explained the reactions of the team.

"So, Uncle Ken still thinks and hopes it's an instrumental artifact," said Stan, "and the way things are going there, I might just leave it at that."

"But Makharam Khan has other ideas. We sat down with him afterwards," explained Jonathan, "and he more or less accused Stan of holding something back."

"Yes, in amongst all the other loose ends and baggage from our day, I've been wondering what to do about him."

"He obviously twigged that we were seeing a pattern," replied Jonathan. "As good as challenged us to go back upstairs and do it again."

"And that line he gave Ken about going over the whole rig up to get the bugs out? Complete bullshit. He knows we've got something here." He thought for a moment. "He might be useful to us, you know."

"In what way?" asked Jonathan as the last of the apple pie went downrange.

"Face it; we're fumbling in the dark. If he can give us some sort of insight; he's obviously the right guy to help with the technical side of this, but..."

"But what?"

"Well, he is so very pragmatic. I don't think he has an aesthetic neuron in his entire body."

"Surely, that's what you want? You want someone who isn't going to take flights of fancy."

"Jonathan, if I were to introduce him to the Music Continuum and the labeled files and the exploding maestros what in hell do you think his reaction would be? What was yours? Jesus, man, it's only *today* that I've seen the slightest inkling that you might be getting it!"

Jonathan felt immediately contrite. He remembered that embarrassing occasion when he had cracked up laughing, and he recalled that he had been dragged all the way this far against his scientific will. True, Stan had told him he relished his role as a doubting Thomas, but even so. Introducing Khan to the crazy world of detonating maestros might be somewhat problematic. There was also the CSIS angle.

"Look," said Jonathan. "What do we really know about Khan? What's his involvement; why's he so interested?"

"Plain naked curiosity, as far as I know," replied Stan. "Why?"

"It's just... I dunno. Nothing I can put my finger on."

"Well, how about this," suggested Sandra. "You tell him as much as he needs to know about the Music Continuum hypothesis—in other words, an extension of the data he has already seen —but leave out anything to do with the other part, which even I still find fantastic."

"Got it in one!" Stan rubbed his hands together. "We should meet with him tomorrow morning and sort it out. I want you along as well Jonathan. What time's your bus?"

"I don't have to be at the bus station until quarter after twelve, so that'll be fine."

"Good. Let's move to the living room."

Jonathan began to feel much better about the afternoon's musical experience. As the memory of it began to fade he likened it to the return to normality after marihuana; how wonderful the music sounded on grass, how easily were all the world's problems solved, how great was the poetry you wrote down quickly on the back of a pizza box. Then you came back, your normality (however you construct it) returned and, well, that was fun wasn't it? And the pizza box went into the garbage.

The earlier part of the evening was spent in quiet conversation, and when the light had all but faded from the sky, they put on their shoes and took a walk down to the close shore of Lake

Ontario. It was clear evening and over in the west a crescent moon was lying on its back over the jutting towers of downtown. It was awe inspiring to contemplate such a huge inland mass of water and to realize that, in all its vastness, it was one of the smaller Great Lakes. The age-long workings of geological time were brought very close then.

Jonathan slept in Peter Ward's room; the son was no longer tied to the home of his upbringing—he had his own small family far away to the west and north—but they kept his room just the way it was until he was better settled and could take his stuff away. They may leave the nest, but half their baggage gets left behind.

He and Stan took the subway downtown after breakfast and goodbyes, and arrived at the Medical Sciences Building a little before nine-thirty. Stan had phoned Khan at home last evening to ensure he would be at the lab and to ask him to book a meeting room. Privacy was needed and neither the lab offices nor the cafeteria was conducive to the upcoming discussion. It was clear to Jonathan that Stan really didn't have any idea of how to conduct the meeting, let alone what the results might be. With Khan sniffing at the trail it would be impossible to put him off, yet revealing only as much of the hypothesis as absolutely necessary might lead to ridicule and worse. He was on the entire brass section of a dilemma.

Makharam Khan was there ahead of them in Meeting Room 2 on the third floor and the ubiquitous cups of coffee were already cooling to drinkable temperature. They busied themselves with milk, cream and sugar, postponing the inevitable as long as possible.

Finally, Khan slapped his hands together and with an open, quizzical expression started the ball rolling. "Okay, it was you suggested we meet Stan. So, you must have something to tell me."

Professor Ward paused for a long moment while he put his thoughts in order.

"Look, Makharam, I'm going to put forward a hypothesis. You are going to find it absurd, laughable and highly fantastic. I want you to understand that it is *only* a hypothesis; it explains the facts we have observed, but is just one of an open-ended series of possibilities."

"I am all ears," relied Khan, smilingly indicating his own generous appendages in a quite unselfconscious way. "Go for it. I am primed for the ridiculous."

"Then, you have come to the right place." Stan took a deep breath and plunged in. "The energy that we see disappearing while music is being played is being stored somewhere else. Every time a piece of music is played, the creative energy necessary for its interpretation is added to its 'file'," and here he indicated the file by curling his index fingers. "Okay so far?"

Khan nodded. They could see by his expression that his judgment was on hold, but there was evident excitement in his gold/brown eyes.

"At some point the 'files' get full. You will remember the total lack of a reading when Jonathan played that piece by Mozart? Why? Because that file is nearly full, and is not accepting energy at the same rate. Okay?"

Khan nodded again.

"When Jonathan played the piece by Bruckner, the energy flow reversed, did it not? We saw a net gain on our monitors." Stan paused to let this sink in, sipping at a coffee that was now ready to drink. "Bruckner's file was overflowing. This is what I am terming a reflux."

Khan nodded again, and neither Stan nor Jonathan could discern any change in his expression or demeanor.

"I term the 'place'," again the curled digits, "where the energy goes the Music Continuum. I have no idea where it is, or if we can even talk about a 'where'." He sat back. "Now, at this point, just sit there, don't say a damned word, and drink your coffee."

They sat in silence while Khan gently nodded his head, his chin between a thumb and a curled forefinger. Presently he sat up a little straighter and did as told, finishing his coffee in several long gulps. It may not have been play-acting, but the tension he wound up in the two men facing him was worthy of the finest theatre ham. Finally he spoke.

"It's perfect!" His eyes shone. "It's ab-so-lutely perfect. Look, I knew this wasn't a glitch in my machinery, but I also knew the last thing Uncle Ken needed was any kind of hassle. Then, when you reported the negative results, you could see the relief on his face. Now, yesterday's demo has pissed him off all over again. Poor bastard's on a teeter-totter. You may not agree with me, but I don't think the rest of the team need to know about this."

Stan took a long time in replying. There were ethical and

practical situations to be weighed very carefully. He nodded.

"Yes, I agree that this is better left between us, although I am really reluctant to be duplicitous. On the other hand, revealing what I... we... believe to the whole team would be highly counter-productive. A knife edge, eh?"

"Yep. Disbelief, derision, scorn. And, more to the point, derailing the publication of the great work. A huge amount hangs on it."

"Let's agree on a low profile. Jonathan?"

"Sure. It's taken me forever to come round to accepting these crazy ideas, but I go as far as accepting a hypothesis that fits the facts."

"Thing is, Makharam," said Stan, "how is that you are so ready to agree with my crazy notions when this guy had to be dragged screaming? I understood you to be a much more pragmatic kind of fella."

"Just like Jonathan, I guess. What you've put forward fits the observations. Of an infinite array of answers, this one simply fits the bill. But, make no mistake, Stan, I've been chewing on this thing ever since you first saw it. Right back to Subject 27, the fiddle player."

"So, when you told Ken you were concerned about acoustic pick-up in inductance coils..."

"Yeah, it was a line of horseshit. We were working in a noisy environment; we made no attempt to be silent, so why would music have any effect at all?" Stan Ward nodded and smiled, recalling his skepticism and then reassessing Khan in his estimation. "And we were working in an electrostatic cage, so it couldn't be a loss to the outside, and it couldn't be a leak to ground either, of course. Checked that first. So, it had to be something intrinsic, if you know what I mean?"

"You're a crafty one Dr Khan. Why didn't you talk to me before?"

Khan looked a little embarrassed. "I was a bit stuck with the ethical issue. Sure, I wanted to explore this much deeper, and I knew damned well that you thought you were on to something, but the rest of the team..."

"Yes," said Stan, "it was a tough time. I'm still very unhappy about it."

They sat in thought for a moment or two, while Jonathan finished the last of his cool coffee. He broke the silence.

"Makharam, what form does this reflux energy take?" he

asked. "You talk of energy in the abstract, but what are you actually seeing on your equipment?"

"Ultra high frequency. Jonathan, when you're playing, you're radiating microwaves."

This was too close to home. The fear was back in Jonathan; he broke into a sweat, and gripped his hands tightly together to stop their shaking. This couldn't be real. He took a few deep breaths to calm himself.

"Okay," he continued when he had slightly more control over his thoughts, "tell me how do you visualize this... what is it... space or location that Stan's describing?"

"It's difficult to put into non-mathematical terms, so how about I say it's a dimension-4 geometry with a fourth axis at right-angles to the three Cartesian ones? If, in fact, it *is* a spatial dimension."

Jonathan nodded; he had encountered multi-dimensional geometry in his studies, but he had hardly imagined a real application for it. But, as Stan had demonstrated a few weeks ago, he had no problem with imaginary numbers. So, postulate an imaginary space and draw conclusions.

"It *has* to be a spatial dimension..." he began, then paused as he realized this would be revealing too much. He knew it to be a spatial dimension, perhaps folded—how else explain energy entering it from the brain of any musician anywhere in the world, and emerging somewhere completely different—but Khan was not privy to this, the even less sane half of the hypothesis. "...I mean, geometrically speaking," he concluded lamely.

"Jury's out," replied Khan. "So, Stan, Jonathan, where do we go with this?"

"Well," replied Stan, "we've got the mixed results from yesterday to look at, and I agree with you that we should go back to the lab and run them again. Jonathan, you have time before your bus?"

"Plenty of time to run through them all," he replied after a pause. He was half afraid, half enticed. Would he feel that same attraction/repulsion again while playing the Bruckner? Only one way to find out.

They rode the elevator to the third floor and went straight to the lab. Ken Livermore was seated on a tall stool at the bench outside the cage working on a pile of print-outs. He looked up as they came in the door, and smiled with his mouth.

"Ah, come to get the bugs out finally?" he asked in a hearty manner that fooled nobody.

"Just the same tests we ran yesterday, Ken," answered Khan. "I've been working on the problem and I'm pretty damn' sure where the bug is."

Professor Ward and Dr Rycroft were astonished at the ease with which the man told lies, and how very convincing he was. At one level it was quite amusing, and it was difficult not to react visibly.

As before, Jonathan sat in the familiar chair and worked up his instrument while all the connections were made. On the cue, he ran through the pieces he had played the day before, watching out of the corner of his eye as Ward and Khan pointed at the monitors and compared notes. Livermore slipped in quickly at one point between sessions, and watched for a while with them. They conferred briefly and then he returned to his print-outs, closing the metal mesh door behind him.

Now came the Bruckner. He raised the oboe to his lips and began to play. In only a handful of measures he was transfixed and that same wonderful/awful sensation came over him. He saw Stan looking nervously at him over the top of the monitor, then returning his attention to the screen. He caught their stifled exclamations as the results appeared. This time, with hindsight to help him, he withstood the siren song and managed to stop playing before he became completely immersed. Even so, it was a hard break and he was left with a longing and an ache that persisted.

"Right," announced Khan in a loud voice, all business. "Just as I thought. I've downloaded the results to my USB key, so I'll check 'em over on my computer. Let's head for my office. Bring your stuff Jonathan."

It was necessary to download the results because, for screening purposes, the instruments in the cage were deliberately excluded from connection with the lab's local area network.

"Okay Ken, it all looks good," said Stan as they exited the cage. "We shouldn't need to do anything more."

"Good, good," he replied appearing relieved. He shook hands with Jonathan. "Goodbye Mr Rycroft; it's been very nice to meet you, albeit briefly. I hope you have enjoyed your little exposure to human physiology."

Jonathan suppressed the gross image this conjured up and made his smile into one of mere friendliness.

They seated themselves in Makharam Khan's domain, along

the corridor and round a corner from the doors to the lab and Ken Livermore's office. The room was surprisingly devoid of the almost ubiquitous clutter of the other academic offices, perhaps a harbinger of a younger generation who were doing the greater part of their work on the computer. Jonathan's mind was still filled with his exposure to something wider, greater, deeper, and he was now only slowly returning to the grey, one-dimensional real world.

Stan peered at him solicitously. "How's it going, my boy? Is it the same as last time here?"

"Yes, just as powerful, but this time I kind of willed myself to stop. But, what the hell is it that I'm feeling only here? Why only here in the lab? What is it?"

Makharam had only seen a fainting, perhaps hypoglycemic Jonathan after yesterday's playing session, and had no clue as to what was being exchanged between them.

"What is what? Something I'm missing? You mean, what you felt?"

"Yes. I'm not just 'feeling' it; I'm getting this enormous surge of... something... Look, I just can't explain it to someone who hasn't been there. Stan, you remember what I said: enticing, repelling... very powerful. Just when you were seeing the reversal on the monitors. What you *saw*, I *felt*."

"So, some sort of aura? Stan's reflux?"

"Yes, yes, but only when I'm here, in the cage. It doesn't seem to happen anywhere else. Didn't happen last night. I just don't get it."

"Only when you're here? *Here*! In the electrostatic cage?" Khan suddenly slapped his hands together in glee, and laughed sharply. "Yeah, yeah! Don't you *see*? The cage screens you from all outside electromagnetic radiation, right? Normally, what you are feeling so intensely *in the cage* would be moderated, dissipated, diluted when you played outside. In the cage you're screened from the noisy electromagnetic spectrum of the real world, so the reflux has much easier access! No competition."

"I'm sorry, but I just don't get this," replied Jonathan. "You're saying that we are normally surrounded by noise—electromagnetic radiation—so we don't pick up much of the energy coming back out. But, in the cage it's easier?"

"Exactly!"

"Oh, shit, let me get my head round this. I am perceiving the reflux from overfull files..."

"But in the cage," finished Khan, "the experience is purified, if you like. More intense."

"Doesn't that imply that before the electronic era people's... musicians' brains were much more attuned?"

"Yes," replied Stan, "to a certain extent. But remember, the reflux is a recent phenomenon, and really powerful because those files are now full."

"But you argued earlier that musicians get a benign feedback all the time, regardless of how full the files are."

"True. You know it yourself; your addiction to music, for want of a better term. And by the same argument, it would be easier to perceive before the modern era, wouldn't it? A fuller musical experience? Raises some very interesting philosophical speculations, does it not?"

"Yes," sighed Jonathan, back into brain overload, "but not for here and not for now."

The idea that present-day aesthetic experience was dulled and blunted by the industrial environment was just too complicated to entertain.

"But here is an interesting point," observed Stan. "Look, at this: you are in the electrostatic cage when you experience... what you experience. In its full concentration, without external influence, yet it does you no *physical* damage. Right?"

Then he suddenly realized where his line of reasoning was taking him and stopped abruptly. Khan hadn't missed the sudden curtailment, although he didn't pursue it.

Too much experience and too much information had flooded Jonathan in less than twenty-four hours. He couldn't take any more in. He felt drained and exhausted, and the last traces of musical ecstasy trickled away leaving a dull hollow. If what I'm feeling in the cage is what maestros feel, then they die in rapture; so why doesn't that make me feel any better? Imagine the obit: 'He died doing something he loved.' No, that's absolutely no consolation whatsoever.

"This is going to take a hell of a lot of thinking about," he replied abruptly. "And right now my brain hurts. I'm going to get on a bus and go home."

He picked up his overnight bag and oboe case.

They walked down the stairs to the first floor together, and while Makharam Khan headed to the cafeteria for a reload, Stan walked his musician as far as the steps to the path. The old man placed his hand on Jonathan's shoulder and gave it a squeeze.

"Nearly let the cat out the bag back there. What I was going to say was, the conductor is totally exposed. He is not playing a musical instrument, so that part of his brain that mediates the energy cannot do so! Imagine the force that must pass through him! Jonathan, I believe most sincerely that you will be protected in a way the conductor cannot be. You can be a *live* canary!"

He saw by Jonathan's expression that you can only force in so much information before risking a reflux, so he said no more but gave the shoulder another light squeeze.

"You've been through the wringer. I can't even imagine what you feel like. But look, if you don't want to continue with this jaunt, you have only to say so."

"Stan, I'm in this now, and I would feel like shit if I didn't go through with it. I don't know where the hell all this is going, but I want to be there."

"Give me a call when you get home and sorted out. Bon voyage!" And he turned and went back up the steps.

By Wednesday Stan Ward's student researchers had crunched the numbers, and now there was a definitive list of the Top 50 orchestral pieces and a worldwide program for the rest of the year. A comparison of this larger work with Kate's initial stab at a Top 20 showed gratifying correspondences.

Bruckner's Fourth was high on the list.

In retrospect, it was simply a failure of communication; the musical experience in the cage had told Jonathan that Bruckner Four would become an issue, Stan's students now knew where in the whole world this piece would next be played, but not one of them had all the information. And even if they had, was there anything they could have done?

Jonathan had returned home on Tuesday sick and tired, haunted by the experience in the lab, and burdened with Stan's request that he continue the beguiling and dangerous playing sessions. His mind was in turmoil, his continuing absences in Toronto were playing hell with any rhythm to his practicing and playing, and bloody Graham Swann was making noises.

He turned his back on the whole mess.

Throwing himself totally into his comfortable other world of making music, he spent that week playing hard and leaving social life—what there was of it—out of the equation. The thought of his continuing distance from Kate stabbed at him when the defences slipped, so his formula was simple: plunge yourself in up to your neck, Jonathan, and work and work. Practice the damned oboe, switch to the cor anglais just for the love of it, then back again to the oboe; eat, drink, sleep, play the music and stop thinking. Just stop thinking.

Thank God—thank God in heaven—that you can get lost in your music.

Another evening session of intense music-making was suddenly interrupted. The little Skype flag winked in the corner of the screen; incoming from Stan. The other universe was asserting itself. He set the warm oboe down beside him and clicked on the icon.

"Jonathan! Have you seen the news? It's on the CBC."

"What is? No, I haven't; I don't have a TV."

"Another maestro has died. Check it on-line. In Warsaw."

"What were they playing?"

"It doesn't say, blast it!"

"I can soon find out. Gimme a few minutes and I'll call you back."

He quickly opened his browser and located a website for cultural life in Warsaw. Scrolling down the venues he found the calendars of performances for the month for all orchestras in the city. He clicked on the calendar for each orchestra and checked its program for yesterday evening, and soon located what he was dreading he would find.

His heart sank. Bruckner's Fourth. What else? He called Stan.

"Stan. Bruckner Four. I feel like shit."

"Oh my God! If we needed any more proof, this is it."

"I knew! I knew! *God damn it, I knew*! Why didn't we do anything?" Tears of frustration sprang to his eyes.

"What could we do? Be reasonable! Phone 'em up and tell 'em not to play it? And on what grounds?"

"So now we think we can predict! Big deal! What in Christ's name do we *do* about it?"

"I don't know; I'm as frustrated as you are."

"Stan, we have just got to do more than sit here and make predictions! Shit! Somehow we *have* to get to the third prong, the preventa... preven*tive* strategy. "

He fumed for a moment, slapped back into reality. In truth there was nothing they could do, except sit by and watch. They had the terrible, impotent power of being able to single out a human being and say 'you are going to die horribly at this time and this place.' And Stan was right; a phone call coming from some little Ontario orchestra: 'don't play such-and-such or you'll blow up.' It was laughable. But there must be some way of marshalling officialdom to take this seriously...

"I'll try to think of some way," he continued, "some strategy, to get recognition. I dunno."

"Here's another thing," said Stan, mercifully deflecting his thoughts. "Makharam Khan has made the intuitive leap; perhaps it was my little slip about the danger, but anyway he's aware of our interest in dead maestros. I told him to call you; he's absolutely buzzing with ideas. All too far over my head, mind you."

"Okay. I can't see what he has to do with it," sighed Jonathan, "but I'll listen to what he has to say. But look Stan, there's something else; I can't keep on dropping down to T-O, at least not as frequently. It's playing hell with my schedule, and our second oboe seems to think my chair ought to be his. Don't know what we can do. Anyway, sorry to give you extra crap to deal with."

"We'll think of something. Don't worry. Talk to you again soon. Bye." And Stan's image winked out.

I need to talk, thought Jonathan, and Kate's my sounding board and leaning shoulder...

Kate was sitting in her easy chair after supper, wondering how long it would be before duty drove her to get the fiddle out and start her evening's practice. Apart from her set of routine exercises, she had in mind some parts from a couple of trio sonatas in Arcangelo Corelli's Opus 2; challenging and could be lots of fun, even playing on one's own. Just had to get up the drive to get out of the chair and open the fiddle case. She had got as far as lifting the violin out, while thinking how nice it would be to have someone other than Liz to practice with, when the phone rang.

"Hi, it's me. Can I come round, bounce a few ideas off you?" He sounded urgent.

She agreed with, she thought afterwards, a little too much alacrity. He had been totally immersed in the job, and they had hardly exchanged a word since his last Toronto jaunt, so it would be good to test the waters. She was tired of the holding pattern they were flying, and of taking second place to a ghost, but she knew to be patient. What else could she do?

She hadn't put the phone down for more that two minutes when it rang again.

"Hi Kathy, it's Dad. How are doing my love?"

The phone conversation was long, first with her father who gave her perhaps more information than she needed about the farm and the neighbours and the Wheat Board's loss of monopoly, then with her mother who was more concerned with the intimate details of life. She heard the doorbell ring and with the handset pressed to her head ran down the stairs, opened the door and motioned Jonathan in. They went back upstairs, Kate leading and still talking, and she waved him to a seat. While he sat fidgeting in his chair she concluded the call.

"Bye, Mum... Yes, I will. Bye."

She put the phone down on the coffee table, blinking her eyes.

"Tears?" asked Jonathan as he stood up.

She nodded and wiped her eyes with her knuckles. "Nothing. My folks. I don't see them as often as I should. It's not fair; it's cheaper to fly to London or Paris than it is to friggin' Saskatoon."

"Well, at least you can talk to them on the phone."

"Oh, my God, I'm so sorry! What was I thinking?"

She hugged him; he put his arms around her just briefly then quickly broke the hold. He was wound-up and agitated.

"Listen, there's all kinds of stuff I need to talk to you about but I have been kind of in a different zone. When I got back on Wednesday I was nearly in overload." He paused and leveled his gaze at her. "I'm sorry... I just need..."

"It's okay. I know where you're at; you know where I'm at. So, spill the beans. What did you and Stan cook up?"

"First of all, Bruckner Four. You know it was high on the list? Well, there's been another death. Stan just told me about it; he saw it on the CBC. We predicted it, Kate. But we didn't move! We knew it was hot, but we didn't *do anything*!"

"Oh no! Oh no! But what *can* we do? We can't go on like this, *knowing*..." She sat down with her face in her hands.

"I know, I know. Jesus, don't I know!" He took a deep breath. "Look, I told you, didn't I, that Stan's students had done a much bigger survey on the web? Well, it confirms your results, only it's statistically a lot more reliable because of vastly bigger data set. Okay, now what happened was this," and he described the results from the set of tests, the resultant secrecy and the involvement of Makharam Khan. This took a long time; she made some tea halfway through and they continued their talk in her little kitchen.

"But, I've saved the weirdest thing until last. Sit down in the other room with your tea and see what you think."

He sat for a moment, across from her, with his hands clasped together and a faraway look in his eyes. He was back playing the music.

"When I played the Bruckner in the lab it was... it was like nothing I have ever felt before. You know, once in blue moon, you get right into the music, and it's like you're on autopilot, and you can't even remember how you got to the end?" She nodded, remembering those rare, sweet occasions. "Well, imagine that feeling only magnified a hundred times. It's like a deep well, Kate, and you could drown in it. It scares me, but I have to do it. See, only those files that are ready to reflux give this sensation, so I need to play lots of stuff on the top of the list to find out which ones are next. And I'm frightened!"

"Oh, Jesus, Jonathan, what have we got ourselves into?"

"God knows. And now we're into it we can hardly back out, can we?"

She nodded, lips closed in a thin line. "I feel so deadly guilty and frustrated. I know I shouldn't, but knowing what we know... Does Stan have any idea where to go? Sometimes I think he sees it as some sort of game, just an intellectual exercise."

"No, he's as frustrated as we are. The other day he said to me: 'where in God's name do we go from here, and while we dither, they die'. But, he's as short of ideas as we are. I'm thinking, maybe, some sort of official recognition, but we don't know anybody; no idea what to do, how to go about it."

Their eyes met and their thoughts ran parallel. How did we get into his, what are we going to do, but always 'we'.

He smiled. "What a tangled web we weave."

She laughed lightly. "I just don't feel like Ariadne."

"Thanks for being my sounding board, Kate." A silence. "And thanks for just being here. It means a lot and... oh, words, words, words." He stood.

"Bye. Go," and the little peck on the cheek that he carried with him all the way along the evening-cool, tree lined East Gladstone back ways to his bare apartment.

When Jonathan got back to his place and opened the laptop he saw a Skype message from Makharam Khan. What time was it?

Nearly ten. Call him now? Oh, why the hell not.

"Makharam, you called. Is it too late?" He was looking into an electronic workshop the like of which he could not have imagined. Behind Khan were racks of instruments bejeweled with coloured lights and festooned with wires. The corner of a workbench could be glimpsed with tools on a wall rack.

"Never too late for me. Admiring my workshop, I see. This is my home shop; even better than U of T, though I say so myself."

A voice called off camera, and he replied over his shoulder that he would be there soon. The voice sounded familiar.

"Looks like a great workspace. What can I do for you? Stan said you'd call."

"Yep. I wanna talk microwaves and higher math." Jonathan was immediately wary, wondering how much Khan knew about his research work. Stan certainly wouldn't have blabbed.

"So, what about them? Microwaves, I mean."

"Jonathan, Stan accused me of being a crafty one, but you? Of course I've Googled you; saw all sorts of publications on microwave transmission. Don't tell me I've got the wrong Jonathan Rycroft!" He laughed.

Oh Christ, out it all comes again. All that reflux energy pouring out from wherever the hell, and why does it have to be at the microwave fucking frequency? My life is full of just too much weird shit.

"Okay, guilty as charged. Stuff I published while at U of T."

"Stan's filled me in on what I didn't already guess... No, no, it's alright..." as Jonathan made to apologize, "I'm cool with all that. You guys had your reasons. Now listen, you've done some multidimensional geometry, right?"

"Away back, and I won't say I was really into it even then."

"Well, I think we've got a little keyhole here. And, you know, Stan may be only a physiologist..." soft scientist implied "...but he's got one hell of an intuitive grasp. I love the idea of a hidden dimension; straight out of S F, but rock-solid possible."

"It took me a hell of a long time to come round to it, but if it's the best hypothesis we have..."

"Right. Now, look. All your work on microwave transmission; I wanna pick your brain."

How in hell am I going to avoid getting sucked in to this, thought Jonathan. Fear was creeping up his spine. Makharam obviously needs my expertise on the stuff I was doing in secret. Is he fishing, or is he innocent? Ah, fall back on officialdom.

"Look, Makharam, I admit I did further work on microwave transmission, but I am covered by the Official Secrets Act here in Canada, so beyond what I published at U of T, I am simply not allowed to discuss it."

"Exactly! Obviously weapons research." Jesus, that's how easy it is to say something without saying it. CSIS would be delighted. "Now, look, I've done a whole lot of calculations here, and I think I'm on the track of something."

From that point Jonathan's wariness of Khan began to evaporate. It was becoming obvious that the man had no nefarious intentions; he was just too open and guileless. The red flag the CSIS operatives had raised was clearly bullshit.

"Okay." He came to a decision; he would cooperate quietly and screw officialdom. "What are your calculations based on?"

"The key issue is the frequency! We know the frequency to a tee, so we can extrapolate. Anyway, I've done a ton of figuring, but it's with good old paper and pencil. How about I scan this stuff and send you a PDF? I want you to look it over, see if I'm on the right track."

"Sure," agreed Jonathan, suddenly realizing that his old research life, so carefully tidied away in a trunk in the attic of his mind, was now firmly and securely a part of everyday experience. Funny, in some ways it was almost a relief not to keep expending the effort continually shoving it back and closing the lid.

"Okay, I'll fire it off right now. Can you call me tomorrow?"

"Sure." What harm could it do to look over a few calculations, he thought. But what a great way to set me up and trap me. No, no, he's just too gung-ho to be anything but what he is.

Makharam disconnected and probably went to join the familiar voice Jonathan had heard in the background.

My God, my past life comes back to haunt me. That's what Makharam's implying; the same mechanism that can blow a chicken to bits can funnel itself through a little mathematical keyhole in non-space and destroy a maestro. All those calculations I did back there in the microwave lab come home to roost.

Roost? Shit, this is so ironic.

Chickens... Wonder if they felt the rapture before they felt the rupture?

Bedtime.

There simply wasn't time between getting out of bed, making a cup of instant coffee and finding some stale muffins, to read Khan's PDF of calculations, and besides Jonathan just didn't want to plunge right back in again. Another part of his old life was running parallel to this one, and there was only so much parallel processing his CPU could handle. After this meagre breakfast he headed downtown with his laptop and oboe for a real coffee before reporting for rehearsal. With a tall medium-roast at his elbow he felt more able to deal with microwaves and shit. He opened the laptop, found Khan's e-mail and downloaded the attachment.

Yes, it all came back as he scanned the densely reasoned calculations; he could follow well enough Makharam's mathematical path; he was a clever lad, but then again Jonathan knew that already. Such genius wasted in physiology; this guy could have been recruited by his government to blow people to pieces!

It was all a matter of frequency and capacitance; the ability of bodies to hold a charge, the tuning of transmission, the focusing. It was all there, although there was much in the math that needed discussion and revision. A second set of calculations concerned what Khan had designated the m-Axis, his more rigorous term for the extra dimension visualized in Stan's Music Continuum, but here he soon got lost in a mathematical branch that he had never really cottoned to. Jonathan sat in thought, sipping occasionally at his medium-roast, wondering where Makharam was taking this. Not just an academic exercise, he thought, but what then? Lightning conductor...

He checked his watch. Holy shit, music called! He grabbed his oboe case and laptop and hot-footed down Main Street to the concert hall, arriving just minutes before Kulikofski opened the score folder. His first notes were not his best...

The rest of the day was a grind, punctuated by the lunch break and lots of idle and empty chatter, just the thing to bring the tension down to manageable proportions. He had a couple of words with Kate—nothing earth-shattering—but resolved to take her aside later and talk about microwaves and secrets and death. It would be tough, but my God it might just feel better. Seeing her, thinking of her, brought out the spectre again, but he could face it now and that's what counted most.

"I've got something I want to tell you," he said as they sat on the low stone wall at the edge of the terrace, with the lake at their back all golden in the late afternoon sun. She smiled at him in that way she had that was so like... her... He paused, determined not to be ambushed by the ghost, and taking strength in how far he had come with this lovely, patient woman who deserved a lot more than he could offer.

"So! I had just finished my post-doc work at U of T when I took a job in microwave research..." and he told her of his naïve aspirations about changing the world, freeing it from reliance on fossil fuels, and then of the descent into secret research. "And that was the point where I couldn't go on. Couldn't. The explosion... the look on their faces, in their eyes... So, I quit right then and there, got into my car... we got into my car... No, sorry..."

She took his hands not caring who might happen to be watching. "It's okay. You're fine. I'm really glad you've told me this."

So this was it! The missing piece of the puzzle from the hotel room in Toronto; the 'machine that worked', his anger and the accident.

"So, the continuing story," he resumed when he had overcome the ambush. "That day I cut out on Stan? My God, that poor guy has had a lot to put up with. Never knew what a basket case he was dealing with. Anyhow, he raised the subject of dead maestros, and I just couldn't deal with it. I couldn't... and I just lost it. It was like everything ganged up on me. Had to get away..."

Her pressure on his hand redoubled. Oh Jesus, Jonathan, she thought, I want you so bad it *aches*.

"Then," he continued, "you've heard of Stan Ward's colleague Makharam Khan? Sure. He's their electronics whizz. Well, he's horned himself into the secret—poor Stan, I think he feels besieged—and he's been doing some calculations along the same lines as my research. The mechanism for... for doing what's happening to the maestros is similar to the stuff I was working on. I suspected this 'way back, but I just didn't want to go there, but now... Well, the irony of wanting to escape into research, only to find that it's taking me right back to where I was. Jeez! Anyway, let's just say," he smiled at her so openly that her heart ached, "I've come a long way since then."

She squeezed his hands, harder.

"What Khan is doing? Is it a way forward?"

My God, he thought, she is perceptive; I've only just got there myself.

"Yes, it might be, but I just don't know how."

They rose, picked up their instrument cases and headed to their respective homes.

"You know, there is absolutely no need to use the cage in the lab," observed Stan to Sandra over their after dinner coffee. "Jonathan can quite easily do all we need in any screened space, provided it's well grounded. Besides, we've got to stop bothering Ken. He thinks we're done and there's no way I'm disabusing him of that happy intelligence."

"So, what do you suggest? We build a bloody great cage in our basement? Imagine if the police raided us: 'Ello, 'ello, 'ello, woss all this then; who 'ave you been confining in 'ere?"

"Don't be bloody silly," he laughed. "I was actually thinking of having Jonathan build one up at his place. When we Skyped last he told me he can't keep taking off and coming down here. Too disruptive to his playing, and second oboe's getting ideas."

"You know what, Stan. I like East Gladstone a lot, and as my Department is right in the middle of summer doldrums, why don't we decamp up there for a week or so? Take in some concerts, boating on the lake. That would be really nice."

"Excellent idea! The publication is out of the team's hands, nothing but maintenance work in the lab. I wouldn't be missed." A wistful expression crossed his face. "Not that my presence is all that relished anyway these days."

"Oh, cheer up, you old bugger. It's just the post-partum depression of completing the magnum opus. Once the academic year's in full swing you'll be right back in it. Give Jonathan a call and tell him we're going to drop by."

"Yes, I'll do that. But it's more than that, my love. It's the frustration of knowing what we know but being unable to do anything. But Makharam seemed to have some enthusiasm about it, so maybe there's hope there. My God, I'm glad he's joined our little party. Never realized, working with him all these years, what a razor he is!"

He got up and went upstairs to the computer in the office.

"Jonathan. Am I disturbing you?" He could see the lad was just laying down his instrument; probably been playing right off the screen.

"'S alright. I was doing some Haydn for the oboe. You got me at the end of a piece. What's up?"

"Look, let me know what you think of this. Sandra and I would like to come back to East Gladstone for a week or so. Stay at the same place as before if it's available. How would it be if you were to construct an electrostatic cage in your place—doesn't need to be a big one—then we could do our research there with you. Could you do that?"

Jonathan looked dubious. "Well, I suppose I *could.* Have to think about this." Yet another imposition as this damned project crept deeper and deeper into his life. "What's involved, really?"

"Angle iron, chicken wire, nothing you can't get at Rona or Home Despot. Don't even need angle iron really; a wood frame would be fine as long as the mesh covers the whole thing. Fine mesh; one centimeter squares maximum. And a secure ground, too. Can you get down to the basement in your place?"

"Sure, that's where I keep my bike and skis and stuff. Why?"

"You'll find a big thick copper wire clamped onto one of the water pipes. That's your ground. Can you connect to it?"

"Don't see why not, but the cage'll have to be in my bedroom; can't have people peeping through the curtains, they might get ideas."

Stan laughed. "Sandra said exactly the same thing! Okay, why don't we do some booking, and perhaps you could look into the construction project?"

"Will do," he sighed. "Hey, Makharam called last night. He sent me a whole bunch of calculations. Seems he's really getting into this. Do I have permission to feel a little optimistic?"

"He's a bright boy. I was saying to Sandra just now how glad I am he's with us, although I must confess I was highly irritated and mighty suspicious at first. No, I don't know what he's up to. He talked sums with me, and I was soon lost. Still," he slapped his hands together, "one thing at a time. We'll make our arrangements and be in touch."

"'Kay. Talk to you later."

If I had thought a couple of months ago that I would be building a God-damned cage in my bedroom and playing the God-damned oboe in it and communicating with the fifth dimension or the sixth or whatever the fuck number it is, I think I would have checked myself straight into Penetanguishene.

Now, where was I? Ah, yes, the lovely Haydn oboe concerto in C major, regardless of who actually wrote it...

Intermezzo

SYMPHABOMBER STRIKES AGAIN
Juan-Carlos Lopresti
The symphonic music world has been rocked again by the death on Wednesday night of another maestro during a classical concert, this time in Warsaw. Janos Bertil was struck down in the middle of the concert to the horror and confusion of the audience and the musicians. This latest grisly death brings to a dozen the conductors mysteriously murdered at their podiums by this maniac. Will such scenes of carnage become commonplace in the concert halls and auditoriums of the world until this terrible terrorist is captured and brought to justice? The death has cast a pall over the music circles worldwide, and all classical concert performances in Warsaw have been suspended until further notice.
Reuters

TWITTERING TWITS
@Nimrod

There dying cos there OLD. Spose it takes energy to stand up there and wag a stick. Its there own fault.

@Sax-fiend

Its not the physical energy, Nimrod, its the emotional energy. These guys really get into it.

@Nimrod

I bet their heartrates right up there. Its a wakeup call to step down.

@Sax-fiend

Taking things too seriously. None of them is getting any younger. Old white guys.

@Nimrod

They cant step down their addicted to all that adolation. Like a drug.

@Slidehorn Boy

Have you seen the faces they pull when their conducting? You watch the faces its really offputting.

@Sax-fiend
Are they really in raptures, or just a show?
@Slidehorn Boy
Maybe thats why Miles always had his back to the audience? Dint want people seeing him ugly when blowing his horn.
@First Trumpet
But its not just heart attacks idiot. These guys are seriously coming to pieces.
@Sax-fiend
Yeah, like real explosions.
@Nimrod
Maybe the musical taste Gods have had it with the 18 hundreds. Thunderbolts from the heavenly esthetic police.
@Slidehorn Boy
Hey, how many of these dudes have to fall down dead before the cops step up to the plate?
@ First Trumpet
Its not just falling down dead I tell you. There blowing up.
@Slidehorn Boy
But why just the classical dudes? You dont hear about rock stars blowing up.
@Nimrod
They just croak. Theres always extenuating circumstances, like drugs and booze.
@ First Trumpet
Drugs and booze dint make nobody blow up.
@Sax-fiend
You guys just too worked up. Look its a question of supply and demand. When their all gone or too chicken to conduct itll all stop. Simple.

A Symphonic Poem

Makharam Khan phoned before the Haydn was even halfway through. The saw-tooth wave pattern that graphed Jonathan's life was by now well established, and where normally he would ignore the call and keep on playing, the last few weeks had set a new standard for urgency and intrusion. Whether he liked it or not, music was taking a back seat to all the other bullshit he had got himself involved in. As long as it doesn't start to show on the concert platform, he thought, I can wing it. He laid the warm oboe down.

"Hello Makharam, I wondered if you'd call me before I got round to calling you. What's up?"

"Have you checked over the stuff I sent?"

"Sure have. You're on exactly the same track that I was on, back when I was doing this stuff. But, I can't get a handle on your n-dimensional math; never was my thing."

"That's not important. The key thing is the microwave stuff. Are you with me on that?"

"Sure. As I say, nothing there that doesn't surprise me, although we ought to sit down and run through your stuff. There's one second-order function in... well, anyway, it would be good to go through it at some point. But, where are you going with this?"

"Simply put, I'll just bet if we put our heads together we can come up with a way of dissipating the force; a way of channeling it harmlessly to ground!"

An absurd image suddenly sprang into Jonathan's head.

"Oh shit man, are you suggesting that the maestro conducting *La Bohème* at La Scala—like the great Lucca Forza—just steps up to the podium with a bloody lightning conductor screwed onto his head? Is that what you're saying? Wouldn't that just go down well with opera fans!"

He laughed at this ludicrous image, but he also laughed because it had provided an insight to just the hint of a thought that there might be a way forward.

Khan cracked up as well, and for a while their laughter passed backwards and forward through servers, antennas and circuitry in the cloud of cyberspace. A figure appeared over Makharam's shoulder, drawn to the laughter. It was Celia Wong, the team's biochemist.

"Seriously, Jonathan, if I come up and visit, can we sit down and work some things through?"

"Please! Any time. Well, let me have a look here. Just a minute..." he minimized Skype and pulled up his calendar. "Okay, sorry about that. I'm free tomorrow all day, and then mornings until the weekend. How are you fixed?"

"The lab's quiet. Frankly, the write-up's done, the tweaks are all tweaked, and it won't be long before I have to find something else to do. Unemployment looms. So, I can come by tomorrow, say ten, ten-thirty? I'll drive."

"Sure. And while you're here, you any good with staple guns and chicken wire? Stan wants me to build a cage."

"Christ, what a laugh! Sure. You don't have a car, eh? Okay, we can go and pick up the stuff in mine."

"Great. Twenty-five Sanders. I'll be waiting for you."

So, what was this; a ray of hope? Was he thinking of tuning, frequency matching? If you can turn it on, you can turn it off.

Tomorrow should be interesting. Meanwhile, picking up the oboe, sorry to keep you waiting Franz Josef, but what's another few minutes in a couple of centuries?

"How much does Celia know about all this?"

It was Friday and Jonathan and Makharam were sitting in the sparse living room at 25 Sanders with papers, calculators and two laptops spread out in front of them. Khan looked up from his notepad.

"It's just that I noticed her in the background during our Skype yesterday."

"Almost nothing," he replied.

"Let's keep it that way, shall we? No, wait, I didn't mean it to come out like that, wouldn't accuse her or you of..."

"It's okay, I'm cool with that. She knows I'm working with you—could hardly keep that secret in my little apartment—but she's sure it's just working the bugs out of the system."

"Okay. Reason I'm concerned is, if this got back to Livermore he'd be so pissed, and quite rightly. I know Stan's concerned as well that we're being underhand. So, at the risk of putting your... relationship in jeopardy..."

"No problem. I don't like the sneaking around either, but what else can we do? Celia's fine; quite frankly, we don't talk much biochemistry or electronics when we're out of the lab."

He picked up some of the papers, changing the subject completely.

"Y'know, this Music Continuum of Stan's, that's a physiologist's term. As you've seen, I'm calling it the m-Axis; much more hardcore scientific. Now, let's bang our heads together, shall we."

They spent the rest of the morning in deep discussion with much calculation, reference to computer files, and note taking. It all came back to Jonathan—the microwave research, the intense activity, the secrecy—but he no longer felt pain and fear; his past was becoming reconciled with his present in a way that, even a couple of weeks ago, would have been unthinkable. And the parallels between his research and Khan's thinking were intriguing.

"I hope you realize," he stated at the end of one particularly fraught piece of higher math, "that I am breaking Canadian law by even talking to you. This shit," and he waved his pencil over the top page, "could land me in prison. Seriously. So, wherever all this goes, you my friend can take full credit and I will pretend I never even met you!"

They concluded the first phase of their work at about twelve-thirty, deciding to head into town for a quick lunch (Jonathan's fridge was almost empty) and then drop in to Rona for some building supplies. By four that afternoon Jonathan's bedroom was graced with a rather crudely constructed electrostatic cage, just big enough for a chair and a small table, while a thick copper wire passed through a suspiciously new looking hole in the floor to the basement below. But, once it was built, Jonathan felt a deep reluctance to try it out. That could be shelved until Stan was here. It unnerved him.

In the meantime, more mathematics.

And as they worked together head-to-head through their calculations a new appreciation and understanding grew between them. That day, an intense session of applied mathematics laid the groundwork for a long and close friendship.

It was nine in the evening when Khan, surrounded by empty beer bottles and pizza boxes announced, "That's it! By God, that's it! And it is so *damned* simple!"

"Yes, a simple tuned antenna!" cried Jonathan. "A little piece of circuitry that dissipates the charge through matching capacitance. If your m-Axis keyhole mathematics is up to scratch this thing should do what the musician's brain does. Genius, just plain genius."

"Oh, stop it; it'll go to my head. Now, the application."

Khan was grinning all over his face, washing his hands together in anticipation, his golden eyes glowing.

"Come on, spill it. What's so damned funny?"

"How to get your average maestro to apply this little invention? Conservative bastards are they not? Loathe innovation. I just about shit when you talked about lightning conductors yesterday, 'cos even then I think I was on track."

"All right, all right! For Christ's sake cut to the chase, you irritating asshole!"

"Simple. We fit the antenna and the micro-circuitry into... a conductor's baton! Ta-dah!"

Jonathan laughed and laughed, and Makharam joined in. It was relief beyond imagining, it was release of tension, it was the feeling that at long last they were doing something. And it was the blatant symbolism; the one piece of equipment that characterized the maestros could be their salvation. But their laughter died as the same sobering thought hit them both. Jonathan was the first to voice it.

"How do we know it'll work?"

Makharam riposted with, "And who do we test it on?"

"But, first off," replied Jonathan, dampening the bonfire even further, "we have to build the damn thing."

"Ah, ha! I'll head off to T-O right now. Tomorrow morning I'll drop into a music store and buy a baton or two, then back to the workshop for a bit of inspired craftsmanship. I've got a ton of components in stock; won't need anything special. The big deal will be programming the microchip."

"Okay. I'm in rehearsal tomorrow afternoon 'til about five. Can you come back tomorrow evening, about six?"

"So, no concert this weekend?"

"No. Mercifully we have the weekend off." The thought of the up-coming Brahms gave him a rush of shit to the heart.

"Okay, see you tomorrow then," and he was into his coat and out of the door.

Jonathan sat a while, nursing an almost-finished beer and musing on the turns of fate and fortune, before rising, clearing up the mess and getting ready for bed. Sliding between the sheets past the looming cage required some flexibility and athleticism, but he managed and was soon asleep, while dreams of multidimensional geometries danced in his head.

Makharam Khan had a lot of fun buying batons. He had never been anywhere near a music store in his life, and had absolutely no idea what specifications a discriminating baton wielder might demand. However, he did have a good line of bullshit and a bit of a swagger, so he stepped through the doors of the store on Bloor Street West shortly after opening time on Saturday, sashayed up to the counter, and asked to see some batons. The store clerk brought several kinds for his inspection, and he picked them up one after the other and swished them through the air in a style he guessed a maestro might employ. It was a quiet time at the store and soon most of the staff had wandered over to watch the spectacle.

"Now, which of these is made of wood?" he asked after another spell of frantic air conducting. "That's a very important consideration for the discerning maestro, y'know. Natural products will never be supplanted."

The real reason for choosing wood over synthetics was much more mundane; he knew he'd be able to cut into it to install his antenna.

"This one..." the clerk read off the side of the box, "...is straight grained Canadian maple with a genuine Portuguese cork grip."

"Ah, ha! Just the sort of thing Uncle Zubin would opt for, I don't doubt," quoth the *soi disant* maestro and shameless name-dropper. "I'll take six of them. They tend to fly off into the audience," he confided.

Six would probably be enough because you never knew what you were going to encounter when you started cutting them up, and a couple might end up as experimental write-offs. He left the store with the same swagger that had signaled his entrance, box of batons under his arm, while the store clerks eyed each other with raised eyebrows and returned to the business of selling musical items to people who knew what they were used for.

It was not as easy as he had hoped to conceal all his micro-circuitry and the platinum wire antenna in the bulk of the baton, but after much trial and error he had a prototype. The platinum wire had to be exactly 17.4cms long and the only way he could ensure this was to insert it up the shaft. So, the shaft of the baton had to be split longitudinally, with a slot carved out to hold the wire, then the two halves had to be glued back together. He had to split the shaft with a knife, as a saw would leave a wide kerf, and this proved a pain in the ass. Luckily, the straight grained

Canadian maple proved to be extremely easy to split, so all went well. The electronic circuitry was concealed in a hollow under the cork grip, and as there was no battery, the whole thing could be glued back together almost invisibly. Then, so there could be a connection between these gizmos and the conductor's hand, he had to carefully glue a band of thin copper foil around the grip, like a wide metallic equator, solder-connected from below to a wire. Once completed, though, he was quite pleased with his masterpiece, and determined to make another one right away; you never knew when you might need a spare.

Around four in the afternoon he called Stan Ward to update him on progress.

"Stan. Makharam. Listen. Leaps and bounds. Here's what Jonathan and I have hatched up..." and he described in detail the magical baton and its hoped-for properties. Stan sounded surprised, absolutely delighted and over all mystified.

"I'll be going up to East Gladstone tonight," continued Kahn, "and then we'll see if Jonathan can persuade their conductor to try it out... You are? Wednesday? What time?... Oh, sure. Gimme a call when you get there and we'll all get together. I'll probably be back at Jonathan's then. Be the third trip in a week. Ciao."

Khan slipped both his batons into the side flap of his laptop case, grabbed two granola bars from the kitchen cupboard and headed down the elevator to the basement garage. He had agreed to be at Jonathan's place in East Gladstone by six, but there was no way he would make that deadline at this time of day. Just getting to the 401 would be bad enough.

It was nearly six-thirty when Makharam Khan finally rang Jonathan's bell. They shared Jonathan's remaining bottle of Smithwick's in the living room, while he admired the workmanship of prototypes one and two. He was quite dubious that something so apparently simple could claim to be effective, but its simplicity had about it an elegance that came of hard number crunching and abstract mathematical thought. There were lots of examples in everyday life of deceptively simple devices that concealed a world of sophistication and development. He thought of his 8gig USB key and his MP3 player.

"So, next week I'll see if I can get our stand-in maestro to give it a whirl. But I don't know what effect we'll see, if anything. And none of the stuff we're doing is high up on the list anyway."

"Well, according to the Oracle of Mount Stan, there is always some feedback, so who knows? Gotta start somewhere. But, of far greater importance, is there any food in this house?"

There wasn't, so they walked into town to find something. They ate quickly at a small internet café along Main Street, and then it was time for Makharam to head back to Toronto.

"Getting to know that road," he laughed as they began the walk back to Sanders Street where his car was parked.

"Tell me about it!" replied Jonathan, having seen it from the bus more times than he would care to think about.

"Stan and Sandra will be up here on Wednesday afternoon, did he tell you?"

"Yes, he called me this morning, said they'd booked the place they were in before, probably stay over the weekend."

"Great. So if your guy has tested the baton by then I'll head up here and we can report to the whole group."

They walked the rest of the way in companionable silence until they reached the car. Khan swung in, started the engine, and with a brief wave headed south around the lake.

At midday on Tuesday, just before the first rehearsal for the upcoming weekend concerts, Jonathan lurked in the corridor leading to the concert hall with Makharam Khan's second masterpiece most appropriately up his sleeve. He wished to accost Stefan Kulikofski before he appeared on the stage for the afternoon's session. With the Brahms symphony impending and the concertmaster still running rehearsals from his chair, it was critical to get him back on the podium and get the baton tested. He stepped forward, but his overture was forestalled.

"Ah, Jonathan. Just the person I wanted to talk to. Now look, your absences are getting to be an issue. I know Stephanie Carol is a good player, and Graham does just fine at first, but as our official first oboe you have a certain responsibility. In all honesty I don't think we can continue this way."

"I'm really sorry. It's been... er... some personal issues..."

"Hopefully on the way to being resolved?" A hint of vinegar.

"I really do hope so, and I'm terribly sorry to disrupt things, especially..."

"Exactly. This is a critical time for the EGSO. This weekend is make or break! We all pull together, Jonathan. *All of us*!"

With this he continued up the corridor. Jonathan hung back for a few moments. The poor bugger was tortured with the fear of a spectacular failure. The other two items on the program—pieces by Mozart and Weber—were easier, thank God, but it would only take one failure... He followed the concertmaster into the hall and surreptitiously slid the baton into his oboe case.

The following day, at the same time and at the same place, Jonathan plucked up his courage again.

"Stefan," he began, as Kulikofski came through the door. He was even less sure of what he was going to say, now he was actually broaching the subject. "I don't quite know how to put this, but a colleague of mine—a scientist at the University of Toronto—has come up with a baton that he says will protect maestros from the sort of deaths we've been seeing." It was lame, and he knew it as soon as he had spoken.

Naturally, and hardly unexpected, Kulikofski stared at Rycroft in silence as if he had just stepped out of a still-smoking flying saucer, and had waggling green antennae.

"I know it sounds far-fetched," he continued. Kulikofski could only nod. "But if you would try it—just use it for one rehearsal maybe—I know he'd be pleased. Frankly, I think his research grant sort of depends on someone testing it for him."

Kulikofski found his voice. "I don't know if this is some sort of joke Mr Rycroft, but if it is, it's in very poor taste." The use of 'Mr Rycroft' put Jonathan in his place. Kulikofski made to continue to the stage.

"No, please," begged Jonathan, "at least someone is trying to do something about this! I do think we should encourage him if we can. What harm could it do?"

Kulikofski spun round. He was within a millisecond of shouting '*Harm*?' and raving about the risk to his life, when the lure of reward crossed his mind. He thought quickly, balancing his fear of the phantom Symphabomber with the attraction of the podium and the siren song of permanent employment as a maestro. If there was the outside chance of something that could get him back onto the podium, and bring the Brahms to an at least satisfactory conclusion, perhaps he would grasp it and take the risk.

"All right," he relented. "Maybe there isn't any harm in giving it a try."

Jonathan handed Kulikofski prototype number two, which had benefitted from experience and was better finished. He swished it around a little and peered at the copper band.

"It's somewhat heavier than I am used to," he stated, implying a sophistication and knowledge of the maestro's craft far exceeding his limited experience, "but I'll see what it can do."

That day's rehearsal went swimmingly well. Kulikofski swaggered at the podium. He was in an excellent mood; he smiled, he advised, he acknowledged feedback from his musicians, and he completed the task of running through their Brahms, Mozart and Weber offerings expeditiously. Once they had come to the end of the session and the orchestra members were packing up their gear, Kulikofski caught Jonathan's eye and with a slight motion of his head, indicated that they should meet outside.

"I don't know what this is," Stefan Kulikofski came straight to the point once they had met on the terrace, "but I believe your scientist friend might have something. I don't know why a mere baton should make any difference, but it appears to. You feel a sense of... what is it? Security, perhaps... I don't know. I wonder if it isn't just psychological."

"Well, if it works," replied Jonathan, relieved but mystified, "don't worry about asking how. Hang onto it, use it again, and let me know what you think."

"Yes, but what if this sense of wellbeing is just masking, and I'm still in danger? What then?"

"I can't answer that, but I believe the designer's on the right track." How could he possibly reveal the truth without looking like someone ready for a straightjacket? Time for some inspired gobble-de-gook. "He assures me that, whatever the mechanism for these attacks may be, this device can neutralize it, and we have to take him at his word."

"Well then, I'll continue with it on that assurance. Thank you, Jonathan. Do you know, I think the Brahms One is feasible now; I really do. And do please thank your friend."

Well, thought Jonathan, so much for field trial number one. It appears to work for him, and he's apparently going to stay on the podium. Although I can't reveal it to one living soul in the EGO—except Kate, of course—I think I've just saved all our jobs. Heady wine! But Stefan liking the thing and wanting to continue using it proves absolutely zilch; feelings aren't data. It feels good; so what?

He walked quickly back home in case Makharam had made the trip in an uncharacteristically short time. Sure enough, there he was sitting in his car and listening to the radio.

"Left town early," he said as soon as he had climbed out of the car. "Couldn't wait to hear the results of the test."

Jonathan showed him into the apartment, and they sat down

while he filled him in on the somewhat equivocal results.

"He was pleased with it—said it made him feel good; secure—but so what? As I said, none of the stuff we worked on today was anywhere on the list—Brahms, Mozart, Weber—so what effect are we supposed to see?"

"God knows. Well, at least he did say something positive."

"Yeah, but it could be purely psychological. The poor guy's just dying to be maestro..."

Makharam laughed loudly.

"Oh, Jesus! You asshole! But, look, if there was any slight chance of keeping him on the podium he'd take it. This could be just a placebo."

"But if he said it... what was it? ...made him feel secure?"

"Sure, feelings. Maybe he was getting a hint of what I get in the cage, but you know what? There's only one way we're going to know if this damned thing works, and that's to test it under live fire. Try it with a maestro conducting a piece that is ripe for reflux. And if it doesn't work..."

A tinny travesty of the *Ride of the Valkyries* emanating from Khan's pants pocket interrupted the thought. He pulled out the phone and pressed it to his cheek. "Stan! Great... Yeah, we're both here... You do? Oh, that's really kind of you both... Okay, around six-thirty. See you." He slipped the phone back into his pocket. "Stan and Sandra arrived in town this aft; they want to invite us all for dinner at some place called *The Simcoe*. Six-thirty. He says they've already called Kate. Looking forward to meeting her, by the way."

Stan must have mentioned Kate to Makharam, because he knew he hadn't.

"*The Simcoe*? It's the town's oldest hotel; very nice restaurant." He checked his watch. "And we might as well head there now. You can leave your car here, it's not far to walk."

Doctors Rycroft and Khan arrived a little early at *The Simcoe* that Wednesday evening, and as the table that Professor Ward had booked wasn't ready they headed for the bar and had a beer each. The bar was old-fashioned in a mannered way that fooled nobody, but the heavy old-world décor, the solid tables of thickly varnished, artificially distressed wood, and the Art Deco lighting fixtures produced a pleasant enough ambience.

"There's some really nice small breweries in this part of the world," observed Khan, sipping his drink as they headed for a table. "This one's got all sorts of things going on in it."

"Yeah, they've been doing some nice stuff for quite a few years now. For a long time we were stuck with just a couple of huge breweries turning out one-dimensional horse piss."

"Tell me about it! Since living in Canada I've started to forget the Californian factory beers. They've come along a bit since then, though."

They had almost finished their beer when they spotted Stan and Sandra coming in the front door and asking after their table reservation. They finished the drinks quickly and went over to greet them.

"This is great Stan, and you too Sandra. I'm so glad you decided to come up here and visit us." Jonathan shook his hand and gave Sandra a brief peck on the cheek. "You staying at the same place?"

"Yes, Ivy Lea. Same room even. Now, this is a working vacation m'boy. Makharam's updated me on progress with the baton —work o' genius, absolute genius—but we have to get all our ducks in a row..." Jonathan had a brief unpleasant flashback, "...then we'll see if there's a way forrard. Ah, this is a nice table; no, you sit near the wall my dear, I'll take the outside. Likely I'll need to get out to go to the gents."

The server passed out menus—"There'll be five of us"—and poured iced water into their glasses.

Jonathan spotted Kate over by the door and waved her over. "Makharam, this is Kate Heinrichs my... colleague in the orchestra. She plays the violin."

Kate was wearing one of her light blue dresses, cinched at the waist with a braided belt of brown fabric. She had pulled her hair back into a pony tail, which gave her face a classical fineness that Jonathan hadn't really appreciated before.

"It's nice to meet you. Jonathan has told me all about you."

This was a standard conversational opening gambit; in fact, she only knew that Khan was working on some possible solution to the problem. And she didn't believe that Jonathan had said much at all about her. Khan looked her over and liked what he saw, and there was no attempt at disguise in his expression. She took the vacant chair and picked up a menu.

"It's so kind of you to invite me," she smiled over at Stan and Sandra.

They ordered their meals and a litre of house red, and for a while music, m-Axis, reflux and death took second place to five people enjoying food and drink and each other's company. Inevitably, when the second litre of house plonk was half done and the dishes had been cleared away, the talk turned to the job in hand.

"So, you two've developed a damned baton that might do the trick?" asked Stan. "It seems ridiculously simple."

"Only if it works," replied Jonathan. "I tested it on our concertmaster today, but... I don't know. He said he liked it; made him feel 'secure', I believe he said, but none of the pieces we rehearsed were high on the lists. I dunno."

"Know what Jonathan thinks, Stan?" said Makharam. "He thinks we won't know if it works until we test it under live fire."

"You may be right. And how the hell will that be arranged?"

"Excuse me for interrupting," said Sandra, "but I'm not really sure what this is all about. Stan's been rather neglectful about details."

"You know about as much as I do, dammit," he rumbled in an aside.

"Me too," agreed Kate. "What is this baton and what does it do? Is that why Stefan was so full of himself today?"

"Tell you what," said Kahn, addressing Kate directly. "Imagine a lightning conductor; now most people think a lightning conductor on a building is so that when lightning strikes it can go straight to ground, but that's not the case. The presence of a thick copper wire going from a point on a high roof down to the ground is actually so that the charge in the clouds is dissipated *before* the big build-up. So, imagine the same thing here; we prevent the big build-up by providing a conduit for the energy, only it's coming out of our little mathematical keyhole in the m-Axis and somehow mediated by the brain. I'm sorry if I have to simplify it for you."

"Oh, don't worry your head on my account," she replied levelly. "If it came to that, I wouldn't have a problem with simplification if you asked for an explanation of all the nuances of *sautillé*, *spiccato* and *martellato* and their application to the violin writing in Richard Strauss's *Elektra*. Different professions; different tools."

Jonathan smiled inwardly; what a smooth and well played 'fuck you', *sautillé* indeed! She scores!

"So," stated Sandra into the slight pause, "the baton is replicating what the brain does automatically when music is being played. Providing a conduit for the energy and taking it safely to ground."

"Exactly," replied Makharam. "Provided it works. The theory is great, but the application..."

"Yes, back to the testing under fire," resumed Stan. "We now have the wherewithal to check for reflux. We can identify the dangerous pieces, but it's a worldwide problem and I know we all feel the frustration of sitting on the Ontario sidelines while it all unfolds."

He sat a while chewing his lower lip, eyes far away, then shook off the mood. "Well, we're not going to sort it out sitting here. First things first; Jonathan, did you test your cage yet?"

"No. Frankly, I haven't had the guts. And anyway, I don't want to do it alone."

Stan picked up his Visa card and payment slip and rose from the table. "So, let's go right now and check what's next on the hit list from the Top 50."

Kate cringed at the image the 'hit list' conjured in her mind. Was she, she wondered, the only one who couldn't lighten up about this. The burden on her mind of all those deaths brought about by the pursuit of all that's wonderful and uplifting was sometimes more than she could bear. She wanted a brief respite from this whole thing, and especially from these three men who seemed to be able to joke about it while playing like little boys. It's all a game for them really, no matter what Jonathan says.

"Maybe it'll be Haydn's *Surprise* symphony, eh?" was Khan's witty riposte. (He had been reading up on classical music.)

"Or the *Clock*, as in time bomb!" shot back Jonathan.

She was sick of the lot of them. "Tell you what, Sandra, why don't you and me go round to my place? How long will you boys be? You can join us later."

"Great idea! About half an hour; forty-five minutes," cried Jonathan. "Let's do it."

So Jonathan, Stan and Makharam strode off to Jonathan's apartment while Kate and Sandra strolled slowly to 46 Simcoe Street. As soon as he got in the door Jonathan threw himself down at the low table, flipped open his laptop and opened the spreadsheet of their Top 50 hits.

"Holy shit!" Makharam raised his eyebrows. "You still using Excel?"

"Shut up; it works. Okay," he announced after a brief search, "on top of the pops right now we have Sibelius's *Finlandia*,

Mahler's Fourth and good old Mussorgsky's *Pictures at an Exhibition*; that one's no surprise."

He brought a cable over to the laptop from an inkjet printer on the floor in front of the fireplace and plugged it in.

"I'll have to print some music; can't take the laptop into the cage. Give me a minute."

As soon as the sheet of music was printed they were ready.

"So, let's test our field equipment at the Medical Sciences Building, East Gladstone Annex," announced Stan Ward rather grandly, and then passing into the bedroom and seeing the actual installation, "Good God, where are the bloody parrots?"

Jonathan slipped self-consciously into the cage with his oboe and sheet music and shut the mesh gate, while the others stood in the bedroom door. It was all they could do to stop themselves laughing at the absurdity of it. While he played the pieces Stan stepped a little way into the room and kept his hand on the gate catch, ready to intervene if things got a little too profound. On the third piece there was an obvious reaction, but Jonathan seemed able to catch himself and not proceed too far, although he could see the struggle this was causing. It didn't take long for Jonathan to establish that the cage was working well, and that, of the three pieces, *Finlandia* was the most dangerously near to reflux.

"Okay, gents," said Stan. "Let's reconvene in the living room and check the calendar for the year."

Jonathan sat down at the laptop again and opened the Excel spreadsheet containing the worldwide concert programs for the year. He pressed control-F and entered 'finlandia' in Find; there were several hits. His heart lurched.

"What's today's date? Shit! The next *Finlandia* is in London *this weekend!* Friday! Two days from now. They're doing a three-day Sibelius celebration. Oh, my God; Royal Festival Hall, Sir Arthur Compton."

For a second time the reality of the threat was brought home to him. Seeing Carlo Mascagni crash to the ground in EGSO's own concert hall was compounded by the horror of imagining Arthur Compton in the same condition.

But, please God, let there be a way to prevent it.

"We've got to get the baton there!" cried Jonathan. "We've got to phone him. And it's Wednesday already. Shit! What time is it in London?"

"Five hours difference," answered Khan, throwing up his

hands. "Middle of the fucking night; one o'clock."

"We have to! We can't let this happen! He conducted us earlier this year. He's marvelous, marvelous. I'll see if I can get his number." He began working his laptop frantically.

"Okay, okay!" interrupted Stan Ward. "Wait now, and let's just think this thing through. Firstly," he counted on his fingers, "what evidence do we have that he is in the line of fire? Why him?"

"Why *not* him? The piece is hot; he's doing it three times! We can't take the chance! Not again!"

"Okay, but let me finish. Secondly," another finger, "we have to contact him, and thirdly—here's the cruncher—we have to convince him we're not completely bat shit crazy. And, finally we have to get the baton into his hands."

"For Christ's sake, Stan!" cried Jonathan, leaping up. "All this frustration and waiting around watching, and now you're playing the academic! There isn't time!"

"I'm not saying that! I'm just saying that before we go off half-cocked, we should think this all through very carefully."

Jonathan was not in the slightest mollified. "Time *is* a factor Stan. Somehow we have to get a courier to send the thing, then we'll need his address..."

Professor Ward stood in front of him, placed his two hands firmly upon his shoulders and stared into his face. He knew that Jonathan was still disturbed by his musical exercise in the cage, and he respected the lad's mental fragility more than ever before. The last thing we want is another crack-up.

"Jonathan," he urged. "There *is* time. We have to sit down and work this thing carefully through. Yes, by all means, locate his phone number because we'll need that, but that can also wait. It's the middle of the night there; let's walk over to Kate's place—a bit of fresh air, stretch the legs—and agree on a careful and considered approach. Okay?"

Jonathan took a deep breath, met Stan's eyes and forced some calm. "Okay. Sorry. You... you're right. It'll wait a while. Let's go."

He grabbed the laptop and headed for the door. Stan was in good shape for his age, but he and Makharam were no match for Jonathan when it came to race walking. Stan's stride was at its maximum stretch while Khan was trotting alongside, more running than walking, when this unlikely athletic trio arrived at Kate's door.

Kate was halfway down the stairs, responding to the three

rings on the bell, when it rang again. "Okay, okay, where's the fire?" She opened the street door and they spilled in, filling the tiny hallway.

"Sir Arthur Compton; this weekend. Festival Hall," panted Jonathan. "*Finlandia*!"

She felt her heart wither inside her. That lovely, lovely man. No, this couldn't be happening. This force, this power... it just couldn't be this cruel. She led them upstairs in a daze feeling faint and sick. Sandra was waiting on the landing, having been alarmed by the commotion down below.

"Now it begins to get critical, my love," Stan told Sandra. "It seems that the latest target is Sir Arthur Compton in London. So, let's sit down and work this through."

"Are you sure? Can you be really sure?" she asked, looking over at their oboist as he paced the small room, face haggard.

Jonathan nodded. "Sure as I can be. There's a huge reflux. I wasn't wrong before."

"Jonathan, sit!" commanded Kate, and with as much surprise to her as anyone else, he obeyed. "I'm going to make some tea." And she disappeared quickly into the kitchen so that nobody would see her tears.

"Now," said Stan into the silence that ensued. "Find his number if you can. I don't doubt he'll be unlisted, but see what you can do. And then, my friends, whatever do we say?"

"In all seriousness," said Sandra, "if someone phoned me with a story like this I would hang up on them. It's got nutcase written all over it. Hysteria over this business is high enough anyway. 'I'm warning you, if you play *Finlandia* you'll blow up'. Just needs a mid-East accent. Oh, shit! Sorry Makharam."

"Ah, 's okay, we Americans can take it. Thick skinned, us."

"No," she continued, "even if you find his number, that simply isn't the answer."

Jonathan had been working at the laptop since the command to sit, and now he groaned. "Crap! I've done the white pages and residential but he's not listed in either. I have the phone number for his orchestra, so we could try that. Nine o'clock their time, what would that be? Four A.M. here. Don't know what else to do."

They sat in silence, each working out potential scenarios. Kate reappeared with a tray of tea, a bright smile upon her face, and all traces of tears completely obliterated. She officiated with the cups and milk, playing for time. She knew exactly what had to be done, and she knew the others did too, although perhaps they weren't quite ready to express it yet.

"Jonathan," she smiled brightly handing him a steaming mug, "you're flying to London tomorrow! Have some tea while you get used to the idea."

He looked at her, mug in hand, and nodded slowly. "Yep, you got it. Nothing else we can do, is there?"

"Not really," she replied. "Even if you phone him, there's no guarantee he'll even agree to see you, assuming he doesn't just hang up the phone. But, if you show up at his door, it'll be all up to your powers of persuasion. It will just *have* to work!"

"It's a hell of a lot of money to spend on a gamble..."

"Jonathan! That lovely man's life is at stake! How much is that worth?" The tears were on the edge again.

"Sorry, I'm really not on the same page yet. You're right." He thought for a moment. "So, I show up at his door? And where exactly is his door?"

"On his business card, of course!" she jumped up and rummaged in a desk drawer. "Now where the hell is it? Where? Ah! Sir Arthur's business card," she smiled and held it out proudly.

"With the phone number as well! Oh, you genius!"

"No, just sensible and foresighted."

"Okay, first thing, the phone. What time is it there? Middle of the night; that'll have to wait 'til later. I can stay up. But even if I call him..."

"It's no good," interrupted Stan. "We agree that he's hardly going to listen. I don't think there's anything for it. We have to fly this gent to London pronto, so to business. Let's get on the web and do some booking. Got yer Visa card handy, my friend?"

Jonathan started searching travel booking websites while Makharam booted up Kate's laptop and began with Air Canada's site. There was a considerable stretch of key tapping and touch pad sliding before they both stopped in frustration.

"Shit, there's nothing out of Toronto. Absolutely nothing!" wailed Makharam. "I just don't get it!"

"I do," put in Sandra. "What's the big attraction in London right now?"

"Oh my, God, the bloody Olympics. Of course! Everybody and his brother's off across the Pond. Now what do we do?"

"The Olympics!" groaned Stan leaning back in his chair with his hands over his eyes. "Flying a bloody baton to the bloody Olympics! How trite can you get?"

Jonathan muttered from his laptop, "Wait. Just checking. US

Airways has a flight out of Philadelphia, seats vacant. Leaving Toronto/Pearson at 3:20, changing in Philly, arriving Heathrow ten A.M.

"You'd better take it," advised Stan. "I loathe going anywhere via the US myself, but needs must."

"Okay, I'm booking it." He clicked away, keyed in his credit card number and continued through the menu. "Right! I'll print this later. All set." He sat back as if a load had been taken off his shoulders, although the reverse was actually the case.

"Tell you what," said Khan, "I can stay here the night—maybe check into your place, Stan and Sandra, if there's a room—then I can drop Jonathan off at Pearson tomorrow morning."

"Great," said Jonathan, closing the laptop. "Now I'd better get back, sort some things out. Dear old Graham's going to love me to bits, but Stephanie'll get a chance to play some good stuff at second. You'd better give me baton number two now; imagine if I forgot it. I'll walk you three back to Ivy Lea."

Kate saw them to the top of the stairs. "Jonathan." He hung back while the others descended. "Will I see you tomorrow, before you go?"

"Best not. I'll be fine, don't you worry."

"No. No, I won't worry. Promise me you'll phone. Promise?"

"Course I will. As soon as I get there. Bye."

And he was down the stairs and out of the door.

The tears came again. For the love of him that she desperately wanted returned, for the aching in her heart that wouldn't go away, for the fate of that dear old man in London.

Jonathan packed his bags as soon as he got home, and made arrangements for Stephanie to sub for Graham. Swann was getting really sick of being fucked around—at least, that's what he said when Jonathan phoned—but Stephanie was happy to be playing so many gigs with the EGSO. Swann was strange, thought Jonathan; he made out he hated being pushed into first oboe, but absolutely relished being there, and then when he got the chance he schemed to make it permanent. Jonathan figured it was a fair deal; often enough, while Swann dealt with the agèd mum in Pickering, he had done all the arranging for Stephanie to sub at second. It should be just quid pro quo.

Their budding maestro would probably be livid as well, but what could he do? He just hoped to God Stefan's euphoria over the new baton would result in a distillate of clemency. Be a shame to lose his job right now.

Even though he knew it was pointless, he stayed up until two-thirty so he could at least try the phone. He read the number off the business card and tapped the keys. His face fell as a tinny voice gave him the message.

In a fake upper crust English accent he mimicked to the room at large, "'Hillew, this is British Telecorm. The number you have diahled is noht in service'. Shit!"

He went to bed and scarcely slept.

Kate checked her phone in the cafeteria during the afternoon break on Thursday. It was more or less routine to check for messages during breaks, as leaving your phone turned on during a rehearsal was close to a death sentence. And if you had a ringtone that sounded anything like anything at all from the classical repertoire, the death would be slow and painful. Ah, there was a message from Jonathan; he must be in Toronto waiting for his flight to Philly. She pressed the key with a light heart, but as she listened to his voice she quickly became horrified.

"Kate, Kate, listen. Call me back, okay. I've been thrown off the flight. Call back as soon as you can, okay?"

With fingers shaking so badly she could hardly manage, she eventually got through and waited while the phone rang. Just when she thought she'd have to leave a message he answered.

"Kate, oh my God Kate, this is so stupid. Stupid! I've been turned back by US Security. I'm on some God-damned no-fly list!"

"How? How? What happened?"

People at the tables were looking her way with curiosity. She got up and walked quickly out to the terrace, phone on her cheek.

"It's CSIS. I didn't tell you. They interviewed me after... after Mascagni died. I told 'em I didn't know anything! Christ, this is so stupid! Stupid!"

"Where are you? Are they arresting you?"

"No, no, nothing like that. I'll be free to go soon, but the shit's going to hit the fan. I'm still at Pearson. Christ!"

"So, so... what...?"

"Listen Kate. You'll have to go to London. Get the spare baton off Kulikofski and book a flight."

"Me! Why me? Why can't one of the guys go?"

"No! You're a musician. You know him. He'll remember you!"

"But there aren't any flights," wailed Kate in agony. "And even if there were it's too late. Too late!"

"Try! Try! Shit! Is your passport up to date?"

"Yes, yes. I renewed it just after our last gig to the States. But I can't..."

"You *have* to! Look, I gotta go; they're taking me for a little more processing. I'll call later. Try! All right, you stupid bastard, I'm talking with my girlfrie..." and the phone went dead.

Afterwards, she couldn't imagine how she had done it, but she had begged Mr Kulikofski to return the baton (promising a replacement as soon as possible), lied to him about a terrible family emergency, and was on the phone to the Wards before the rehearsal resumed. Stan and Sandra agreed to meet her at Ivy Lea right away to discuss the disaster and see what could be done.

She hurried into the lounge of the bed-and-breakfast and found the older couple waiting for her. She ran to Sandra and hugged her, at a loss for words. Sandra's hand patted her shoulder gently. Stan sat down in front of Ivy Lea's guest computer at a side table and began working the web. She knew what he was trying.

"There isn't time," she cried, "even if you could find a flight! So close, so close!"

"Wait a minute," Stan called over his shoulder. "There's a flight out of Ottawa, Air Canada 888, leaves twenty-one twenty-five. And they have a seat."

"But it's at least five hours to Ottawa by car! There isn't *time*."

"Sandra, listen. Drive Kate home; get her packed and ready, then bring her back here. I'm going to call Peter. It's a long shot, but he might know someone around here with a plane. Go! Go!" and he shooed them out of the door.

Before their son had enrolled in the college in Sault Ste Marie and earned his commercial licence he had done a great deal of light plane flying in southern Ontario. Stan prayed that his connections were still current.

"Peter, it's Dad. Yes... Yes... Look, bit of an emergency. I'll explain later. Do you know anyone, anyone at all, around East Gladstone, Barrie, Simcoe, whatever, who could fly to Ottawa in a hurry?"

He waited, drumming his fingers impatiently while Peter, somewhere in the Northwest Territories, looked up phone numbers.

Finally, "Yes, I've got a pen... Good."

He wrote numbers, read them back, and quickly ended the call. He tried two of the numbers Peter had given him and got no reply. The third one answered after five rings.

"No, I really can't. Plane's not fit to fly right now. Tell you what, try Manfred... Oh, you've got his number already? Yeah, he's crazy. Bye."

Manfred's was the fourth name on Peter's list. He came up trumps.

"Sure," said a loud enthusiastic voice at the other end. "I live near the airstrip. Was going to visit sis in Mississauga later today, but I can make her wait."

Stan explained the emergency, hoping to God the details wouldn't put the man off, but the adventure seemed to fire him up even more. Some sort of white knight, Stan thought, and thank you whoever is up there for putting him in our path.

"How far away are you from East Gladstone? Great... Perhaps half an hour."

"Okay, I'll warm the engine up. She's fully fueled, so that'll save us some time. See you soonest."

Stan had just finished booking Kate's seat when the two women returned. Kate was trundling a little black wheelie case and carrying a small bag.

"Okay, you're on AC888 out of Ottawa and an air ace by the name of Manfred is going to fly you there. Have you got everything? Passport? Got the bloody baton? Thank God; imagine if you forgot that. No, no, don't!"

Kate hugged Sandra again tightly, and Stan led her quickly back out to the car. They drove the ten kilometers to Lake St John airfield in less than ten minutes and parked alongside a row of wooden sheds. Peter's friend Manfred was there waiting for them, a solid man in his sixties with a florid face and a fantastic moustache.

"Now, look here," began Manfred, "I can't fly you direct to Ottawa—no way I can stray into MacDonald-Cartier airspace without a transponder—so we'll have to land at Kars, the Rideau Valley Air Park."

"How far is that from Ottawa?" asked Kate.

"Not far; bit south. Twenty minutes, half hour maybe? Here's the phone number of the manager there." He turned to Stan. "Get on to him and see if he can get the young lady a taxi."

"You know this guy, then?" asked Stan, amazed at this man's

apparent knowledge.

"Oh, no, no. It's all in the book; Nav Canada's *Flight Supplement*. Every piece of grass, tar, gravel or water where you can put down a plane in the whole of Canada is listed there. Provided they're licenced, of course."

"But if you don't have a radio..." began Stan.

"Got a small radio I can broadcast on, but that's it. Little planes like this, we fly VFR. Visual Flight Rules. Means we have to keep to small airfields, but it's flying the way it used to be y'see, and that's how we like it. Now, all ready?"

So, after a parting hug from Stan, Kate was led out onto the grass field to the aircraft standing in front of a wooden shed. To her eyes it really looked rather small and frail, and not the sort of thing to do a trip of 350 kilometers.

"Okay," said Manfred. "Throw your case and bag in the back, that's it, behind the rear seat. Now, have you ever been in one of these?"

Kate confessed she hadn't and admitted she had never even seen such a small plane close-up.

"And we can get all the way to Ottawa in this?"

"Oh, sure! She's got a range of nearly four hundred K and we're fully fueled. And the wind's from the west; tail wind. She's an Aeronca 7AC, made in 1947. Only 65 horse, but very economical. Simply built and easy to fly, but you're going to have to help me start her up. No, don't worry, it's not difficult."

He stood her on the right side of the plane just in front of the two-bladed propeller.

"Now, I'm going to turn the propeller counter-clockwise by pulling down on it, like this." He showed her how he would do it. "This will be to prime the engine. First, I'll have you sitting in the rear seat with yer feet on the brakes. Hop in."

She scrambled a little awkwardly into the rear seat, relieved that she had decided to wear pants. He stood beside the plane and leaned into the rear section to point out the details.

"Do up yer seatbelt; there... Now, this plane's got dual controls; everything I've got up front you have here. Now, see these two little pedals; not the big jobs, they're the rudder, don't touch them. There, feet on the little ones. That'll hold us on the brakes, one for each wheel. I'm going to turn the prop for four blades to prime us."

He returned to the front of the plane and pulled down on one blade of the prop, swinging it through 90 degrees, then grabbed the other one and repeated the process three times. He came back and leant in to the cockpit.

"Now, Kate, follow me very carefully because this is extremely important. Keep your feet on those brakes the whole time! When I tell you, I want you to turn this little switch, like so; one click. This turns on one of the magnetos, so the engine will fire. Once it's on you will sing out and tell me. Then I'll swing the prop, and off she'll go. I will step away from the propeller, walk around the wing, and climb in. You'll be holding her on the brakes the whole time. Got it?"

Kate nodded, rather tongue-tied at this sudden and novel experience; hey, she thought, I'm a fiddle player not an aero mechanic. How did I get into this?

"Okay," he called once he was back in front of the plane. "Brakes on!"

She pressed hard on the pedals with her feet, far harder than necessary, but fear kept her leg muscles tense.

He turned the prop over a few times, then called, "Magneto on!"

"Magneto on!" she sang out as she turned the switch, starting to really get into this game.

He reached up and swung the propeller and stepped back as the engine fired and caught. He backed away from the blurring propeller, hair blowing in all directions, walked round and climbed up into the front seat.

"Okay, I've got the brakes!" She gladly eased up on the pedals and the near-cramping pain in her calves subsided.

The interior was tiny, and on all sides it was bare metal with struts, and nuts and bolts and rivets. There was a complete set of controls in front of her; a joystick between her knees and the pedals on the floor. Manfred yelled back to her over his shoulder above the resonant din, "Put the headset on!"

She found the headset on the floor and fitted it over her head, adjusting the clip for comfort, and swinging the microphone in front of her mouth.

"That's better," his voice sounded thinly in the speakers. "We're almost set. Don't touch any of the controls, okay?"

Manfred worked the pedals and stick and Kate's rear controls moved by themselves. As she looked down between her knees she could see rods and cables sliding backwards and forwards. He released the brakes, reached for the throttle at his side, and the tone of the engine rose. The little plane bumped forward as he taxied slowly to the runway. They waited, poised on the brakes for a few seconds, then he reached for the throttle again and the noise magnified ten-fold. It was bump, bump, bump surge, and in a surprisingly short length of time she felt the little Aeronca lift alarmingly upwards, the wings waggled and the ground swung in an arc, then they stabilized, banked and headed east.

The lake spread out below her, and far to her right she could see the buildings of East Gladstone. This was quite unlike any flight she been on before; with the big aircraft you have very little impression of being in the air at all, but here the sensation of flying was immediate and disconcerting. She wouldn't exactly say she was frightened–she was in the care of a man she had only just met, in a fragile thing made of sheet metal and wood, and plunging through the sky in surges and drops–but it was unnerving to have so little control. It was exciting too, because you so seldom get to see the ground from the air at such a low altitude, and she watched fascinated as they passed over small towns, farm fields and tracts of forest.

After a while, as the shadows lengthened and there was less to see, the flight got boring. Manfred was not one for casual conversation, although he made the occasional observation of some landmark they passed over. Kate tried to think of neutral things but a nagging gremlin in her mind kept telling her what a foolish errand this was, and questioning what she would do if Sir Arthur couldn't be found.

The remainder of the flight was spent in a sort of catatonia, strapped into a resonating metal box that never stayed stable. She looked at her watch repeatedly, calculating how much time remained before she would miss her flight. Eventually, Manfred announced that he could see the airstrip at Kars, and that he was going to take a circuit left, making his descent over the Rideau River from the east. She heard him in her headphones: "Joining downwind... turning final for a full stop." She didn't know who he was talking to–if anybody–but assumed it was part of the flight routine.

The little Aeronca landed with several bumps decreasing in severity, then taxied round to park in front of a row of sheet metal sheds. Manfred cut the magnetos and the noise mercifully died, leaving a slight hissing in the ears and a blissful clarity. They climbed out and Kate retrieved her case and bag. In the falling evening light the place looked deserted.

She shook hands with Manfred. "Thank you so much for doing this. We couldn't have made it without you."

"A pleasure! Peter's a pal, but he sure owes me one. Now, I'm not leaving you alone in the wilderness. We've got to get you to MacDonald-Cartier pronto, and I have to find a place to stay myself. Can't fly after dark. I know a guy in Manotick who can probably put me up. Now, the big question is, do we have transport further...?"

As he spoke, a man emerged from behind one of the sheds and strode towards them. "Hello, I'm Ian; Ian Davis. Stan Ward called me. I manage the air park. He asked me to find you a taxi, but quite honestly, it's just as easy if I drive you myself."

"Oh, that's really kind!" said Kate as she shook his hand. "This is Manfred, my valiant pilot."

"Once you've dropped Kate off, any chance of passing by Manotick on your way back?" asked Manfred as the two men shook hands.

"No problem. This way."

Ian Davis led them round to his car parked behind one of the sheds and they jumped in. Kate sat in the back with her belongings beside her. She quickly phoned Jonathan to tell him she was safely on the ground in Kars and heading to Ottawa. The reception was poor. He was on the second of two buses back to East Gladstone and had already been in touch with Stan and Sandra. He told Kate they had done some hotel surfing and that they would text her the name and address of a hotel not far from the Royal Festival Hall.

"No idea what it's like, but you're damned lucky to get anything at all. They booked you a room online. If it's a fleapit I'm sorry. Cost a fortune..." The call ended abruptly.

She then phoned Stan and told him of the kindness and good luck she had encountered in Kars. He wished her bon voyage while Sandra called goodbye in the background.

She looked at her watch yet again in an agony of impatience; she wasn't sure how long there was between boarding and departure, so she couldn't even guess the odds. But she had no idea of the route or distance anyway, so all she could do was sit in a tight, nervous ball in the rear of the car and watch the trees, houses and fields flash by.

"It's 888, isn't it?" called Davis over his shoulder.

"Yes, yes it is. How are we doing for time?" She knew the answer; why ask?

"I won't lie to you, it's tight. Let's hope the Ottawa police aren't pulling any speed traps."

Minutes later Stan's text came in with the address of the hotel in London. After an eternity of nearly thirty minutes the car pulled up at the Departures door. The two men leapt out, hauled out her bag and case and stamped impatiently through the slowly rotating door. She was pulling out her passport as she followed them. They located the Air Canada desk and she was appalled to see that there was no line-up. They must have already boarded! The agent behind the counter took her passport and tapped the computer keyboard.

"Let's get you through as quick as we can. I'll call down to hold them, but you better hurry." She pressed the passport into Kate's hand with the boarding pass tucked into it.

Kate turned to Manfred and Ian and thanked them as best she could, unable to find words that could fully express her gratitude.

They waved to her as she passed through the gate.

Mercifully, the security check went smoothly, the walk to the boarding gate was relatively short, and the agents waiting for her whisked her down the jetway. As she walked quickly down the aisle of the plane to her seat, trundling her wheelie case, she had the strong impression of disapproval from some of the passengers, who assumed quite rightly that she was the cause of the delay. She almost fell into her aisle seat, sweating, heart racing and immensely relieved.

She tried to get herself comfortable while the larger gentleman beside her commenced a process of studiously ignoring her when he thought she was aware of him, and peering surreptitiously at her when he thought she was not. She settled in to her seat, knowing now that this whole enterprise was in the lap of the gods. Take-off followed soon after, and once the flight had leveled to its cruising altitude, the smells of dinner began wafting down the cabin.

The airline meal was a diversion, and she actually quite enjoyed it. She had chosen a small plastic bottle of factory red wine that claimed to originate in France, and had found it drinkable. She was unused to food served on flights, as her previous jaunts had been only as far as Saskatoon. And because she had never been across the Atlantic jetlag was just a word. The meal finished, the hours began to drag. She was far too keyed up to relax; although she closed her eyes and tried to think of nothing, it was beyond impossible. And the seat was so narrow and tight that she could scarcely stretch out. So she tried the in-flight entertainment system, first the movies, none of which appealed, and then the music selection, which was uniformly awful; and had there been anything worth seeing or listening to, the sound quality of the silly little ear buds would surely ruin it. She made an attempt at the book she had brought with her, then the Su-doku in the in-flight magazine, but none of it worked. The dinner began to not sit well. She was exhausted already and to make matters worse her period was starting. Thank God for an aisle seat.

The trans-Atlantic flight is usually a boring necessity, but to her it became an absolute purgatory. Finally, when she thought she might go mad with anxiety and boredom, the captain announced they had started their descent into Heathrow. This was the beginning of another harrowing period when the plane cruised in dipping banks and circles over most of the Home Counties as it jockeyed for its landing slot. Finally, the plane touched down and taxied, seemingly forever, to its stand. The seat belt sign bonged off, the flight crew welcomed them to Heathrow, and the little cabin window was streaked with grey rain. Kate experienced further delay with the usual selfish assholes who *will* wait until the line along the aisles is actually moving before belatedly retrieving their jammed-in luggage from the overhead bins.

Customs and passport control was cleared and, as she had only cabin baggage, she passed quickly through the arrivals area. She went first to a money change booth and got ripped off in service fees as she collected a wad of colourful pounds that didn't fit properly into her wallet.

Kate found the huge variety of aboveground and underground transportation far too confusing, and there was a long queue at the information desk, so she decided to sacrifice some of her hoard of pounds and take a taxi.

She watched with stinging dry eyes as the scenery of her first European city passed the rain streaked window of the cab. This was not a good way to meet such an exciting new place, she thought; it was grey, tired and grubby and so, she felt, was she. The low clouds didn't even have the guts to rain properly; just a thin miserable drizzle that made things look slick and slimy. She got the impression that, far from washing the buildings and roads, the rain was actually making them dirtier.

The taxi driver was of a garrulous nature but he got short shrift from Kate, mostly because she could scarcely understand a word he said. It was more a question of rhythm than accent, she thought, but either way the mostly one-sided conversation soon dried up. She had no energy to concentrate. Interminable traffic passing rows of tiny houses and corner shops eventually gave way to larger and more imposing buildings, until eventually she arrived in Belgravia at the address she had given the taxi driver.

It was an imposing building in the Georgian style, with an extremely forbidding wooden door flanked by wrought iron carriage lamps. The door was accessed by a flight of stone steps from street level. As she paid off the cab the weather decided it did have the guts after all; the clouds opened. She quickly picked up her case and bag, and was wet before she had got halfway up the steps.

What if he's not here? What if there's no answer? What will I do? With her heart beating almost painfully she swung the substantial brass knocker down with a resounding thump. It probably wasn't more than half a minute, but to Kate it felt like ages as the rain pelted down, before the door opened slightly and the familiar face peered out.

"Sir Arthur Compton?"

"I am he."

"It's rather difficult to explain sir, but it's rather urgent."

"Yes, yes, what is it? You're not one of those blasted journalists, are you?" He sounded impatient and irritated.

"No, no, I'm not. I'm a musician. It's about the deaths of all these maestros..." As soon as the words were out of her mouth she realized her mistake. Why didn't she have the presence of mind to rehearse her speech before coming here?

"You *are* a journalist! Damn it, I disconnect my bloody phone and you come pestering at my door! I just don't have time for this." He made to close the door.

"No, no, please! I'm a musician, really! We think you're in terrible danger. I only want to help." The door opened again slightly. "I'm from Canada—just flew in—I'm a violinist with the East Gladstone Symphony Orchestra. Kate Heinrichs. You conducted us once."

"I do remember that, but what of it?" he asked warily with the door still just ajar. "Explain yourself quickly or I will be obliged to contact the authorities."

"Look, my boyfrie... colleague in the orchestra, he's... we've been working with some researchers from U of T—the University of Toronto—and they have come to the conclusion that certain pieces of music are causing the deaths. Oh, for God's sake, I'm just not explaining this well."

She was tired, dehydrated, jetlagged and cramping. His expression of hostility and incomprehension caused her suddenly to collapse inside. What am I doing at this stranger's door, in the rain, in this great big dirty city? The further away from East Gladstone she was, the more absurd this whole thing seemed. The expression on the old gentleman's face made her see through his eyes how ridiculous she must appear. And why did it have to be *now*, when I knew how my body would feel? It all welled up and spilled out and she began to cry.

When he saw the tears and the rain-dampened clothing the old conductor's heart melted a little and, intrigued just slightly more than irritated, he ushered her gently into the house. He put her case in the hall and led her to a sitting room; he sat her down in a chair and pressed a handkerchief into her hand.

"It's all right; really," he said. "I have no idea what this is all about, but if you've come all the way from Canada in such a terrible rush, it must be important to you."

She nodded through her tears. "I know I've made a complete mess of explaining this to you..."

"Well, you just sit there for a while and compose yourself. I'm going to get you a nice cup of tea, and perhaps a few biscuits."

She looked around the tall ceilinged room with its bookcases, chandelier and grand piano and felt small, foolish and rural. She hated herself for appearing like a silly little girl; where was the sophisticated musician with the fine tastes for music and wine and art? Again she asked herself: what am I doing here sitting in this great man's house, so far from home on this fool's errand? Her jetlag was cultural; it had nothing to do with the mere difference of a few hours. Suddenly plucked from her comfortable world, she was tiny, lonely and vulnerable.

Sir Arthur came back presently with a tray of tea and set it down on a table beside her chair. Kate had dried her face quickly with the handkerchief while he was gone, and had tried to do something with her hair, although she knew she still looked mess. As she watched this patrician gentleman stooping to pour her tea, asking after milk and sugar and Digestive biscuits, she was again struck with the hopelessness of her mission.

"I do remember you now," said Sir Arthur, looking at her closely and nodding his head slightly while he put down the teapot. He smiled. "You were hatching plans to kidnap me."

Kate nodded, glad she had spoken up and thanking almost-divine intervention that she had asked him for his card that day. His recognition of her seemed to have dissolved some resistance, and that gave her new heart.

"However, young lady," he continued, "I simply do not understand what you are talking about."

"They died while playing certain pieces of very popular music. I *wish* I could explain it more clearly! But, the calculations show that *Finlandia* is a danger. Whoever conducts *Finlandia* is putting himself in terrible danger!"

"But this is madness! How could music be dangerous?" His hostility began to return and only the presence of tea moderated his behaviour. "I've never heard of anything so ridiculous!"

New resolve welled up as his anger rose; she was again in front of that reception desk clerk in Toronto and acting the perfect bitch.

"You *must* accept what I say! You have no choice! Listen, exactly one day before the death of Janos Bertil in Warsaw we predicted that Bruckner's Fourth Symphony would become dangerous. We *knew*! Damn it, we *knew*!"

"You predicted this?" She had got through. He sat for a long while pursing his lips and nodding his head slowly while Kate drank some tea. Oh, it was so-o-o good! But she couldn't face the biscuits.

"And you propose what?" The animosity returned. "That we change the entire program of the Royal Festival Hall at the last minute on the say-so of an agitated young lady from a small town in Ontario? Is that what you are suggesting?"

"No, no. It's... we... the scientists... have perfected a baton that will alleviate the problem. I have one here."

She took the baton out of her shoulder bag and handed it to him. He took it with a look of utter incomprehension, disbelief once again covering his face, and held it at arm's length as though awaiting a venomous bite. When she looked at his face and saw the baton in his hand, she realized anew how absurd this must appear. She knew he was on the verge of dismissing her and sending her packing out of his house.

"And just where did you and your, ah, friends purchase this item?" he asked with acid sarcasm. "Diagon Alley?"

What kind of madness had been delivered upon him this rainy Friday morning by this bedraggled specimen?

The perfect bitch disappeared and again the tears came, an emotional roller coaster quite out of her control. The old conductor's heart was newly softened. He looked down at this tired, damp, disheveled young woman and he was filled with pity. He had a daughter, about her age. What harm can come, he thought, from humouring the young lady and using her damned baton?

But wait: the series of mysterious deaths—the so-called Symphabomber—has not yet been explained. The attacks are random and worldwide. How would it be if a young, attractive and impassioned actress were to show up at a conductor's house and persuade him with tears and pleas to use a baton of her providing? He wondered if the unlucky thirteen who had already died could have told a similar tale, softened by the sobs of a lovely young girl. But surely, the killers would hardly concoct such a cock-and-bull story; would they not simply provide the conductor with a baton as a free sample with no obligation to purchase? Besides, you could hardly hide anything bigger than a tuppeny banger in there anyway. No, his heart and reason told him that this young lady was the genuine article. He made his decision.

"My dear, I have never in my entire life heard such a load of unmitigated bollocks. I don't believe one syllable of what you have told me, but I'll tell you what I'm going to do. I will use your damned baton when I conduct tonight. I promise." And he waved it about, weighing it in his hand.

Kate applied his handkerchief to her face again. "I'm sorry, I am not usually so stupid. It's been... a bit of a trial..."

"As I say, I promise you I will use your baton, and here..." He turned to a side table and wrote quickly with a fountain pen upon the back of a business card. "Give this to David at the box office and he'll see you get a good seat. You do know where the Royal Festival Hall is?"

She took the card and nodded.

"Well then, you get yourself on your way." He led her to the front door. "There's a taxi rank just at the end of the road, on Sloane Street." He pointed the way. "Ask the taxi driver to find you an hotel... Oh, you have one already? You are most fortunate with all this sportive nonsense going on. Then get some rest, a nice hot bath and you'll be as right as rain."

She was on the sidewalk when he called her back.

"Just a mo. Look, give this to one of the ushers after the concert and ask him or her to find Sebastian for you." He came down the steps and handed her another card. "Sebastian will help you find me backstage; after all, you'll want a report on your magic wand, won't you, Hermione?"

He smiled and returned to the house.

The taxi took her swiftly to the hotel that Stan had booked, in a narrow road off Waterloo Station. The driver had pointed out the Royal Festival Hall on the South Bank of the Thames in an accent that was almost incomprehensible—it sounded like Raw-festi-vlauw—so she was able to get her bearings. She checked in and took the ancient elevator up to her floor. She was feeling dirty and feverish.

As soon as she got into the room she parked her wheelie, threw her shoulder bag onto the bed, threw off all her clothes and went to check the bathtub. It was an ancient cast iron job on lion's paw legs and when she turned the taps they cried chugga-chugga-bugger and discharged a thin stream of cold water. She waited with her hand under the spigot, adjusting the taps until it began to flow warm. She couldn't wait for the bath to fill, so she pulled the vinyl shower curtains around, stepped in and luxuriated in the water streaming off her body. She found soap in the dish attached to the wall, tore off the paper wrapping and soaped away the frustration, humiliation and tiredness.

Once satisfied she went back into the bedroom carrying a spare towel, which she spread out on the bed. She laid herself down still wet with her arms away from her sides, legs apart, and allowed evaporation to cool away the fever. Presently, she rose, dried the places where evaporation hadn't reached, and went back to the bathroom to attend to herself. She thanked God she was well supplied; the thought of mooching around the Waterloo backstreets looking for a drugstore that had feminine products she might recognize was daunting.

When Kate put on clean panties and a bra from her case she felt a thousand times better. She threw herself down on the bed in her underwear and flipped her phone open.

"Hi Jonathan, it's me in big, strange London." Oh, if you could see me now!

She hadn't called him before because of the five-hour time difference, and truly she hadn't wanted to anyway because she knew she would break down and cry. Now she felt stronger; clean, optimistic, mission half accomplished, so she told him briefly of her adventures and promised to call back later after the concert.

She fiddled with the bedside alarm and set it for five-thirty in the afternoon, laid down on the side of the bed not dampened by her towel, and fell into a quick and deep sleep.

Kate woke to the alarm clock and spent some seconds surfacing and remembering where she was. She hadn't eaten since the breakfast on the plane—a 'fruit' salad that was mostly water-melon except for one grape, some synthetic orange juice and a very dry muffin—but she was still too keyed-up and worried to eat. She dressed quickly, put on minimal make-up, and headed down in the elevator, remembering to take her coat with her.

"Do you have a map of London, please?" she asked at the front desk on the ground floor.

"Certainly love," replied the middle-aged woman behind the desk. "This one's just central London, see, would that be awright? Look, it folds up nice and small."

She thanked the lady, spread the map out on the desk, located the Royal Festival Hall on its outer, unfashionable southern edge and saw that it was, indeed, a very short walk from where she was. The rain had ceased, but the streets were still wet and the sky frowned down on her. She set out slowly, getting herself used to the pedestrian crossings with the traffic going the 'wrong way', the noise, and the constantly moving crowds. She marveled at the huge Ferris wheel that dominated the South Bank, watched the river traffic and heard trains rumble over Hungerford Bridge to Charing Cross. As she walked she held an on-going dialogue in her mind with Jonathan, discussing all she saw with him, and remembering with anguish the imaginary dialogues he conducted down by the lake that was so far away. It was hard not to resent having to share him with the ghost who took such greedy slices of the pie, but here she had him all to herself.

She arrived early at the concert venue, but was glad to sit in the foyer and take in the scene around her. I wish I'd traveled more when I was younger, she thought, but there never was much time what with the farm and all. She was hit with a sudden pang; she should have called Mum and Dad, just to tell them where she was going, but it had been driven from her mind. She resolved to call as soon as she was back home in East Gladstone.

After a short rest on a soft bench in sight of the box office, Kate got up and walked over to the wicket. She passed the card Sir Arthur had given her through the window and asked for David.

"That's me. Come to the right window. Less see... How about

slap bang in the middle, ten rows back? That suit you?"

"That's wonderful. Thank you. You've been very kind."

"Don't thank me; thank S'r'Arthur. He likes 'is guests to get a good view."

Mercifully, *Finlandia* was first on the program because by the time the orchestra members had seen to their warm-ups, the concertmaster had taken his bow, and Sir Arthur Compton had appeared from the wings, Kate was once again a nervous mess. But as soon as the first rumbling bars swelled out she knew in her heart that all was well; she knew without knowing how she knew that this day Sir Arthur would be safe from harm. Perhaps it was her wound-up emotional state, perhaps it was the brand new and strange ambience, or perhaps it was her secure knowledge that all was well; the tears streamed down her cheeks and she didn't care who saw it.

Never before had she experienced so much emotion from this, one of the oldest of the old favourite chestnuts. It was as if she was hearing a concert for the first time, had never been a run-of-the-mill second violin doing exactly this day after day. The music fed her as if she was new; it filled her with an inexplicable childish joy.

In the intermission, after a rapid and highly civilized bathroom break—where she discovered that British architects had solved the gender conundrum—she bought a sandwich and a coffee from the bar. Even though her stomach was far from right she felt she ought to eat something.

Kate returned to her seat in a state of warm, almost cocooned, contentment. She didn't really remember too much of the second half; jetlag, relief, fatigue and joy crowded out mere sensory input. At the conclusion of the concert she sought out Sir Arthur with the help of Sebastian, and was shown to a small dressing room in the rear of the building.

Sir Arthur Compton regarded Kate Heinrichs appraisingly with raised eyebrows, rolling the baton slowly between his fingers and nodding slowly. She wished she could read his mind, at least to break the tension she felt under his gaze. Doubt crowded into her mind again, driving away joy. Finally, he spoke, and what he said came out well prepared from his long appraisal.

"I don't know what sort of magicians you and your friends are. In all my years of conducting music I have heard and seen many strange things, but I have never had the sort of experience I have had tonight. I don't know what this thing is," poising the baton horizontally between his two index fingers, "but the fear of stepping up to the podium is no longer there."

Kate was so filled with relief and awe she couldn't speak. She just stared at the great conductor with mouth slightly open and eyes wide.

"We'll say no more now, Ms Heinrichs. Come to my house tomorrow for lunch. We have a great deal to discuss. A great deal. Around twelve, shall we say?"

She found her voice. "Thank you. Thank you so much for listening to me. I'll... I'll see you tomorrow."

Kate wafted back through the streets to her hotel, rose in the elevator to her floor in a daze, and called Jonathan as soon as she was back in her room. She gave him the incredible news, tired beyond imagining, and then quickly turned off her phone as soon as she had finished speaking.

She quickly threw off her top clothes, and crashed on the bed into dreamless sleep while London honked and hooted and rumbled all oblivious outside her window.

Jonathan had been overjoyed when Kate had phoned earlier on Friday to tell him she had arrived in London and that the first leg of the baton relay race had been accomplished. They had talked very briefly—she sounded exhausted—and she promised to call back after *Finlandia.* He kept thinking about their parting on Wednesday evening, standing on the landing of her apartment, when she had asked if they would see each other before his flight. Every time he played the scene in his mind it looked worse, and he wondered how he could have been so unfeeling. The rest of the day he spent walking by the lake, sitting in cafés on the main drag, wandering the town, waiting and waiting.

Since his return from the abortive attempt to leave the country, he had displaced Graham Swann from first oboe—pissing him off all over again—and rendering Stephanie re-unemployed, while returning to the orchestra as if nothing had happened. The first thing he did was to take Stefan Kulikofski aside and press upon him the first of the magical batons, the one that had been refused entry into the United States. Encouraged, invigorated and relieved Kulikofski swore he would conduct the orchestra on Friday—tonight—and on Saturday as well. There really *was* something in these batons. But what...?

Now he was footloose, with his whole mind centred on a city some five-and-a-half thousand kilometers to the east. Around five-thirty, at a point in his random wanderings just beyond the windmill, the phone rang. He grabbed it out of his pocket on the first ring. It was her!

"Kate, Kate, oh God it's so good to hear from you... It did? Oh, that's incredible! He did?... But... Oh, wow! We didn't dare hope. Wait 'til I tell the rest... So, lunch with him tomorrow? Ooh, you must have made a good impression. Phone us then... we'll all be waiting at Ivy Lea, what'll it be?... about nine? Great." He took a long pause while he marshaled his thoughts. Too long. "Look Kate... I just wanted to say..." God damn it, she's gone; thought they'd finished! He called back immediately, but her phone was off. Damn! Well, at least he had heard her voice.

He hurried back into town to tell the Wards the good news. While walking swiftly by the lake he called Makharam and shared the news. He was almost deafened by the whooping at the other end in Toronto, and just hoped that Celia was nowhere in earshot.

It worked, it worked! Jesus, it worked! But what does it really mean? It's all just feelings...

Jonathan stopped quickly by his apartment, collected his oboe, and hurried to the hall to lend his support to the Brahms concert and the CBC radio airing. He was an old hand; the one thing that seldom happened to him before any gig was any hint of nervousness. Tonight, to his great surprise, as soon as he took his place on the platform of the East Gladstone Centennial Centre he had an attack of what he could only describe as the heebie-jeebies. What if Kulikofski chickened out; what if he stopped believing in the baton; what if he lost the damned thing? And what the hell would be the repercussions of the country-wide airing of a complete dog's breakfast? Such uncertainty simply didn't happen to him; rigid control was what he was all about. So why was he sitting here on the stage, shuffling and reshuffling his scores and fiddling with his reeds like a bloody newbie? Concentrate for Christ's sake man! As he willed himself to focus on the task in hand and banish all his foolish misgivings, the thought of Kate asleep in a strange bed far away, floated across his inner eye. This was getting ridiculous. He breathed deeply and slowly, willing his heart rate down and forcing the distractions out of his mind. By the time the maestro had appeared and taken his bow Jonathan was again the consummate professional.

The Brahms Symphony No. 1 was spectacular, although the consummation was long in coming because it was featured in the second half of the program. The Mozart and Weber went well enough, but the musicians all knew that the true test was in the second half. When it came to the moment, Stefan Kulikofski conducted like a true maestro, and all the hard work they had done in the preceding weeks was repaid with interest. Although the audience were completely unaware of the sub-text, the liberating feeling of having your conductor back safely on the podium—and, with him there, job security—caused all the musicians to far excel themselves. The audience only knew that they had witnessed a truly great moment in the history of the East Gladstone Symphony Orchestra.

Kate awoke on Saturday morning to sunshine streaming in the window, making the dingy glass panes glare yellow. She remembered having woken and taken a bathroom break in the night, but she had fallen back asleep and it was now half-past-nine. She went ruefully through her small supply of clothes and unfolded the only dress she'd brought, one of the pale blue ones she liked so much. It wasn't too creased and with the help of a damp face cloth she got it looking quite presentable. When she had showered and dressed she took the lift down to the ground floor and sought the breakfast room. There was a fine variety of foods in the buffet, and it appeared you could have a Continental breakfast of just pastries, fruit, yogurt and such like, or go the whole hog with the sausages, bacon, eggs, mushrooms and fried bread. Her stomach heaved at the thought. Her digestion was still not right, and as she would be lunching in Belgravia (my, how swish *that* sounded), she ate a simple light breakfast, followed by a cup of mediocre coffee that didn't sit well.

Kate decided to set out early for Belgravia and to walk the whole way. The sun was shining, she desperately needed to stretch her legs and calm her stomach, and who knew when she would have the time and leisure again. She had checked her route on the little tourist map and saw that it passed by several memorable places.

She walked over Hungerford Bridge on the pedestrian way beside the train tracks, pausing several times to look down on the heads of the passengers in the pleasure boats and shuttles passing beneath her, then went slowly up to the Strand, and thence to Trafalgar Square. As she stood there looking at Nelson's Column, the fountains, and the façade of the National Portrait Gallery she found it hard to believe she was actually standing here, seeing these things. It was more real than real. The internal dialogues continued as she enjoyed the sight of the legendary pigeons, fewer now since their feeding had been outlawed. She strolled slowly through Admiralty Arch and encountered the vista of Pall Mall with Buckingham Palace at its end. When she drew near to the Palace after a long slow walk she noticed the flag was flying, remembering that this was the sign the Queen was in residence. She went slowly up Constitution Hill to Hyde Park Corner, and thus to the northern limits of Belgravia. She arrived at the house unfashionably early and decided to walk around the square until noon, pausing every so often to sit on a park bench in the square and watch the world go by.

At exactly twelve on her watch she rose from her seat, crossed the road and walked up the steps to the big front door. Just a day ago, she thought, and look how the world has changed. Ooh la la, I'm lunching in Bel-gravi-ah!

Sir Arthur opened the door himself and showed her in. This time they went further back in the house, and into a small lunch-room that looked out onto a long, lush garden. Lunch was laid out on a glass-topped table; an assortment of small sandwiches and cakes dominated by the same teapot and cups as yesterday. The baton lay beside the tea tray. A tall and handsome lady of about Sir Arthur's age with high cheekbones and deep set eyes rose from her chair to meet her.

"Welcome to our home," she said in a melodious tone with an eastern European flavour. What a gorgeous voice, thought Kate, she must be a singer.

Sir Arthur performed the introductions. "This is my wife Katrina. And, Katrina, this is the magician I told you about, Kate Heinrichs. Or perhaps Miss Granger would be more accurate! She fronts this group of wizards in Ontario."

"Please sit down... here, in this chair you will see better to the garden. So."

"Do help yourself to a sandwich or two," Sir Arthur urged as he poured her tea.

Dammit, the man had even remembered from yesterday how much milk she liked and that she took no sugar. She helped herself to a very small cucumber sandwich; as neutral a filling as possible because her stomach was still dodgy, although she hardly wanted to appear impolite. This was a bit of a mistake as she discovered there was some smoked salmon lurking under the cucumber. The tea helped.

"Now," began Sir Arthur, wiping crumbs from his lips with a napkin, "there is a great deal I need to know."

Here it comes, thought Kate; just how do I even begin to explain the last few months? Jonathan would have been so much better as a spokesman. She nodded and awaited hard times.

"But," he continued, "I don't know if I *want* to know what this is all about, and perhaps you cannot explain it to me anyway, but let's just say that your appearance at my house yesterday has taken an enormous load off my mind. I no longer fear stepping up to the podium.

"With this," and he picked up the baton and conducted a few imaginary bars, "I know—God knows how—that I am safe from harm. So... how?"

"It's a heck of a long story, and I don't think you'll believe much of it, but you remember I told you yesterday that certain pieces of music had become dangerous? I know you don't believe it..."

"Correct. Unmitigated bollocks, as I said yesterday."

"...but the fact remains that my scientific colleagues have identified a flow of energy out of... well, somewhere... that has lethal force."

His expression convinced her that she wasn't getting anywhere. Then she thought of Jonathan's argument about Stan's hypothesis.

"Look, there's a physiological basis for energy disappearing from the human body while music is being played; the scientists at the University of Toronto have established that. So, there's energy pouring out, then reappearing, with these terrible results. There could be any number of explanations to connect these two phenomena, but our hypothesis is that certain pieces of music have been played so often that the energy must come out."

His expression was one of applied forbearance and patience. "Let us, just so we can move along, assume my reluctant acceptance of what you have just said. So! What kind of information sent you rushing from Canada in a huge panic, showing up like a drowned rat, thrusting a baton into my hand and begging me to use it?"

"We have compiled a list—our Top 50—of popular pieces of

music. Our analysis shows strong trends. I told you yesterday about Janos Bertil in Warsaw with Bruckner's Fourth. Very high on the list was *Finlandia*, and we saw that you would be conducting it, not once but three times. We test these suspect pieces—I really can't explain how, because I don't understand it—and our tests show us if they're... ready to pop... if you see what I mean?"

"So, *Finlandia* was, ah... ready to pop?" He placed round, rolling, sarcastic emphasis upon the phrase.

My God, she thought, this is tough sledding, but he's alive and well, and that's really all that counts.

"And, what I am feeling," he continued, "is this energy coming out and passing through my body in a continuous trickle, rather than all at once?"

She nodded. A roguish expression crossed his face.

"Hmm. Bit of a setback for an old gent like me. Us old chaps prefer it to come out in one big rush, rather than little trickles."

They laughed and Katrina reached over and shoved his shoulder. "Behave yourself in front of this young lady!"

"And your wizard friends then devised this baton, a conductor for the conductor so to speak. And so now all is well." His applied levity was clearly a thin veneer.

"We could wish! We've saved your life—at least we think we have—but we can hardly go around the world shoving batons into maestro's hands and begging them to use them."

"Well, I'm not so sure. If you were as persuasive with them as you were with me, you might just pull it off!"

His face then took on a serious aspect and he rose from his chair and came round the table to her. He placed a hand on her shoulder.

"In all honesty, Kate, whether or not I believe one tenth of what you have told me, the truth of the matter is, I do believe what you said just now; I do believe you have saved my life. And that's what counts the most. And I am forever grateful."

She couldn't help herself; she stood and hugged him, and he hugged her back, father to daughter. Presently she sat, a little embarrassed, while he returned to his chair, but she saw that Katrina was smiling at her and her husband, and the sun shone in from the garden behind her, green and golden.

"So, really, it's a question of where you go from here, isn't it Kate?"

"Well, first of all, back to my chair with the EGO, then we'll see."

"EGO? I thought it was EGSO?"

Kate coloured at her faux pas. "I'm... I'm sorry... slip of the tongue..."

He smiled, and the smile spoke volumes that could now be left unsaid. Their eyes met and complete agreement passed between them.

"I meant, of course, regarding the magic baton. Do you have a... reading... of who or what is next?"

"I don't know but Jonathan... my... the colleague I'm working with is doing the analysis." She laughed. "I'm just passing the baton!"

"And a very nice relay racer, too. Now, look. What we should do is this." She was delighted by the 'we'. "We should call your... colleagues and discuss the next steps. I don't know what I'll be able to do, but I can try. If there's any persuading that needs doing, you can count on me. This silly little toy," he waved the baton about, "has taken a vast load off my mind. You and I are duty bound to share it. So, let's go up to the office and call 'em. Do they have Skype?"

Kate was nonplussed; this revered, traditional gentleman of the old school was wired? Wonders would never cease. Then she thought of Stan Ward and felt a little embarrassed at her presumption.

Sir Arthur caught her expression. "Not such an old fossil after all, eh?" he smiled. "Look. You have probably perceived that I am a caricature of myself; you see, it's something that happens to us English gents. Probably something in the water. But it's only skin deep, if that. Come on, let's get connected. See you in minute my dear."

She sat in front of the computer in his office while he pulled up a chair and sat with his head just over her left shoulder.

"I hope he has his laptop with him. I promised I'd phone, but I don't know where he'll be."

The connection was made and in a short time Jonathan's face appeared briefly on the screen, followed by blurring and sickening movement as the laptop was repositioned. The picture settled with Jonathan in the centre and Stan and Sandra on a chesterfield in the background.

"Hey Kate, we're all here at Ivy Lea. Lucky I brought this with me; it's better than the phone 'cos I can see your face. Where the hell are y... Oh, Sir Arthur! I'm sorry, I didn't see you there."

"It's fine," replied Sir Arthur. "We're in my office."

"Stan, Sandra, this is Sir Arthur Compton. Stan's a professor at the university; our team leader, you could say."

"Pleased to meet you." They waved. "Now listen; as I have told Ms Heinrichs, I have really no idea what this is all about, but I do recognize the effectiveness of your solution. I am indeed convinced that you have saved my life—although I'm damned if I know how—and I owe you an enormous debt of gratitude. But for the immediate future, we clearly need to know when and where you predict the next attack to take place so that precautions can be taken. As I have told Kate here, I am willing to help in any way I can."

"This is more than we could have hoped for. Thank you!" Stan Ward called from the background. "We have a list, we have some predictions, but we'll need to do some more work."

"As soon as you know, you *must* call me. Now, who is responsible for designing this wonderful baton?"

"Well, Jonathan..." began Kate, before he interrupted quickly.

"No, no, it's another member of our team, Dr Khan. He's not with us at the moment."

The less anybody knew about his role in this the better he liked it.

"Well, look, Kate, you can give me his Skype address, e-mail, phone number, whatever, because I need to know as much as I can about these damned batons. Meanwhile, who's next; when and where? Key questions."

"We'll get onto it right now," replied Jonathan. "And thank you; thank you so much."

"It's me who should thank you!" He paused. "Well... I'm sure Kate can tell you all the details later. Goodbye for now."

"See you soon, Jonathan," said Kate. "I'll call you later about my return flight. I think I'll come back tomorrow if I can."

"Okay, bye." Kate didn't miss the slight shade of disappointment on his face, and felt that he would have said much more in a private phone call. Well, that could wait until later.

They returned to the lunchroom with the golden view of the garden. Katrina Compton had made some more tea, which Kate accepted gratefully, although she politely refused any more food.

Sir Arthur picked up the baton again.

"Bloody marvelous. The wonders of technology. Y'know, when I was a lad all this..." he spread his arms wide "...was pure fantasy. Click, we're seeing your chap in Canada; click, we're booking flights around the world; click, my bacon is saved by an electronic doo-dah that might just as well have come out of a flying saucer!"

"Please keep that one, because you never know."

"Prophylactic qualities, eh?" Swish, swish. "Although you might not want to market it quite like that." He got another shove on the shoulder for this. "Everybody should have one. You'll have to open a factory."

His perceptiveness floored her. The further development of this project had never entered her head, and suddenly it was all rather strange and unsettling. I'm just a violinist... How to even begin...?

"Our old maestro... er, conductor was a member of an international organization. Perhaps that would be a good place to start?"

His expression seemed to show otherwise.

"Well, I'm not really in contact with most of those chaps. I call 'em the High Flyers." He paused a moment, weighing Kate up before coming to a decision. "Well, this may be talking out of school, but frankly, most of them are just too damned fond of themselves. No, let me clarify; I am very fond of myself as well, of course. In fact, I think I am my favourite person, but I don't go around trying to convince other people of it. Certainly, I have the bottle to stand up in front of eighty highly talented and accomplished individuals and tell 'em how I want 'em to express themselves. So, yes, I have the big ego too, and the side to go with it, but it's my business and nobody else's. That being said, I might be able to exert some influence if necessary. It's an issue of vanity. Just have to find a way to massage their... ah... EGSOs!"

"Well, I don't know how to thank you," she smiled. "We'll all get working on this. I'm sorry, but it's all rather strange and new, and I'm not sure how it will all pan out. And now, I really should get back and sort things out. I have an open ticket so I should book my flight."

She stood.

"But you should stay in London for a few days; stay here with us. There's so much to see, so why not take the opportunity?"

"It's kind of you, really, but I'm tired and I just want to go home."

"So be it. Too late for your flight today, so do see a little more while you can."

"Yes, please," urged Katrina, "do take a little time until you leave as a tourist. We want you to think well of our city."

Kate took her leave with thanks and promises, and walked slowly and gently in the direction she had come. Indeed, there was time for a little sightseeing and the weather was keeping fair and mild. But she felt flat, drained and lonely. Yes, time to go home.

Mission accomplished.

Symphony No. 4 in G Major

As soon as the Skype connection was broken Jonathan, Stan and Sandra leapt to their feet and joined together in a triple hug. They called Makharam in Toronto and gave him the good news with more rejoicing. They agreed to get in touch as soon as Kate returned, and then arrange to meet. Clearly, they had their work cut out for them. It was essential to identify the next item on the list and prove, with a playing session in the cage, that it was indeed ready to reflux. And then there was the issue of a supply of batons. He and Makharam really hadn't thought this through; the demand for them (assuming the end-users could be convinced of their efficacy) was potentially enormous. Jonathan decided to shelve all these issues until later because there was something much more pressing on the immediate horizon; his presence in the orchestra. There was the trial-by-fire Brahms tonight and he had some work to do on the scores.

"So, Kate might fly back to Ottawa tomorrow," he said as he stood up. "Just wondering how she'll get home from there; probably have to take a bus."

"Oh, God help her!" cried Sandra. "Don't talk to me about transport in Ottawa; I had to take a humanities grant application up there last year. They have a bus station that's nowhere near downtown, they have a train station in the middle of the industrial east end, and an airport that connects with neither of them. And, wonder of wonders, the taxi companies are rolling in money. Oh, and a light rail spur line that goes from nowhere to nowhere. And it's a Sunday, of course."

"So, bus isn't a good idea?"

"No, you can't get here from there anyway," added Stan. "If she took a bus, she'd have to change in Toronto. Why not have her fly to Toronto on the Air Canada shuttle; there's one every hour from Ottawa. We can all go down tomorrow afternoon and pick her up at Pearson. If she's worried I'll foot the bill."

"It's okay, she's going to call me later, so I'll check it with her then book a flight. Don't worry, it'll go on my credit card. But thanks." He made for the door. "And now I have to get moving."

"Then, there's the matter of our homework assignments," sighed Stan raising the irksome topic. "Have to test the Top 50 list. Hate to be so melodramatic, Jonathan, but someone's life might well depend upon it."

"I know, I know," he replied with his hand on the doorknob. "But I'm doing a big concert tonight, and I absolutely have to play some music this afternoon. It is really, really critical. Last night was terrific, but we have to do it again, and it's got to be as good, if not better. I may be only guessing, but from my previous reading, I don't think either Mahler's Fourth or *Pictures at an Exhibition* is ready yet. We might have some breathing space. At least, I hope so."

"Okay, why don't we wait until after Kate's back?"

"I guess that's best..." Was he gambling with someone's life, or was there, in fact, enough time? How reliable were his feelings as a guide? The weight showed in the sag of his shoulders.

"It's so tough on you, isn't it?" sighed Stan, wishing he could understand even slightly what the lad was going through every time he did this.

"Yeah. I love it and I hate it. No, not love exactly; it's more... I dunno, lust maybe. Oh, words are just useless. And what worries me is, I can't see any end in sight. How long do I have to keep doing this?"

"Wish I knew. See you tomorrow afternoon, then?"

"You coming to the concert tonight?"

"Wouldn't miss it. We'll stand up in the middle and wave at you. Might even whistle if you're really good."

Jonathan gave Stan's shoulder a little squeeze and went out of the door.

He left Ivy Lea and walked quickly home, feeling guilty at the second place his practice sessions had been taking, worried about his shifting priorities, and determined to get back to music with a will. As soon as he got home he sorted out his music and plunged in. There was some stuff in the Brahms that could be even better. He left the phone on the table beside him, but only Kate's voice would be allowed to displace his attention from the oboe.

She phoned around midday, just when he was thinking of pausing for a little liquid refreshment. He seized the phone on the first ring and started in, trying to follow the script imprinted in his mind from long repetition, while she listened in silence.

"Look, when I left on Wednesday... I feel really bad I didn't want to say goodbye. It's..." the script was shredding "...I don't want you to think I don't care... didn't care... 'cos..."

She was getting used to intervening, slowing him down, and she did this now, not putting words into his mouth, but making words superfluous. She placed a phantom hand gently on his arm and told him that everything was just fine. Relief washed over him, then gratitude. Practicality returned quickly.

"AC888 into Ottawa tomorrow? I'm going to book you on the Ottawa/Toronto shuttle at, let's see..." he opened the Air Canada website and checked the schedules "...four o'clock. I'll book it now. We'll all be there to meet you. Bye."

Oh God, I can't wait to see her...

That evening's concert was better yet. How they could have improved upon Friday's offering, which had been aired across the country, Jonathan didn't know, but he was confident they had. When it comes to judgments of that kind, rational comparisons fall away in deference to feelings, sensations and the heart's thoughts of the moment. Collectively, they knew how good it had been, how together they had achieved surpassing excellence, and that was what mattered most. Such musical moments exist in the 'now' and can never, ever be recaptured.

Early on Sunday afternoon Jonathan joined the Wards at Ivy Lea, and together they set off to Pearson Airport to collect Kate from her Ottawa shuttle flight. They got there early and were at the arrivals gate with time to spare. Watching the monitors and waiting for her flight arrival to be signaled was agony for Jonathan. Now he just wanted to see her, to thank her, to... to just know she was there.

He spotted her before she saw him; he stepped forward and enveloped her in his arms right in front of the sliding doors before she had a chance to let go of her wheelie case or drop her shoulder bag. The bag dropped to the floor and the handle of the case swung out sideways as she wrapped her arms around him. Irritated travelers diverted around them.

"Gads," observed Stan laconically to Sandra from their post against a far wall, "that's the first time I've seen them as much as touch each other. The plot thickens."

The younger couple came over to where they were standing, Jonathan wheeling Kate's case. Kate was pale and looked tired and travel worn.

"Look Kate," beamed Stan, "we'd like to have you two stay over at our place tonight. It'll be better than that drive back up to East Gladstone."

"I can run your stuff through the wash," suggested Sandra, seeing the doubtful expression on Kate's face, "because I'm sure you didn't take too much with you."

Kate glanced briefly at Jonathan and then back to the Wards, and they could see the doubts in her mind.

"We have two guest rooms," Sandra assured her, "and we'd love you to stay."

That settled it. She was tired and felt sick, and the thought of a soft bed only a short drive away did the trick.

"I'd love to, but I'm afraid I won't be very good company, if you don't mind."

Stan retrieved the car from the parking lot and met them at the arrivals door. Their house in The Beach was a good distance, across the other side of Toronto from Pearson, but the traffic had mercy upon them and in forty-five minutes they were in the door. Sandra took charge of Kate, showed her the bath and the spare bedroom, and took away her clothes to wash. When she peeped into the spare bedroom Kate was asleep under the sheets.

"I don't think she'll sleep long," she told the others, "and it might be an idea to wake her soon anyway. She won't have changed her sleep patterns over just a couple of days, so she'll be back to normal pretty quickly."

"Sure," said Stan. "Maybe wake her in an hour. Time supper for about seven-thirty?"

"Sure. Her laundry should be through by then. Have to see what's in the fridge. Might just do a monster omelet with some cheese and ham and stuff."

"Look," said Stan, "I've got this bottle of champagne, and I'm damned if we haven't got something to celebrate. How about we call Makharam and see if he can come round later this evening? I think we should fete our two geniuses and our brave, intrepid courier as well. What do you say?"

"Great!" cried Jonathan. "Let's do it!"

"Stan, get that bottle into the fridge," directed Sandra, "and I'll see what materials I can find to make an omelet into a feast. Jonathan, go sit down in the living room and take it easy. If you're lucky, Stan might even crack out his Laphroaig."

Stan called Makharam Khan and invited him round for eight o'clock, then retrieved his precious whisky and poured two generous glasses. Just over an hour later a freshly minted Kate Heinrichs appeared at the door of the kitchen.

"I feel a thousand percent better. It's amazing what a quick snooze, a bath and a complete change of clothes does. And for the first time in a few days I am really starving!"

"Well, then, my dear, you've come to the right place. Go and sit with the gents and I'll call you all to the table as soon as may be."

It was a simple and excellent meal. Kate went over all the things she had seen and done in London, describing in detail the meetings with Sir Arthur and the mystical encounter with *Finlandia*. For all her appetite, the omelet was not far from cold by the time she got around to it. While she spoke the Wards couldn't help but notice the way Jonathan hung on her every word, watching her face as she described her adventures.

They left the dishes just where they were and moved into the living room. It was not long before the doorbell rang and Khan was ushered into the house. There was much hand-shaking and congratulation, and kisses on both cheeks for Kate and Sandra. The champagne cork narrowly missed a vase and two framed family photos, but such was the skill of the opener, only a whiff of white vapour escaped the neck.

Professor Stanley Ward was the first to propose a toast, holding his flute of bubbly aloft.

"Firstly, to Kate Heinrichs, our brave courier, without whom none of this would have been possible; to Doctors Makharam Khan and Jonathan Rycroft, for an invention that passeth all understanding; to Sir Arthur Compton *in absentio* for his anticipated future support; and of course to Dr Sandra Ward for devotion above and beyond, and so on and so forth. Cheers!"

And they hoisted their glasses.

"And here's to Professor Stanley Ward, Emeritus," shouted Jonathan into the din, "for leading us on the craziest wild goose chase in the annals of science or music!"

They drank again. Then Makharam Khan raised his glass. "Here's to Sir Arthur Compton, once again! I have been in communication with the gentleman, and I believe that great plans will unfold. Early yet, but I have great ideas."

And that was all he would say. More bubbles went downrange.

"And now," announced Stan when all the champagne had gone and a reflective mood had settled on the company, "we deserve a special treat."

He stooped down to the liquor cupboard under the bookshelves. Jonathan fully expected the Laphroaig or the Lagavulin to be brought out, but instead there emerged a squat cardboard tube.

"And now, let's pour ourselves a little Edradour, shall we?"

He began to slide the bottle out of its protective sheath, and noticed Kate's expression.

"What's *that* face for, my dear? Have you never tasted real Scotch whisky?"

She admitted she hadn't, and wondered if it wouldn't be wasted on her. Frankly, with tiredness from travel, the emotional hammering she had taken, and the champagne still working, the last thing she wanted was a further chemically induced loss of control. Still, perhaps a little sip would be fine and—who knows? —she might even get to like it.

"This," announced Stan to the company, holding the bottle aloft, "is the rarest of things. We bought it last year at the distillery itself in Pitlochry. It's the smallest distillery in the Highlands and ye only make the pilgrimage there if you want the best!"

He poured half an inch of the glorious liquid carefully into five tumblers and passed them reverently around. He held his glass before him, commanding their attention.

"Here's tae us,
Wha's like us,
Damn few,
And they're a' deid,
Mair's the pity!"

Sandra smiled a secret smile at him. "Aye, Stan, ye do that well... for a Sassenach."

They sipped quietly, taking their time, and Stan again officiated with the precious bottle. Even Kate took a refill.

After a good while, when the Edradour had done its thing, Jonathan remarked, "you know Stan, it's a huge pity... *massive* pity, that you'll get ab-so-lute-ly no credit for all this."

He waved his hand loosely.

Stan Ward sighed and shook his head. "Jonathan, let me put it this way. A hypothesis that excess energy produced by musicians is disappearing into a 'continuum' containing labeled files—which is nowhere describable or discernable in the entire sidereal universe—and is then blasting out and vapourizing tuxedo-clad fops, might not exactly be on top of the editorial pile in the offices of *Nature* or *Scientific American* any time soon. As long as this is the domain of crackpots like us, the bloody m-Axis will remain unreported."

He paused with an inward expression, perhaps regret, perhaps resignation.

"A pity really, because evidence of its existence constitutes Humanity's next great leap forward. It's in the same class of phenomena as the Higg's boson, quantum foam and the dark matter between the galaxies."

"Yeah, right between them... All that dark matter..." sighed Jonathan.

The remainder of the evening passed quietly and gently, but this was just an intermission. The future was unclear.

Jonathan and Kate needed to be back in East Gladstone on Monday to resume their musical lives, as rehearsals would begin again on Tuesday. Stan and Sandra would not be going back up to the lake; it was the end of their vacation. Although Stan insisted he could drive the young couple to East Gladstone, they were both adamant that they take the bus. In the end he drove them to Edward Street bus station and, amid further but futile protestations, bought their tickets for them.

"It's the least I could do; don't be silly! Now, Jonathan, I'm sorry to say, the project must go on. We need to identify the next on the list and then discuss our strategy further."

The last thing Kate and Jonathan wanted to think about was the bloody project, but lives depended on it. They were becoming martyrs to responsibility.

"Okay, I'll give you a call. Thanks for everything Stan." They shook hands, Kate kissed Stan on the cheek, just above that tickly beard, and they boarded the bus.

This early on Monday morning the bus was almost empty, so they took a pair of seats near the rear and quite isolated. They sat in silence for the greater part of the northward leg through Greater Toronto, gently holding hands and lost in their thoughts. It was only when the bus was accelerating onto Highway 401 that Kate spoke.

"What's the story with your passport? Can you travel?"

"Right now, no. They didn't take it, but it's flagged in some database. Still, I'm not planning on going anywhere." He sighed and rubbed his eyes. "It'll sort itself out. Least of my worries at the moment."

"We're not exactly doing any international travel with the

EGO, that's for sure. Those two gigs in Albany and Syracuse? We lost money on both of them!"

He nodded and was silent for a while, frowning, watching the speeding vehicles on the feeder lanes as they approached the turn-off for Highway 400 north.

Presently she turned her head from the scenery drifting past the window and looked into his eyes. "So, this thing with CSIS. Aren't you still in trouble with them?"

"No. Don't think so. Sure, I've used some mathematical tools I developed during the secret work, but they don't know that. And if they've been spying me and Makharam—which I'm sure they bloody well have—all they'll see is me helping to design a baton. Harmless. And deniable."

"It must be horrible to know you're being watched."

"Happens all the time on the stage."

She laughed while he smiled, then his expression turned serious again as a cloud briefly hid the sun.

"Kate, I need your help. I have to sit in that damned cage and identify some reflux items, and it's as much as I can do to drag myself in there. Could you come round to my place and just be there? Could you do that?"

He had come to this very reluctantly; he didn't want her seeing into his bedroom, but there was nobody else.

"Jonathan, of course I could." She squeezed his hand a little. "When? This afternoon?"

"No, it'll have to be this evening; want to collapse and do sweet nothing this afternoon."

She was on the verge of asking whether he wanted her to be around doing sweet nothing with him, but she sensed a pulling back from that fabulous hug at the airport. Once again, it was bide your time.

"Okay. Sure. Right after supper, then."

"Good. Get it done. We're on deck again tomorrow. Can't even remember what we're supposed to be going over."

"The Orff, of course! *Carmina Burana*."

"Yeah, of course it is! Christ! How could I forget? See, I just want to get this God-damned business with the batons and crap over and done with. I'm fried. And I was so friggin' high after the Brahms One..."

He was quiet and withdrawn for a kilometer or two of featureless Ontario farmland. Then the frown returned. "You know what it is about that cage? I've been thinking about this. That home-made piece of junk in my bedroom; it's just sleazy. Worldwide influence, life and death, and it's all centered on some piece of Rona hardware store crap in a small-town bedroom. Sleazy."

He sounded so tired. With all her sudden, exciting and frightening travels she hadn't really thought of all he'd been through; the humiliation of being turned back at the border, the worry about his passport and future travel and the anxiety over the invention. And, of course, the tug-of-war between her and... *her*. She said nothing, knowing there was more to come.

"You see, it's never ending. It's never going to stop and we're stuck at an impasse. It's no good trying to convince maestros of the need for these fucking batons, so it's on a piecemeal basis; I identify the pieces, we hope we can get Sir Arthur to persuade the potential victims to use the baton, then if that works we'll have to ship them out all over the bloody world. An even if all this works, who's going to manufacture them all? Makharam has done a great job making a couple of 'em, but he's not going to do it forever. It's never ending and I'm tired."

"We'll work it out," she assured him, with no clue as to how that might be achieved. "Somehow..."

"It's all very well to celebrate like we did," he continued, "but we don't really know if the damned batons even work. Feelings; it's all feelings. I just feel like saying screw 'em; if they want to blow up on the podium, let 'em."

"Please don't say that," she begged. "I know you don't really mean it. Think of Sir Arthur!"

"I know, I know. You're right, of course. We don't have any option; at least, I don't."

"We're in this together, and you know it. And there's sure to be something we can do!"

"There is. Let's watch the scenery go by, and let the future take care of its sweet self."

And they did that.

They went their separate ways at the bus station. There was a smell of rain in the air, so neither of them lingered long but hurried before the clouds should arrive. Kate headed home to enjoy a day of little structured activity, while Jonathan loafed around his apartment too distracted to engage in anything. He almost wished he had asked her to stick around, but it was just too damned complicated. The afternoon dragged to its end, and just as he was wondering whether he should call her, Kate rang at his door. She came in quickly bringing a breath of rain into the apartment, propped her violin case against the wall, and shed her wet coat and hat.

"Nasty out there; had to hurry."

There was a late summer storm coming in, and they were particularly spectacular when they drove across the lake from the south west.

"Here, let me take those; hang 'em up behind the door. See you brought your fiddle with you."

"Yes." She caught and held his eyes. "I want to feel what you feel. Get an idea of what it is you have to do."

"That's... that's really kinda brave of you. Er... look, why don't we do it right now and get it over with?"

"Fine by me. Lead on." She opened the case and took out the bow and instrument.

She followed him into the tiny bedroom, dominated by the electrostatic cage, and placed her violin and bow on the bed. He surreptitiously watched her face for signs of amusement, noting how she looked around the bedroom, and wondering with embarrassment what was going through her mind.

My God, a bedroom and a cage and a beautiful woman; what would the shrinks say?

"Good grief! The stuff we've got ourselves into, you and me!" she cried, lightening the mood considerably. "If I had believed when I won the East Gladstone audition that I'd be alone in some guy's bedroom with a metal cage..."

"You'd have run screaming," he completed. "Yeah. Sometimes I wonder... Well, never mind. I've got the first oboe part from Mahler's Fourth and bits of *Pictures at an Exhibition*, so I'll just do it. Keep an eye on me and just, well, stop me, okay?"

He sat down in the cage and closed the door. She watched carefully as he warmed up a little then began to play a few bars from the Mussorgsky. She noticed nothing about him that appeared in any way remarkable.

"Nothing doing there. I kinda wondered how *Pictures* made it so high on the list, but we'll have to watch it. Now for our old pal Mahler."

Again, he chose a few bars from the sheets in front of him, and this time Kate could see that he was off somewhere else. How long do I let him go on, she thought, and do I just barge in?

However, he seemed now to have developed the knack of knowing how far to go and before too long he put the oboe down and opened the door. He looked ragged and irritated.

"I can't keep doing this! Jesus!" He took a deep breath. "The Mahler's hotter than I thought, so I'd better check our database then e-mail Stan."

They returned to the living room and he sat down at the laptop, and pulled up the Excel spreadsheet of future concerts.

"Oh, for Christ's sake, an orchestra in Geneva! Wednesday! I'd better e-mail the results to Stan, and cc Makharam. See this is it," he cried. "How do we handle this? Great theory! Great intellectual exercise! But now the rubber hits the road. Who are we? Why are we doing this? We can't keep scrambling around. It's driving me bats!"

He slumped down over the keyboard with his face in his hands. Kate came and sat beside him and wordlessly put an arm around his shoulder. Presently he sat up, opened his e-mail and composed a brief note to Stan Ward:

'Stan: Mahler 4 problematic. Check spreadsheet Geneva Wed. Suggest you have Sir A send his baton. Keep me posted. J.'

"That's all I can do. It's like having a huge weight on your back. Bloody Sisyphus."

"I know. Sometimes I can't sleep for thinking about it. I was so ecstatic after London, but now the load is back again." She felt near to tears and suspected he did too.

"It's all so pointless!" he cried, leaping to his feet. "How the hell do we know if this isn't a total pile of bullshit? Feelings! That's all we have to go on. We have no hard data."

"But I was there in London, and I am convinced... Sir Arthur was convinced that the thing works."

"But we don't *know* it worked. Maybe *Finlandia* wasn't ready to go yet, eh? Maybe somewhere else in the world some poor asshole's going to stand up with a stick to conduct Sibelius and get blown to buggery for his trouble. And all because we were *wrong*. It's all feelings, and feelings are not science."

"But they're feeling exactly what you're feeling in the cage. What's the difference?"

"Just because *I'm* feeling it doesn't give it any more value, for Christ's sake. It's still useless as evidence!"

"Well, what else *can* we do?" she shouted, standing in front of him. "It's all very well for you to say it doesn't work. What more proof do you need?"

"You just don't get it, do you? *We have no proof at all.*" He stressed every word. "Not a single shred. All we know is that something *didn't* happen, not that something *did*. That is not evidence! And what happens if we find that even with the magic baton this bugger in Geneva still dies? And then his family finds out that, just before the event, we sold him a crock of shit. What then?"

"Oh come on! You can't be serious."

"I *am* serious. If he doesn't die we won't be any the wiser, but if he does die we'll have proof that it doesn't work. And lawyers breathing down our necks!"

"Oh Christ, that's just so negative..."

"Do you have anything better?"

"No, no, you know I don't." She was near to tears.

"No," he sighed, "I know you don't." All passion was suddenly dissipated by her tone, the catch in her voice. "No. I'm sorry, but this is just killing me."

He flung himself down on the chesterfield, head in hands. She stood across the room from him, arms folded, back rigid.

He looked up from his hands. "I'm sorry, I truly am. I just can't bear the thought of coming so far and having nothing to show for it. Nothing. Knowing they're dying..."

She softened and came to sit beside him.

"Okay. I know; all that elation and joy for nothing. Ashes. But it's got to work. It's got to."

"Yeah. A lot hangs on it."

They sat for a while side-by-side. Presently she took his hand and he returned the pressure.

"Tell you what," he sat up straighter. "While we're feeling like shit anyway, let's bite the bullet. Let's go on the web and download some fiddle bits from the Fourth, just to give you a taste. But I don't think you're gonna like it."

He located some very old and dog-eared looking facsimile sheets on a website. "This'll do. Let's see what we have... What about the scherzo from the second movement?"

"Isn't that *scordatura*? Let's see." She leaned over the laptop, pressing close to him so as to get her eyes square to the screen. "Yeah, it's pitched a tone higher. Let's find something a bit more straightforward."

He downloaded and printed a PDF of some parts from the first movement; a single page would be more than enough. They returned to the bedroom, she picked up her violin and bow from the bed, and this time it was her turn to be enclosed. Again, a few warm-up notes, a little tweak of the D string, and off she went. He noticed right away that she found this more than enjoyable, but he held off intervening right away. It was only when she got to the bottom of page and started again from the top that he thought enough was enough. He opened the door and placed his hand on her shoulder; he had to shake a little to get her attention.

She stopped playing, looked into his face as if examining a stranger, then an expression of almost anger appeared. This soon passed and she rose from the chair, came out of the cage and the bedroom, and sat herself down in the living room, fiddle held by the neck, bow loosely in her hand.

"Get me a drink will you?"

Without a word he went through to the kitchen, uncorked a half-enjoyed bottle of Chilean red, and poured her a generous glass. He did a more modest one for himself and brought the bottle in with him. She seized the glass gratefully and took a mighty swig.

"So, that's what you go through? Fuck!" He couldn't remember if he had ever heard her swear before; it stirred him.

"My God, Jonathan, this is awful. I had no idea. It's... what is it... it's addictive and it's dangerous. It's just the feeling I always have, but multiplied and distorted. I don't know... Shit!" And she took another long swig.

"It'll pass. When I first felt it I thought music would be ruined forever. But, mercifully, it passes. I'm sorry, I shouldn't have let you..."

"I *had* to, and I'm glad I did! Pour me some more!"

They sat for a long while in silence nursing their glasses.

She was in exquisite mental and bodily agony; they had shared a monumental experience and they were now as close to each other as they had ever been. She wanted so desperately to take him in her arms and join him utterly and completely, but she didn't dare make a move.

After a while she stood up to leave.

"I'll have to help you with this; you can't do it alone."

"Thanks Kate, but let's not even talk about it now. Okay?"

"I just wish all this," she waved her hand in the general direction of the bedroom, "would just go away." She placed her hands on his shoulders and looked into his eyes. "It was horrible and magical. But whenever you need my help, you know where I am."

He nodded. "Sure do."

She put the fiddle and bow away in the case and collected the music sheets. The tiptoe, the peck on the cheek, the swift exit, the lingering scent of her...

The all-day rehearsal on Tuesday concentrated on the instrumental parts of Carl Orff's *Carmina Burana*, a set of 24 mediaeval poems set to music in the 1930s. This was a huge undertaking for the EGSO, requiring solo singers, choruses and additional instruments, including a huge mess of percussion, and would mark the opening of the fall season. It was a perennial favourite on the concert repertoire, and always guaranteed a good house. Today was a session for just the orchestral players, and it was only on Friday that rehearsals would become more and more complex as choruses and soloists found their way to East Gladstone. Unusually, Wednesday and Thursday were free this week.

The usual group were sitting at their usual table in the concert hall cafeteria between the afternoon sessions.

"Holy moly, I just adore playing this stuff!"

"Don't you love those constant rhythmic changes? That bit in *Were diu werlt alle min*? All over the planet!"

"Oh, just wait 'til we come to the accelerandi in *Tempus est iocundum*! Then we'll have fun."

"And, you know what? We could handle the usual classical stuff without the baton, but not this."

"Yeah, old Stefan's a key figure, eh?"

"The condom we all need!"

"Funny, but just since the Brahms One he's been a different animal. Wonder what happened?"

"It's not as if the Symphabomber has let up or anything."

Jonathan and Kate eyed each other, sharing the secret of their newly confident leader. The baton had transformed him, and there was orchestra scuttlebutt that the Board members were more than pleased with his performance.

Indeed, EGSO's presentations of *Carmina Burana* would prove to be the icing on Stefan Kulikofski's promotion cake, and thereafter he would be able truly to call himself Maestro.

Kate and Jonathan met briefly on the patio after the rehearsal. The sun cast their shadows long on the terrazzo and a slight evening breeze moved the water. She wanted to walk home with him through the busy East Gladstone streets, to walk with him to his door, to come inside with him... She was on the very edge of asking him when a shadow crossing his face stopped her.

"They couriered the baton. Stan and Makharam. Got a text. It's on its way to do whatever the hell it's supposed to do."

"It must work! It *must*!"

"Let's not go there again. Please! I have to go home."

"Maybe see you tomorrow?"

"Sure. We could meet for a coffee. Gimme a call. Bye now."

He strode away into town, the slope of his shoulders and the set of his back painting the tension of body and mind.

Jonathan stretched and yawned. He had slept dreamlessly, but the usual waking ritual had to be performed; the ghost at his shoulder must be pushed aside to take her place in the attic of his mind while the day stretched ahead. Busyness and activity helped. But these days off were a boon. No need to get out of bed except to make a cup of the finest coffee; dark, bitter and exhilarating. Then a bit of practice, make a few reeds perhaps, and a little run down by the lake...

The phone blew his plans away.

"Stan! What's up?... No... Oh, that'll be great... All three of you?... Okay, in a couple of hours... Yes, Kate too, of course."

Well, if his plans were shunted off into a siding, at least he'd have the company of Stan, Sandra and Makharam for the morning. What time was it now? Shit, nine already. He held the phone to his cheek.

"But, what's the story?... Oh, come on!... Okay, I'll bide in patience. See you!"

He put the phone back on the side table, edged his way out of bed, and went to put the coffee on. What the hell was so important that Stan couldn't tell him over the phone, and why were all three of them coming? He called Kate while the steam blasted through the grounds, and invited her over.

Kate arrived ten minutes later all fresh and beaming, and hung up her hat and coat behind the door. "So, what's it all about? It must be about Geneva!" He shoved a cup into her hand.

"No, that's not 'til tonight." He checked his watch. "Well, this afternoon for us."

"What then?"

"Dunno. Do what I'm doing; wait with bated breath."

"Do they know how to get here?"

"Yup. Stan has the address."

They sipped their coffee and chatted. He had thawed a bit, so while they talked she sensed a coming closer, a forging of the little liaisons in thought and attitude that build for the long haul.

A little before eleven o'clock the front door bell rang—pointlessly—as Makharam Khan burst into the hall, trailed closely by Sandra and Stan.

"Listen, you'll love this." Khan's beaming face presaged great news. "I've been doing a lot of thinking these last few days. Told you I was in touch with Sir Arthur; what a nice guy, eh?" He flashed a look at his watch. "He wants to talk to us a bit later on."

"Yes," interjected Stan. "At noon our time."

"Okay. So Stan and me have had a great confab. Eh, Stan? Now, here's the scoop; I've decided to become baton supplier to the maestros of the world. Ta-dah!"

Jonathan ushered them in to the room, realizing how small it was when filled with a boisterous crowd.

"But, how are you going..."

"Here's how it works," he interrupted as he threw himself onto the chesterfield. "We've got Stan's student team on side, so we can continue piling up the stats, then all we have to do is check our top two or three hits and set the machine into operation!"

"Machine? What machine?"

"Listen. We do the stats. Then Sir Arthur contacts the potential victim, uses that old-world Limey charm, and we make and ship the baton! Now, here's the thing. The data on Mahler's Fourth that you sent Stan? As you know, yesterday Sir Arthur's baton was winging its way to Geneva care of DHL, while flowery recommendations from that gentleman have already been received. But that's just the start. If this spikes the guns we'll *really* know we're on track!"

"You're... you're making *more* batons?"

"Yep! Made a couple more from scratch, and now I've contracted a small woodworking firm in Don Mills to make more, and the installation's easy. I'm calling my outfit—you'll love this—m-Axis Batons!"

"Oh, this is incredible!" Jonathan was floored. "This is just... Holy shit! But, Jesus man, I didn't think you could find the time for this, let alone the interest."

"Interest? Sure! I've even registered the URL and I'm building a website, ready in a couple of days; it's www.mAxisBatons.com. My card!"

He flourished a business card, probably printed yesterday at Staples, which described Dr M. Khan as CEO.

"I'll be in business in no time because, let's face it, it's a captive market. Sir Arthur's got some international organization interested. He says it's a vanity thing; once one of 'em has one, they all have to. It'll be the Stradivarius of batons!"

"Oh, the High Flyers of the maestro world!" chimed in Kate. "The subtle old bastard!"

"But," continued Khan, "they only pay if they're satisfied with the product, and of course they will be. Alternative: they'll be dead. The first two were freebies, but from now it's income. Of course, there's the question of your share in all this."

"None!" said Jonathan very quickly. "None at all. It could be serious trouble for me. No, no, Makharam, it's all yours and welcome to it."

"So, we'll need some sort of agreement, in case I become a millionaire." He smiled around at his collective audience, already savouring his projected wealth.

"No, nothing in writing; nothing whatsoever. You'll have to take my word for it that, when the time comes, I won't sue for my share of your Caribbean island and Lear jet."

"Okay, it'll be your loss." He hardly looked regretful.

"But how you can devote enough time to this?"

The huge load was lifting. Kate watched him from her seat on the chesterfield beside Stan and delight and joy and disbelief swelled in her.

"Easy. It's my sabbatical year coming up anyway, so I've got all kinds of time, but there's more to it. To be quite honest with you, the magnum opus at the lab is with the publishers, and my role as the go-to guy for electronic gizmos is near the end. And Celia's done her bit too, so she'll be back to the Department of Biochemistry and looking at new stuff to explore in her area."

"I'm done as well," said Stan wearily. "The team's been together for nearly ten years, and I think we're all just a bit tired of each other. For the physiologists—Ken and Robin, and maybe John—there's all sorts of new stuff to explore. But for me? No, not really... A life of indolence might be quite appealing."

"We're going to take a little down time," explained Sandra. "Stan and I are going to the Hebrides. We'll be six weeks in and around Stornoway, visiting all over Harris. Hiking, taking pictures. It'll be a marvelous break."

"Fantastic!" cried Jonathan. "Wait, wait, let's get some coffee and tea going!" He hurtled off to the little kitchen and clattered away industriously. Steam roared and cups and spoons tinkled.

"My God, you have no idea what this does for me," he yelled through the kitchen door. "But what about secrecy? You simply *can't* keep this under wraps." He poked his head into the living room, tea towel draped over his arm.

"We'll deal with that as it comes," replied Makharam. "As far as I can see, the truth is so whacked-out nobody will ever believe it anyway, and your music business—I hope you'll pardon my saying so—is so full of the most astonishing and counter-intuitive bullshit, matched only by the credulousness of its purveyors. I would imagine, in the realm of incomparable Stradivariuses" (a small frown of disapproval from Kate) "flutes with personality, and heaven-inspired musical genius, a magic baton would go down a treat."

"But what if someone takes one to bits and finds all the inner gizmos?" asked Kate, getting up from the chesterfield and going to help carry the drinks.

"So what? Without a knowledge of the science—the math and all our crazy dimension-4 stuff—the components in there won't make any sense at all! And who could possibly know how to program the chip? Only me. I was thinking about patenting it, but I don't think it's possible. Can hardly describe the function to the Patent Office, eh? But here's the thing that'll really make you hoot. Inside every one there's a little label that says 'Time to re-order: By opening this baton you have rendered it useless'."

Jonathan laughed. "Wow, I just don't believe this! Time to celebrate." He raised his coffee cup over his head. "Cheers!"

"Saved the best bit 'til last!" smiled Stan. "The test you did on Mahler's Fourth? That's the last time you'll have to do it. We're rigging up a cage at Makharam's place, and I've got my Celtic fiddle player—good old Subject 27—who's willing to run the tests. All in-house!"

"Oh, my God!" cried Jonathan. "Off the hook! Oh, my God!"

He put his face in his hands while the news sunk in. Presently he looked up and his eyes were moist. "So, all we need now to make the party complete is a word from Geneva. Will it; won't it?"

"Sir Arthur has promised he'll call, day or night, as soon as he hears anything," replied Makharam, "so I'm afraid we'll just have to wait and see."

"But it will! It *must*!" cried Kate. "Otherwise all this..."

"...is for nothing," continued Jonathan soberly, eying Kate warily. "But it's weird science, you know, where a supposedly positive result is inconclusive." He sighed. He and Kate briefly locked eyes. "Well, we just wait..."

They drank their coffee and ate the cookies that had emerged with it (from God-knows-where, thought Kate, knowing a little about the state of the Rycroft larder).

"Okay, Jonathan, open up yer laptop," ordered Stan, checking the time. "We have to talk to our man in the UK."

Jonathan hauled in the sole kitchen chair and sat on it with the laptop on his knees. Kate, Makharam and the Wards clustered behind him on the chesterfield, hopefully within camera shot. Sir Arthur must have been waiting for the call, so quickly did his image appear on the screen.

"Excellent! Excellent!" Sir Arthur rubbed his hands. "I can't stay long but I wanted to speak to all of you. Now, you know, of course, that I have joined wholeheartedly into this nonsensical business of yours. As I have told you, I persist in my view that your explanation of the phenomenon is complete bollocks. But... I am absolutely convinced of the efficacy of your remedy. Now, does that not sound contradictory?"

Jonathan was the first to speak. "It is contradictory, but we have to learn to live with it. We were just discussing the frustration of feelings and thoughts compared with hard evidence."

"Of course, you scientific chaps need the numbers, don't you? If you can't measure it, it isn't there, eh? Well, I am content to go with my intuition. I know what I felt when I used the damn' thing, and I am prepared to help others in similar straits. If what's-his-name in Geneva 'feels' it works, then that's fine with me. So, in a nutshell, we have an excellent team in Makharam, Stan and me, but I do feel that, as word spreads, it will be less and less necessary for me to be its advocate. I can just visualize everybody wanting one. You know what they're like, eh Kate?"

She smiled. "Oh, yes, it's all to do with their EGSOs!"

"Exactly so. Anyway, must fly!"

"Thank you again from all of us," called Makharam, leaning over Jonathan's shoulder.

"You are most welcome. And as soon as I hear anything at all from Geneva I will certainly call. *Au revoir*!"

And he was gone. The team members eyed each other, filled with a new realization that a whole new chapter had opened.

Stan leapt to his feet, slapped his hands together and offered Sandra his hand. She waved it off and rose from her chair. "Got to get moving, now you've got the news. I hear the call of the Isles. Flights are booked for tomorrow, but we have all the packing, and time presses!"

At the door Kate gave both the Wards a hug.

"What's this?" cried Stan. "Are you crying, girl?"

She nodded.

"Good God! We haven't been diagnosed with some fatal disease! We're going to Scotland, not palliative care! You have the face of a consumptive orphan in a Victorian penny-dreadful."

"No, no, I'm *happy*! It's just that you two and Sir Arthur and the Hebrides are all so beautifully woven together..."

"Ah, the lady's a Romantic! She weeps through joy. And," here he looked directly at Jonathan, "cherish her: she walks in beauty like the night..."

"...of cloudless climes and starry skies," continued Jonathan.

Kate laughed and blinked her eyes as she and Jonathan saw them to the door. Makharam Khan swung an arm briefly around Jonathan's shoulder, squeezed then followed the Wards to the door. "See you old buddy. We'll Skype you immediately the news comes from Geneva."

As soon as the door closed they fell into each other's arms in the hall, a mingling of closeness and shared joy. He returned her hug, solidly and sincerely, for the first time since that greeting at Pearson Airport. They separated slowly and returned to the living room.

"Oh God, the immense relief!" he cried. "It's a load shifted."

"I am so happy for you, Jonathan. Won't it be great if the thing really works? It *has* to!"

He bit back the 'yes, but' on the tip of his tongue. "I'll call you as soon as I hear anything."

"I know you will. Look, I've got to go into town right now, but how about I drop by tomorrow? Would that be okay?" Even though the hugs were solid, she was still tentative; still didn't feel confident enough to take more than a subtle, gentle line.

"No rehearsal; another day off, eh? And then it's back to old *Carmina Burana* on Friday. I'll be around, so why not?"

"I'd love to." She rose and collected her hat and coat, already looking forward to the morrow. "I've got to meet with Liz Straker and some of the other strings tomorrow morning for a playing session, so some time in the afternoon?"

"Great! See you then."

She kissed his cheek and was gone before he could call her back. He had almost wanted to ask her just how important it was to go into town right at this very moment.

It was three-thirty on Thursday afternoon and Jonathan was annoyed. Why was it every time he really got into his practice sessions there was some damned interruption? If he was just doing scales it was no big deal, but not when he was into something solid for Christ's sake.

The only interruption he would have welcomed would be a word from Geneva, but he had heard nothing. Still hanging in suspense.

The interruption was the door bell. He was working with his cor anglais, having played through Donizetti's Concertino in G major for the sheer enjoyment of it, and then tackling *The Swan of Tuonela* for the same reason. He would never play cor anglais in public, and the joy was therefore his alone. Sibelius stopped in mid bar, and so in this version the swan suffered a premature death and Lemminkäinen got off scot free. He placed the cor anglais down carefully on the chair and strode over to the door, preparing to refuse the bloody *Watchtower* or to buy any modeling clay chocolates for the local kids' soccer team.

Kate was standing at the door looking gorgeous. He'd forgotten. Or had he really? She was wearing tight jeans and a fawn sweater, and again her hair was caught up in a ponytail, instead of in the headband or flowing free about her shoulders, and she had brought her violin case. He smiled and swung the door wide.

"I heard the lovely swan singing when I was outside, and I had second thoughts about disturbing her, but..." she shrugged.

"It's okay, she's dead and it's lovely to see you. Really!" as he detected a small hint of doubt around her eyes. "I don't mind breaking off. I thought it was the bloody Jehovah's Witlesses, so I was prepared to do battle. You're a beautiful alternative."

"Why, thank you kind sir! Anything from Geneva?"

"No, not a word. I called Stan this morning but he hadn't heard anything. I checked the web, of course; the concert was fine, but that doesn't mean a damned thing. Well, I guess we can only wait."

"Hey, look what I brought you."

A trace of perfume crossed his face as she walked in and sat herself down in the living room. She opened her case and extracted two sets of score sheets held together with paperclips.

"It's the Bach C Minor concerto for oboe and violin. Like to give it a go?"

"Oh, I love y... this is great!" he cried, then coloured immediately and got extremely busy arranging a place to rest the scores so they could both read them. "Here, let's balance yours against this book, and I'll put mine over the laptop screen. Will that suit? There."

His hands were shaking.

There were a few stops and starts before they got on track, but it was not long before they were able to play as if they had done this for ages. They played the first movement through twice, the second iteration much better than the first.

This is it, she thought as she played. This is what it's all about. I knew it! I knew it as soon as we sang *Mingulay*. Before that even; when I first met his eyes. This was her prayed-for sharing for life and it filled her with immense joy.

"That was marvelous," he exclaimed as they set their instruments down on the low table beside the laptop. "We've got to do more of this. You're so kind and... It's just what we... I... needed to..." he sighed and rubbed his face with his hands.

"We'll do it again."

"They said they'd call. Christ, why don't they get in touch? Maybe I'll give 'em a call now."

She took his hand. "Wait. They'll call when there's any news. I just want to think of us. It's a lovely afternoon, and there won't be many more like it this year, so why don't we take a little picnic supper down to the lake? Push reality away for a bit. Like we did just now. You'll have your phone with you."

She watched the thoughts crossing his face, and saw him reaching the conclusion she wished and prayed for. "I'd love to," he smiled, bewitched, and this time he meant it. "But I'm not sure what we're going to eat, as you seem to have come completely empty handed."

"Well, I was halfway here when I thought of food, I must admit. But then, I thought, Jonathan's bound to have something in his kitchen." The expression on her face was downright mischievous. "Let's have a look in your fridge and see what we can find.

We can pop into the LCBO on the way," she called over her shoulder. "They have this cooler chest. Have you seen that?"

"Look, Kate," he protested, "you're not going to find a hell of a lot that's edible in there. We might just want to buy some stuff in town..."

"Jonathan!" she cried in mock horror. "You've got a can of Spam in here!"

"Half a can, actually. But what's wrong with Spam? I love it."

She was back on the prairie farm of her childhood, watching nature in naked action.

"When you slide it out of the can it's like watching piglets being born!"

"Nice and pink and slippery. Mmmm..."

"You're disgusting! You don't eat properly; it's not healthy."

"Listen you: I can play the oboe all night, I can walk, run and bike for miles, I have a resting heart rate of 60 and just look how slim I am. So back off."

"Slim? Skeletal, I call it. Well, there's no bread anyway, so you can't bring Spam sandwiches even if you wanted to."

"I could just stick the can in my pocket; bring a spoon..."

She threw up her hands in exasperation. "All right, all right, it was a fool's errand to think there would be anything worth eating in your house. You win; let's buy in town."

"Sure. What's it like out? Will I need a coat?" he smiled. "After all, you're the one who seems to be charged with overseeing my wellbeing."

"Sarcasm is the lowest form of wit. No, it's lovely out there, I told you, that's why I thought this would be such a good idea."

He went to close down his laptop-cum-music stand when he noticed the Skype flag was indicating a call. "Just a moment... Oh, it's Stan!"

He grabbed the laptop and sat on the chesterfield with it, while Kate dropped down beside him.

"It worked! It worked. It *goddamned worked*!" crowed Stan's face on the screen. He was flanked by Sandra and Makharam, all three of them crowded round the computer in Stan's office at home. "The Geneva maestro called Sir Arthur last night. Completely mystified, baffled but totally in awe of the thing! He said it was magic. That's what he said; he said it was magic."

"Magic? But that's what he *feels*! What actually *happened*?" cried Jonathan in an agony frustration. He slumped forward, hands together at his forehead in an attitude of prayer. "Is this effect real? Are we seeing a *result* here?"

"Yes, yes, and yes!" yelled Khan. "Here's the clincher: ever think to play the same piece *after* it's popped? No? Obvious ain't it, now you think of it? Well we did—good ol' Celtic Subject 27—and the reading is reversed. *Reversed* man! Energy going out as per usual."

"Good Christ! How stupid of us! *Of course*! Stupid! Stupid!"

"Yes," put in Stan, "dropped the ball on that one, didn't we? All I can say is, we've been so wound up that we just weren't thinking clearly."

"But now it's so obvious," replied Jonathan. "Remember, after *Messiah* in Rio, when you said it was no longer a threat? You knew 'way back then, didn't you?"

"No, no. I didn't *know*. I suspected. At that point it was all supposition. And," he smiled ironically, "you weren't exactly sold on the idea yourself."

Jonathan nodded, remembering his cynicism. "Yeah, but later we could've... Bruckner Four in Warsaw..."

"Yes, I know we could have. But we didn't. Okay? It could have been sooner, it could have been later. It was later, that's all."

"God, Stan," replied Kate at Jonathan's side, "we were all so bloody worried; no wonder we weren't thinking straight."

"But," cried Stan, "look to the future! What else do we now need to support the hypothesis? Energy appearing before; energy disappearing after. File full; file empty. Absolutely cut and dried. My God, there's work to be done here. Just think; the research potential is absolutely enormous. Jesus, it's only the convergence of brain and mind, that's all. There's work for a generation here."

"So, no retirement in the cards for you then, Stan?" smiled Kate from Jonathan's side, thinking of the woebegone face of two days ago.

"Lord, no. This old dog's got some mileage yet."

"Yeah," said Makharam. "He's heading up the m-Axis Batons research division. We've got it all sorted out."

"Yes, and then there's the anomaly of why only the conductor is affected. What is it about physically playing that gives immunity? And then there's..."

"Enough!" interrupted Sandra. "Enough, you silly old bugger! Wait 'til after our vacation. You're taking a forced leave of absence, my dear, like it or not."

"All right. All right. You know damned well I won't have to be dragged screaming to the Isles. It'll be wonderful and, who knows, we might even make a side trip to Islay and acquire some of the best *uisge beatha* in the world. For which you, Kate, seem to be developing a taste."

Did the sun choose to shine through the front window at just that moment and illuminate the chesterfield and its occupant, or had it been shining all along, unnoticed before this sudden turn in the flow and tide of the world? No, there's no such thing as divine intervention; the world just put on a brighter face, that's all.

"Oh, I can't believe this!" cried Jonathan. "I'll call you back as soon as it's all sunk in."

Time slowed down to a leisurely stroll. The room was clearer and brighter, everything stood out with sharp clarity; the warm sun-dance from the varnished wood of Kate's violin, the bright white reflections on the oboe's silver-plated keywork, the curled cream paper of the Bach score, the smile on her face, the curve of her cheek with its soft sunlit down, that upturn of her lips, the delight and love in her eyes. A tableau finely painted on a thin sliver of time.

"Now, where were we?" asked Jonathan, as the world accelerated to its usual pace. "Ah, yes, picnic bound. Shall we?"

And he held out his hand to the lady.

She said nothing, but stood up and came over to him and they hugged again tightly.

They walked slowly into town, arm in arm. Since her return from London and their brief sojourn in Toronto they had been like this, easy with each other, perfectly comfortable, but not yet fully together. Now the Bach C Minor concerto and the wonderful news from Stan and Makharam had done their work; their closeness was redoubled.

They bought a chilled bottle of Niagara Riesling in the liquor store, choosing one with a screw cap, then went into the A&P almost next door and bought simple cheeses, plain bread and some fresh celery and carrots. Kate picked up a package of disposable plastic glasses against her better nature, and stole a plastic knife from the food counter. They giggled like children.

The paths down by the lake were marvelously unpopulated. They walked slowly hand in hand to the little beach beyond the windmill and found a small patch of grass to sit. They ate their modest little supper and enjoyed their chilled wine while the sun continued its slow descent. They sat for a long while beside each other, arms around shoulders, contentedly quiet and looking out over the lake. They both knew that here, in this place and at this time, something was going to change forever, but they were almost shy.

Presently, he took her hand in his, and still looking out across the water, said quietly, "You are *you* now. You're not her. I'll never, ever forget her. You know that. But now I have you. When you were away... when you went to London... I was closer to you then than if I was sitting right beside you. Can you see that? But it was agony..."

She nodded, not wishing to break any spells. Gulls cried high up in the air, and the voices of a few children could be heard far away. A kayak passed swiftly across their line of sight.

"It was then, when you were away... You're so good for me..." She shushed his lips with her finger.

They stood and walked slowly down to the edge of the water. The air was cooling. The sun sank behind the windmill, throwing its vanes into black diamond-paned relief, and night unfurled her dusky bedroll up the eastern sky.

He placed his arms around her and brought her close; her arms went around him. Their lips met. The kiss lasted for a measurable fraction of eternity.

She broke slowly from him, looked into his eyes, and murmured gently, "Jon?"

He clasped her close again. His head was on her shoulder, mouth beside her ear.

"Yeah, Jon."

Da Capo

It's a small thing; a little over a foot long and weighing only a few ounces. But it has enormous power. Inside there's a little microcircuit and a platinum wire and some capacitors. It's a pragmatic little key to a tiny hole into another dimension. It lets the incomprehensible through in small doses from wherever that other place is. We're not supposed to understand it, any more than we can really understand music. Accept it; it just works.

Is it a gun; a sword; a whip; a magic wand?

Of course not.

It's the maestro's baton, and it's manufactured and distributed by m-Axis Batons of Toronto, Canada.

It's a lightning rod.

On second thoughts, maybe it *is* a magic wand...

www.ingramcontent.com/pod-product-compliance
Lightning Source LLC
Chambersburg PA
CBHW031945090426
42739CB00006B/94
* 9 7 8 0 9 8 6 7 8 7 9 2 8 *